The Chinese Women's Movement
Between State and Market

The Chinese Women's Movement
Between State and Market

Ellen R. Judd

STANFORD UNIVERSITY PRESS
STANFORD, CALIFORNIA

Stanford University Press
Stanford, California
© 2002 by the Board of Trustees of the
Leland Stanford Junior University
Printed in the United States of America

Library of Congress Cataloging-in-Publication Data

Judd, Ellen R.
  The Chinese women's movement between state and market / Ellen
R. Judd.
     p.   cm.
  Includes bibliographical references and index.
  ISBN 0-8047-4405-x (alk. paper) — ISBN 0-8047-4406-8 (pbk: alk. paper)
  1. Women—China—Economic conditions.   2. Women—China—
Social conditions.   3. Women in development—China.   4. Zhonghua
quan guo fu nè lian he hui.   5. Women—Government policy—China.
I. Title.
HQ1767.J83   2002
305.42'0951—dc21   2001049505

This book is printed on acid-free, archival quality paper.

Original printing 2002
Last figure below indicates year of this printing:
11   10   09   08   07   06   05   04   03   02

Typeset at Stanford University Press in 9.5/12.5 Trump Medieval

For CHRISTINE EGAN
(1946–2001)
who loved life, family, and friends
and brought joy to everyone who knew her

Preface

This book arose as the unexpected product of the efforts of numerous Chinese women to explain to me the changes in their lives during the reform era, as well as the changes in the role of the official women's movement in China from the late 1980s. I have attempted to listen closely to their voices, but I expect they will find my views remain some distance from their own. I hope, nevertheless, that they will read in these pages faithful accounts of their resourcefulness in working under challenging circumstances to improve the lives of women in rural China.

The fieldwork reported here was conducted from 1988 to 1995, with generous support from the Social Sciences and Humanities Research Council of Canada through a SSHRCC–Chinese Academy of Social Sciences Exchange Grant, 1987–88; a SSHRCC Canada Research Fellowship, 1987–92; and SSHRCC Research Grants, 1990–91 and 1992–96. Within China, the research was made possible by staff of the Shandong Academy of Social Sciences, the China Shandong International Culture Exchange Centre, the Shandong Women's Federation, the Qingdao Women's Federation, the Jining Women's Federation, the Dezhou Women's Federation, the Lingxian Women's Federation, and various levels of government in Shandong province. I am especially indebted to the women of the rural community of Huaili and to all those who accompanied me and made my visits to Huaili possible. The research was further enriched by numerous members of women's organizations in Jinan, Qingdao, Jining, and Lingxian, and by scholars in women's studies in various locations in Shandong.

Within Canada, writing began while I was a Visiting Scholar at the Centre for Research in Women's Studies and Gender Relations (which also granted a research allowance) and at Green College, University of British Columbia. I benefited from office space and a collegial environment in the Department of Anthropology and Sociology, University of

British Columbia, due to the courtesy of Graham Johnson and Richard Pearson, and from the assistance of the librarians at the Asian Studies Centre, University of British Columbia. Geri Boyle was instrumental in making the months in Vancouver feasible and enjoyable. Publication of this volume has been generously assisted by the Faculty of Arts and the Office of the Vice-president (Research) at the University of Manitoba.

Among those whose comments, criticism, and information have contributed to the study over the years, I would particularly wish to acknowledge Isabel Crook, Lü Jingyun, Lü Xiuyuan, Janet Salaff, Jack Scott, and Yuen-fong Woon. Assistance with library research was provided by Paula Migliardi, Shaun Mulvey, and Yang Jun. Roxetta Wilde typed and formatted portions of the text. Chris Egan assisted with the map, and with everything else.

An earlier version of part of Chapter 3 appeared as "Rural Women and Economic Development in Reform Era China: The Strategy of the Official Women's Movement," in *Feminist Fields: Ethnographic Insights*, ed. Rae Bridgman, Sally Cole, and Heather Howard-Bobiwash (Peterborough: Broadview Press, 1999), pp. 264–81.

I am grateful to Muriel Bell at Stanford University Press for her interest in and support of this project throughout its long gestation period. John Feneron has been helpful and efficient in guiding it to publication, and Sharron Woods has been meticulous in her editing. The index was prepared by Linda Gregonis.

I remain solely responsible for the interpretations presented here and for all remaining shortcomings in this study.

Contents

Map and Tables

The Chinese Women's Movement
Between State and Market

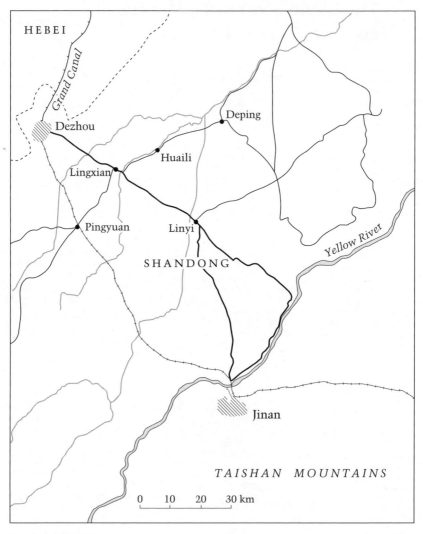

Huaili and Environs

1

Introduction

W hen China embarked on its rural economic reform, change for women was not part of the program. The reform was conceptually a strategy of gender-blind political economy designed to generate economic growth in the countryside and the nation. But the implications of the reform as it unfolded were much more far-reaching. Every facet of rural social life was affected, and this meant that gender relations were recreated and the lives of women actually or potentially transformed.

As men left the countryside, or at least found work outside, women assumed increasing roles in agriculture. In contrast to their traditional role marginal to agriculture—as expressed in the classic phrase, "men till and women weave" (*nangeng nüzhi*)—women were doing roughly two-thirds of the nation's agricultural labor by the 1990s. The small rural enterprises whose productivity was driving the Chinese economic success relied heavily upon the work of young rural women, especially in the key textile and light consumer goods sectors. Household-based enterprises mushroomed throughout the countryside, and these were commonly based upon the partnership and division of labor of a conjugal couple. For many married women, this offered an opportunity for the use of skills and abilities that had previously had no avenue for expression, while other women lacking skill, capital, or opportunity experienced more difficult circumstances. Young women entering marriage in the countryside found that their economic potential and that of their young husbands gave them an unprecedented independence, and placed them in a stronger position in relation to their mothers-in-law. Other young women left the countryside temporarily or permanently in search of a better life elsewhere. The entire fabric of rural gender relations had become open to obvious and to more subtle processes of change.

Rural women responded to this wider range of possibilities in di-

verse ways, and it has become more difficult than in the relatively ho-
mogeneous past of the collective era to generalize about their conditions of life. As economic differentiation has proceeded, this has affected women—not only in connection with their localities and their
male relatives, but also on the basis of their own activities. Nevertheless, while local communities and households have been transformed,
they remain androcentric and patriarchal. Significant differences in
gender relations and a gender division of labor continue to give rural
women substantial shared interests.

By the end of the first decade of reform, in the late 1980s, the implications of shifting gender relations for women in particular, and for the
recommoditizing rural society in general, had become increasingly evident. In the final years of the 1980s, in addition to the changes women
and men were making in their own lives, an organized response from
the women's movement was gradually formulated and put into practice.

This book had its origins in the efforts of many Chinese women to
educate me about their vision for improving the lives of women in rural
China in the context of reform. This vision was not exactly what I had
expected to find on the part of grassroots women leaders responsible for
"woman-work" (funü gongzuo). Their starting point is the proposition
that the decisive problem for women is that their "quality" (suzhi) is
too low. Although quality may be and often is used in a very general
sense, the main point here is that women have disadvantages in literacy, education, and skills that would enable them to compete successfully and thrive in the marketplace. On the basis of this identification of
women's quality as the decisive factor, a set of programs and policies
have been developed and implemented to raise women's quality (especially in basic and practical education) and to lead women to compete
more successfully in China's "socialist market economy." A defining
paradox here is that it is the official women's movement—the Women's
Federations under the leadership of the Communist Party of China—
that is spearheading this move toward the market.

How an arm of the state—the official women's movement—leads
the move toward the market can be examined in general terms as one
aspect of the distinctive fusion of state and market characteristic of
contemporary China. My concern in this study is somewhat more specific and concrete. I will attempt an "ethnography of the particular"
(Abu-Lughod 1991), in which I will explore this vision as situated in

specific experiences of the reform and in women's various efforts to strategize in the reform context.

Among the varied issues that one might discuss in relation to women's organizing in contemporary China, I will limit myself to the complex of changes I was able to observe and to discuss with the women involved during a series of field trips from 1988 to 1995. The framework of this study is determined by what was present in directly encountered locations of Shandong province during those years. There is a broader significance in that the same policies and practices have been evident nationally in the 1990s in policy documents, studies by Chinese scholars, and in publications by and for Chinese women, especially those involved in woman-work. The contribution of this study will be the grounding of an encounter with this set of policies and practices in the ethnography of a contemporary community.

WOMEN'S ORGANIZING IN CHINA

It is not new that women are organizing in China in the context of larger processes of social change.[1] Women and women's issues figured significantly in most of the major initiatives and movements of the twentieth century. The earliest Communist Party experiments in governing, in the southern soviets in the early 1930s, included an activist agenda on women's rights, especially in marriage. The subsequent Yan'an period (1937–47) saw some retrenchment in this area as the Party consolidated its support among the rural men upon whom it relied in the Anti-Japanese War and in the renewed civil war that followed. Nevertheless, the same period saw the emergence of a major role for women in rural production and in local governance, taking the place of absent men and finding some new openings in the policies of the border regions. The first law of the new People's Republic of China, the Marriage Law (Central People's Government 1975), proclaimed in 1950 and popularized in the early 1950s, directly addressed women's specific oppression in the patriarchal family. At roughly the same time, women were granted at least nominal economic equality through being allocated land in the land reforms of 1947–52. This was followed by increased participation of women in public labor in the collectives, which was partially remu-

---

[1] There is a large and excellent literature on women organizing in China. Among the major works consulted here are Croll (1978, 1981, 1983), Davin (1976), Diamond (1975), Gilmartin et al. (1994), Honig and Hershatter (1988), Jacka (1997), Johnson (1983), Stacey (1983), and Wolf (1985).

nerated through the workpoint system, even if a whole household's remuneration might be given to the (usually male) household head. The
ill-fated Great Leap Forward that began in 1958 included experiments in
collectivizing domestic labor by instituting public dining halls and child
care. While these changes were underway in the countryside, the rebuilding of urban institutions included the creation of employment for
women, with equal pay and a gender-sensitive program of benefits. The
upheavals of the Cultural Revolution (1966–76) did not initially include
particular initiatives on the part of women, although its later years were
marked by the increased entry of women into traditionally male fields
of work, an increase in the representation of women in leadership, and
the encouragement of uxorilocal marriage.

After a brief interregnum, the period of reform that followed from
1979 was not a favorable one for women. In the 1980s, many women in
leadership positions found themselves marginalized, transferred, or retired, while the early reform policies being promoted did not give attention to the needs of women at the grass roots. The 1980s also saw a resurgence of a women's movement in China both within and beyond the
established framework of the official Women's Federations.

All of these changes, reshaping the conditions of life by and for
women in China, have been closely connected with the state, and specifically with the Communist Party, both before and after it formed a
national government. Women had organized for change outside this
framework as well, especially early in the twentieth century, but it was
those who linked women's liberation with the socialist movement who
were historically more influential in China. The resulting approach was
one that kept the women's movement intrinsically connected with and
subordinate to gender-inclusive movements for national liberation and
socialist revolution. For their part, the men (and they were almost exclusively men) who led the Communist Party recognized the commitment of the inclusive socialist vision to women's liberation at the same
time as they continued to hold and implement patriarchal beliefs and
practices. The result has been an uneasy fusion in which some discernible gains have been made through a state-supported women's movement, but with evident compromises.

These gains have not been a simple or direct matter of implementing policy, although state policy in China since 1949 has generally been
more supportive of women's rights and interests than the society at
large, and this has been especially the case for rural women living in

bounded androcentric communities. In considering the prospects for change for women in rural China, it is essential to place the possibilities in the context of these communities and their social structure. The continuing norm in rural social life has been that men remain in their communities of birth while women born there marry out, and women from elsewhere marry in. Despite small numbers of uxorilocal marriages and a recent increase in the acceptability of intravillage marriage, patrilocality continues to structure rural communities. The significance is not only that men remain in the same communities while women experience a rupture, after which they build adult lives at some remove from their natal families. Patrilocality also means that men live in communities in which the outer domain or public life is structured around multigenerational groups of related men. In the various locations in Shandong with which I am familiar, descent within the village can be traced back roughly twenty generations, and villages are often single-lineage communities. Even in the village at the center of this study, Huaili, which is a multisurname village, there is a core lineage of the same depth, and a similar androcentric (but multisurname) core to the village's outer domain. This pattern of forming communities, together with cultural sanctions against women's participation in the outer domain, leave both formal and informal community ties realized by or through men. This situation obtained prior to 1949 on a more directly patrilineal descent-based model, following collectivization as the same communities became vested with political and economic authority, and after decollectivization in the form of administrative villages. The exact boundaries, size, and number of corporate units have varied, but the deep androcentric character has remained through each transformation. Such communities have been markedly resistant to change that would give women rights in marriage, divorce, or child custody—all of which go to the heart of the community's membership—and also resistant to women's fully equal participation in the economic and political life of the communities.

Women, for their part, have most commonly pursued strategies based on family and household. They have nurtured strong ties with children, grandchildren, and, wherever possible (in a situation where most marriages are still semi-arranged), with their husbands. While young married women are discouraged from forming ties with women outside their own household, except with those married to their husbands' closest agnates, they can legitimately assume important roles in the inner domains of their own households. The desire of women to manage their own households independently is one of the major forces promoting household division and the increase in the number of nuclear families. Women may manage or co-manage household resources, make major contributions to household income through raising domestic animals or other household-based activities and, especially in the re-form era, run small household-based endeavors on their own or jointly with their husbands. Although not every women has the education, skill or capital—or the favorable household relations—to do so, many women do find this a more attainable (and perhaps more desirable) goal than entering the outer domain characterized by androcentric domina-tion.

Creating change in the interests of women within such a context has been a formidable undertaking. Much Western writing on the subject to date has addressed the question of the role of the state, and this study is partly a continuation of this scholarship. But this is not to argue that the state has been the prime mover of change in the countryside and that the difficulty has simply been one of local implementation.

My own view of this matter was decisively affected by interviewing the senior generation of women in three Shandong communities about the impact of the 1950 Marriage Law (Judd 1998). My understanding prior to these interviews was that this law, together with the national campaign to implement it, was a threshold event in which the new Peo-ple's Republic made a concerted if only partially effective effort to in-tervene in the familial dimensions of patriarchy, especially by making it possible for women to leave unwanted marriages. I spoke at some length with all the women who had held leadership roles in these three villages in the late 1940s and the early 1950s, a time when women had often filled such roles in the place of absent men, and I spoke with many other women of the same generation. I was struck by their absence of mention of the Marriage Law; even when explicitly asked about it, they did not consider it very significant. Equally striking were accounts of how some young women had resolved their own marriage problems in that era, by leaving unwanted marriages and subsequently remarrying. I was not being told about policy and its imperfect implementation; I was being told how some women had actively changed their own lives. It appeared to me, from the cases described, that young women close to the newly emergent political forces might have been best positioned to make this change, and that the new policies and state structures had

some indirect, enabling role. The women who spoke with me emphasized the women's own actions, and added the observation that these
were women who did not yet have children, or they would not have
been able to take the steps they did.

It has seemed to me that there is a major point to be learned from
this oral herstory. In a peculiar and unconscious manner, given the explicit sympathies of most Western feminist observers with Chinese
women and their movements for change, we may have inadvertently
orientalized Chinese women by allowing them to appear as passive figures responding to equally distorted images of exaggerated state power.
The actual workings of women's agency in modern and contemporary
rural China utilize resources made available by state policies and programs and by organized arms of the state, such as the Women's Federations, but their agency is grounded in the immediate structures of rural
communities, and primarily dependent on the women themselves.

A RURAL COMMUNITY

The departure point for this study is the administrative village of Huaili
in the primarily agricultural region of Dezhou Municipality, Shandong
province. I visited this village on five occasions from 1988 to 1995, and
much of this book is based in the lives of the women of this community.
Although the study also addresses issues elsewhere—in the township
and county in which Huaili is located, in several cities in Shandong, and
nationally—the significance of the issues resides firmly in Huaili and in
innumerable villages like Huaili.

I arrived in Huaili after an extended search for a community where it
would be possible to explore the process of decollectivization. I had earlier been sent to villages that had concentrated on rural industry and,
while this had proved useful in understanding emergent forces in the
countryside (see Judd 1994), I still sought a location where I would be
able to explore the new household-based agricultural economy. The
prospective sites in Ling County appeared rather exceptional, but a
chance invitation to a wedding in Huaili introduced me to that community, and I was allowed to make it a continuing fieldwork location.

Huaili had formerly been a relatively successful production brigade
in the collective era. The village had done well with vegetable cultivation, in addition to grain and cotton, but lacked the advantages of either
close location to an urban center or a diversified non-agricultural base at
the time it decollectivized in 1984. Shortly thereafter it suffered a major

setback with the appropriation of a considerable amount of Huaili's land for a World Bank–supported water control project. This misfortune of location meant that Huaili lost more land than neighboring villages, and for a year the situation was sufficiently dire that no woman married into Huaili. However, improvement in the village economy (and marriage situation) occurred quickly with Huaili's move to maximize some compensating advantages, also related to its location (see map, page xii). Huaili borders on a minor paved highway that brings some traffic close enough to the village to provide commercial opportunities for motor repair and minor commerce, although traffic is not heavy. In addition, the township offices are located not far on the other side of the road, attracting local travelers. The township itself is a walled compound of offices and residences for township staff, but it is small and not a market center itself. A periodic market is located along the wide street that separates Huaili from the neighboring village of Dongjie. It is Dongjie that is the market town, but Huaili also benefits from its presence. Huaili's strategy for development was one of encouraging households to open small shops and other enterprises along the roadside or near the periodic market site, or to engage in any other form of small enterprise that might benefit from these commercial opportunities. An effort at developing some village-based industry (primarily weaving) was also made in the late 1980s, but failed to survive the shakeout in 1990, as was the fate of most of the limited rural industry in the county. Huaili's chosen route in the reform era was a mix of intensive cultivation of the remaining land with promotion of household-based enterprises. The majority of Huaili households attempted and had some success with at least one enterprise. These were uniformly small and rarely involved the employment of anyone outside the household, but generated substantial income for their households. Land remained valued and a basic resource for food, fodder, and tax payments, but a household enterprise was essential for well-being in land-poor Huaili.

In 1988 Huaili had 997 people in 220 households, and the size of the community increased gradually in the following years. There were only occasional, temporary additions to the village, when one of the more successful enterprises sometimes hired an employee from outside. There were always some people absent from the village working elsewhere on a temporary or long-term basis, and most of these were men, although Huaili had not experienced the significant out-migration of men characteristic of some other areas in the 1980s. A few women left permanently prior to marriage, and a few young couples successful in business also left the village. Huaili was not a community that had strong economic contacts outside the village, and there was no established connection with external employment. This situation was beginning to change in the mid-1990s as Huaili developed greater ties and opportunities in the expanding economic region centered on Tianjin Municipality, but for the most part Huaili was reliant on its own labor and resources.

Huaili did not share in the new affluence of villages close to major cities or located in the thriving coastal areas. Although some households had built new homes in the 1980s and 1990s, these were single-story structures built along traditional lines, not modern multistory structures. By the mid-1990s a few households had begun to have radiators and telephones, the latter primarily for commercial purposes. The pace of economic development was uneven, with the early 1990s being difficult for all of Ling County, but there was a discernible trajectory of moderate improvement for the village as a whole. This was built upon continuing intensive cultivation of the modest land base (less than one *mu* per person) and active involvement in a shifting mix of small enterprise. Huaili can be viewed as somewhat representative of the middle economic stratum of communities in rural China, although one village cannot capture the full range of diversity, and Huaili was more commercial than most surrounding villages.[2]

Huaili was, at certain times, slightly out of the ordinary in having a higher level of activity in woman-work (*funü gongzuo*, as the work of the official women's movement is known) than was usual. All villages in China have a nominal structure for such activity, but it is not always very active. Huaili was located in a township where a long-serving vice-head of the county Women's Federation had once worked, and Huaili itself was reasonably accessible from the county seat by road (a half-hour trip). At the time I first arrived in the village, a younger vice-head had briefly made Huaili into an example of what could be accomplished by promoting women's activity in the "courtyard economy" (*tingyuan jingji*) through her regular visits and through concerted effort together with the village women's committee. In subsequent years, Huaili went through a less active period when it had no women's head within the village; it revived its activity later under a new women's head and the

---

[2] For further background on gender and the political economy of Huaili in the 1980s, see Judd (1994).

"two studies, two competitions" initiative; and then it lapsed into a period of little activity apart from monitoring compliance with the birth planning policy. Huaili demonstrated within itself both the possibilities of various initiatives when actively pursued and the fragility of the work and organization.

THE STUDY

The study described here took form during the process of fieldwork, in response to and in discussion with women in Huaili and in the women's movement both there and elsewhere in Shandong. My initial purpose had been broadly to explore the implications of decollectivization and the reemergence of a household-based economy for life in rural China. This necessarily included both women and men and required an understanding of gender relations and the changes that they were undergoing. There was never any question about whether I would work and talk with the men—they were the leaders in each community and active in the outer domain, including interactions with foreigners. From the beginning, I made a point of ensuring that I also worked and spoke with women. I sought out women involved in woman-work or who were active in the outer domain in any other way (such as teachers and former teachers, successful entrepreneurs, medics, and midwives), and I ensured that the diversity of women's household and working situations was represented in my household samples. I also tried to recruit women (as well as men) as research collaborators in each village, and was usually able to do so. I did, of course, have to be officially accompanied in each village and, since this often involved sharing a room, my hosts often found it most convenient to turn to the Women's Federation for a companion to share both living arrangements and daily fieldwork. These women were not only indispensable with the planned schedule of household and key informant interviews, but they also allowed me an insight into their own world of woman-work at township, county, and provincial levels.

A significant element of this study is that it includes both systematic data on women derived from household samples and an in-depth longitudinal examination of the women's movement as it unfolded in and around Huaili. The data regarding women in Huaili has allowed me to look systematically at issues such as women's literacy, education, and employment, and to explore the relation of the women's movement's initiatives to changes in the local political economy and in women's activities.

The longitudinal study of the women's movement began in 1988 with visits to households in which women had been conspicuously successful in the mid-1980s, and with inquiries about the context for this provided by the "courtyard economy" initiative. This was essentially an effort to increase incomes by maximizing the use of two under-utilized resources—women's labor and the space within courtyards. This built upon women's traditional association with the inner domain of courtyards and their long-standing participation in activities such as raising domestic animals, but sought to promote this more widely and on a very much more intensive level in an effort to increase household income significantly. There were some additional implications of this initiative, including strengthening organized ties between women and promoting training in new skills. Women at the grass roots of Women's Federation staff and women within Huaili struggled to find promising economic avenues for women in their community and to organize ways for more women to benefit from these, as they were newly called upon to generate local economic development programs for women.

Local efforts such as this provided the ground from which the Women's Federations proposed their national initiative under the rubric of the "two studies, two competitions" activities (*shuangxue shuangbi huodong*) from 1989. This was referred to as a set of "activities" (*huodong*), in order to distinguish it from earlier mobilizational movements (*yundong*), as part of a general move by the state to retreat from mobilization. Nevertheless, the "two studies," as I will abbreviate it here, did have some mobilizational elements in that it was organized by the official Women's Federations on behalf of the state. It differed from earlier movements in being more voluntary in nature. The Women's Federations sought and where possible reported very high participation rates, but the new strategy was to induce women to participate by offering the prospect of increased income rather than relying (solely) upon administrative or mobilizational recruitment.

The phrase "two studies, two competitions" is a conventionally compressed way of referring to a program literally consisting of four elements: adult basic education (*xue wenhua*); practical technical training (*xue jishu*) intended to generate income very quickly; competition among local women in achieving economic success and gaining recognition (*bi chengji*); and through that economic success, competition in making social contributions (*bi gongxian*). The core of the program, especially as it began, was the effort to increase rural women's income through providing short-term training oriented toward the market economy. The remainder of the program revolved around that element.

In 1989 Huaili showed considerable evidence of the courtyard economy from which the "two studies" grew. This was the year I began to hear the distinctive discourse associated with the new activities, the argument that the decisive obstacle was the low quality of women. In this year, also, I first formulated the idea to look not only at the official women's movement, but also at elements of the women's movement emerging beyond official limits.

In 1990, in addition to following developments in Huaili, I began exploring at the fringes of the official women's movement in three Shandong cities—Jinan, Qingdao, and Jining—by meeting in discussion groups and individually with a selection of members of professional groups and study groups of several kinds and associations for the advancement of women. Here, too, issues of quality and discourse regarding it emerged as prominent concerns. Quality was not only an issue for rural women, but also one for women in privileged levels of government and the professions.

In 1992, when I returned to Huaili again, I found it at a peak of activity in the "two studies." This was partly a matter of the initiative by this time being vigorously implemented, and partly a matter of Huaili enjoying the activity of an unusually effective "women's head" (*funü zhuren*). The women's heads (village women's leaders) in Huaili during these years were, as one might expect, selected from among the more capable and well-connected women in the village, and these women were also the ones most likely to leave for attractive opportunities elsewhere. By 1992, this was the third occupant of the position I had met, and she, too, would soon leave. While still there, she effectively organized women to participate in market-oriented activities and to join in the official competitions of the "two studies." By this time, I was primarily focused upon understanding that initiative in practice, and what it meant for the grassroots women's movement. I continued to visit households systematically, updating material on households visited in the past and adding to the number of households in the study; and I continued to trace developments in the lives of women activists and models of market success.

In addition, I spent a considerable amount of time perusing local records and documents of the women's movement at each level from village through township to county. I had read some of these before, but record keeping for the "two studies" had resulted in an increase in records at village and township levels, and these were extensively made available. The county Women's Federation also granted me access to a considerable quantity of files and reports covering their work in general, and especially material related to the "two studies." I supplemented these with published material in the internal publications of the national and provincial Women's Federations, *Zhongguo fuyun* (*The Chinese Women's Movement*) and *Funü gongzuo* (*Woman-work*), both of which were initially provided to me by members of the Women's Federation and to which I later subscribed. During these years, I also reviewed a range of more readily accessible Chinese publications.

On each of the previous visits I had spent some time with women from higher levels of the Women's Federations—province, prefecture, and county—but beginning with this visit I began to work more closely with women at the county level, in order to contextualize Huaili and to have a better sense of the support available from this crucial local level of the state to women working at the grass roots. In addition to reviewing documents, I spoke extensively with several women in the county Women's Federation, in addition to working with those who sometimes accompanied me in the field.

In 1995 I went again to Ling County and Huaili, primarily to pursue the "two studies" but also to explore broader aspects of the women's movement. By this time, the five years initially envisioned for the "two studies" had concluded (1989–94), and a revised second phase had been launched. The new phase had moved from literacy to higher levels of technical training and from small-scale local projects to integration into local economic development programs. The local plan here was for large-scale production of chickens for export to Southeast Asia, and women were being trained through women's classes in the Rural Correspondence College (*Zhongguo nongcun zhifu jishu hanshou daxue* or *Nonghanda*) to participate in this endeavor. Huaili was not, however, a key point in this project, and the focus of its woman-work had shifted toward implementation of the state's birth planning policy. Again in 1995, I visited households, interviewed participants in the women's movement at various levels, and reviewed documents.

The result of this work has been, I believe, a relatively detailed pic-

ture of the local work of the women's movement, and one that is eth-
nographically situated. It remains an outsider's view and one that is
necessarily limited by that perspective. From the point of view of feminist methodology, it is essential to be fully a participant in the feminist
practices in question to be able to know about them and to be able to
represent them adequately to others. Such a method was never possible
in this study. I have attempted to break through the differences that
separate my own life from those of women in China, but the differences
remain. I have lived in China, as a student from 1974 to 1977, and I have
returned on a roughly yearly basis from 1986 to 1997, in most cases either to conduct academic field research or to participate in gender
analysis and women-in-development work. As a Canadian feminist I
also participated in 1995 in Beijing in both the official United Nations
Fourth World Conference on Women and the NGO Forum. These various ways of being in China all allowed me some interaction with Chinese women and some knowledge of their lives, but the conditions of
my own life were always different—in culture, in middle-class privilege,
and in the work of being an anthropologist.

That this work could be done at all is due to the Chinese women
who helped me understand their lives and work—from the outside.
Those with whom I had more contact knew that I had a life elsewhere
that included feminist action, but I was necessarily outside, by definition as a foreigner, and as a foreigner I could not directly participate in
the women's movement in China. I could not do so because I was tran-
sient in China, but also because it would have been a form of foreign
meddling. China is adamant about keeping foreigners outside (even
when they are inside), and this extends also to the women's movement.
Long-time residents in China and those engaged in the growing number
of internationally supported development projects for women within
China are able to enter more than others into these processes, but the
difference remains real. Learning to live the status of outsider is part of
learning to live in China as someone from elsewhere.

Being outside, there is much that I cannot know about how the Chinese women's movement works from the inside. Consequently, there is
much that remains for Chinese women to tell the rest of the world
about their own movements at the grass roots in the countryside. One
reason I undertook to write this book, despite these obstacles, is that
there is little detailed firsthand material available outside China about
this work, especially at the village level. There is an additional advan-

tage in that this material can be connected with earlier ethnographic work on the same community (Judd 1994), with complementary material added here. Imperfect and provisional as it must be, this account can nevertheless aim to add to international understanding of the grassroots women's movement in China.

Being outside the Chinese women's movement has not meant that it has remained outside me, or that my thoughts have not entered this account. There is no easy separation possible between "here" and "there." I am not attempting and do not claim any form of unrealizable objectivity. However, I do take an ultimately modernist standpoint (see Wolf 1992) and have aimed for an account that approaches the "reality" in and through which these women live their lives. I have also sought a critical perspective on myself as the one perceiving and examining this constructed reality, although this book remains firmly focused on the women of Shandong. There is certainly an implicit assumption here that change in the interests of women (in China, Canada, and everywhere else) is a social good, and that organized action toward this goal can be effective. I also depart from a vision of such change that values it only if it includes all women, especially those who are confronted with multiple barriers and are most vulnerable. I will generally avoid the term "feminism," since its usual understanding in China is that it is a Western construct that privileges middle-class women and market-based concepts of equality. There are important reasons for debating what feminism or a more broadly conceived women's movement might or should be, and I have previously attempted to explore this question (see Judd 1995). For present purposes, I will depart from the particularities of the women's movement in Huaili and elsewhere in Shandong. My preoccupation in the pages that follow is not with whether the women's movement is a good thing, but with how it is conceptualized and acted upon, and with the details of local and particular strategies for change.

The research reported here was conducted under the highly public circumstances characteristic of research in China. It was all done openly and through official channels. All involved knew that they were part of a research project conducted by a foreign academic and that the results would be published. Moreover, everyone was aware of the official people accompanying me during the household visits and interviews. The fact of being part of a foreign research project may well have been less constraining than the knowledge that the material presented

was also part of the local record of the fieldwork. Under these conditions it is not possible to offer anonymity or confidentiality, nor would
it be expected. Nevertheless, I have slightly obscured the location of the
community and the identities of the people; no real names are used, except where citing publications; and I have presented no more about individuals than is entirely public. I did not seek to evade the constraints
put upon me, or to gain privileged access to private or public material.

THE WOMEN'S MOVEMENT

The women's movement in China has a very different shape from that
familiar to readers in the West. Since the establishment of the People's
Republic in 1949, it has been dominated by the institution of an official
women's movement, known as the Women's Federations. These had
first been established in the border regions administered by the Communist Party prior to 1949, became national first as the All-China
Democratic Women's Federation and, since 1957, as the All-China
Women's Federation. This organizational structure, with a lapse during
the Cultural Revolution, has continued with only limited changes to
the present.

The Women's Federations are a "mass organization" in classical
Marxist-Leninist terms, a transmission belt through which the Communist Party is able to reach a particular constituency of the people, in
this case women. It is paralleled by similar organizations for youth and
for industrial workers. The mass organizations are attached to the Party
rather than the government and, although they are in some respects (for
example, financially) in a weaker position than government departments, they are a component of the state as understood here, that is, as
the ruling structure including Party, government, armed forces, and all
institutions connected with those elements.[3]

Individuals do not join the Women's Federations, but all women are
at least nominally considered to fall within its constituency. In practice, women workers are reached through the mass organization for
workers (the trade unions) and, until recently, women in government

[3] The Women's Federations have not been entirely happy with their status on the
margins of state power. Some staff have argued that it would be better for the
Women's Federations to enjoy the advantages of being a government department.
More recently the predominant approach has been to seek to define the Women's
Federations as "non-governmental organizations" (NGOs) for the purpose of receiv-
ing international aid and forming ties with international NGOs.

offices were not targeted. The Women's Federations have very largely addressed questions of reaching rural women, and the majority of their personnel are engaged in that work.

There are several administrative tiers of the Women's Federations, paralleling the national administrative structure: national, provincial, prefectural/municipal, county, and town/township. Although there is a framework for leadership between these levels, the Women's Federation at each level is under the authority of the Party Committee at its own level. There is nothing exceptional about this administrative arrangement in China, but it is worth noting because it means that each Women's Federation is tightly linked with the state at its own level, and that the Women's Federation structure is not autonomous.

The mandate of the Women's Federations is to mobilize women as a whole to pursue the policies of the Party, and also to represent and pursue the interests of women. Priority has historically been given to mobilization for the Party's programs that, as socialist ones, can be construed as including the liberation of women as a goal, so working for the Party and for women are therefore fundamentally compatible. In practice, a considerable amount of the work of the Women's Federations has revolved around working toward general societal goals, such as economic development, rather than working on women's specific issues. Since the Women's Federations have very limited personnel and funds, their incorporation into the general work of the state results in a significant reduction in the resources available for work in the interests of women. Nevertheless, the existence of this structure provides a publicly funded national framework for women, and one that is historically well established.

The work of the Women's Federations is conducted by professional staff, who are assigned to work in the Women's Federations through the usual mechanisms of staff assignment in the civil service. That is, women do not become Women's Federation staff through a commitment to or activism on women's issues, but are assigned to this work, and can be transferred in or out of the Women's Federations. The staff commonly do have a commitment to woman-work, although there is a constant need for orienting the flow of new staff, who may not have given much consideration to this work prior to their job assignments. There is a large absolute number of Women's Federation staff, simply because a Women's Federation is part of the state structure at every level. This can be deceptive, however, since by the mid-1990s (following a general reduction in the civil service) a county might well have only six Women's Federation staff and each township only one or two. Since Women's Federation staff commonly have other work to do as well, especially at the township level, the human resources are scarce. Although the framework is very thin, it reaches through the entire administrative structure, formally terminating at the town/township. Beyond that point, connections are made with village women's heads (funü zhuren), who are outside the Women's Federations but linked with them.

For the most part there has been little in the way of an independent women's movement, since the ground for legitimately organizing in the interest of women was occupied by the official women's movement. Indeed, the women's movement in China is largely seen as the profession of those who do woman-work, that is, women in or connected with the Women's Federations. Women could pursue their individual or household-oriented strategies, which might include courting appointment as women's head, but rural women have rarely organized as women apart from the official channels.

Since the 1980s a more independent women's movement has emerged in the cities—in women's studies circles in universities, in newly formed non-governmental organizations, and in development work. Where these groups have moved to develop a presence in the countryside, they have generally done so in connection with the ready-made framework of the official movement. This has not been a difficult link to make, since the Women's Federations themselves have been experiencing a revitalization and have been eager to extend their scope beyond traditional channels by finding new allies and new modes of organizing.

In part this book is concerned with the strategies of the Women's Federations, but it is actually more concerned with what is happening at the margins of the official women's movement, where that movement intersects with the lives of women charting their courses through a society in transition.

2

The Meanings of Quality

Quality has emerged in this study as the crux of the contemporary women's movement in rural China. The concept of quality appears concretely in programs and in discourse about "raising quality" (*tigao suzhi*) or "developing talent" (*chengcai*), and it does so with a myriad of nuances and implications. In unraveling the multiplicity of meanings attached to quality and strategies to develop it, it will become apparent how quality can become a goal that captures a diversity of intents and visions.

Much of this discussion will involve conceptualizations of women's economic roles and of development. However, it is important to see the political economy in the context of a broader discussion about women's agency. Here the decisive element of the strategy is that it places priority upon qualities internal to women. In its broadest sense, the strategy is one of strengthening women so that they are more effectively able to change their own lives. There are resonances here with international discourse on the empowerment of women, and comparable ambiguities about what this means and how it might be realized.

SPIRITUAL CIVILIZATION

Just what is meant or implied by "raising women's quality" depends, in part, upon the level at which the statement is made and the audience to which it is directed. As is common practice in China, statements at the highest national level are often intentionally broad and imprecise, in order to allow later, more specific interpretations and applications to be localized and diverse. At the most general level, the proposals for women are part of the still larger project of improving the quality of the entire Chinese nation. As programmatically expressed for women at the time when this direction was emerging, the project included what was described as spiritual as well as material civilization:

Socialism does not only aim to realize material prosperity, but also to achieve all-around social progress. Our basic direction is to grasp socialist material civilization and spiritual civilization [*jingshen wenming*] together. The construction of spiritual civilization ultimately demands raising the quality of the entire nation, to develop the new socialist person with ideals, morality, education, and discipline. Do not imagine that a nation without strong spiritual pillars can stand on its own feet among the world's nations. We must deeply absorb the diverse lessons of the past few years in the construction of material civilization and spiritual civilization and, at the same time as we energetically develop material civilization, we must conscientiously grasp the construction of spiritual civilization. Developing education and science is a hundred-year strategy that has great and far-reaching significance for raising society's forces of production and the nation's quality. (Jiang Zemin 1989)

In statements such as this, a continuing focus upon national development is linked with a conception of human development phrased in terms open to wider interpretation.

There are several strands of living tradition in China, each of which serves to resonate with and to reinforce this wider, more open sense of quality. The classical Confucian tradition survives powerfully in concepts of humans as malleable and educable that have persisted and been embodied in modern initiatives for education. The classical view was one that saw persons as moral and political beings, and was not narrowly concerned with technical education (Munro 1977). This approach intersected in the mid-twentieth century with Marxist interpretations of human nature as requiring well-rounded and creative interaction with the material world. These strands fused within the Chinese revolutionary tradition to create practices in which the politically engaged were constantly called upon to strive for higher levels of self-cultivation, sometimes in connection with practices of criticism and self-criticism in rectification campaigns, but also and always as a continuing call for improvement (see Liu Shaoqi 1980 [1939]). The strong emphasis on inner change in the Chinese revolutionary tradition may well have been reinforced by the impact of a formative history in which the revolutionary movement was dependent upon widely dispersed personnel throughout the villages of various north China bases. Individual activists were then called upon to internalize a mode of thought that would allow them to work toward a central goal even when quite isolated (Compton 1966 [1952]).

In contemporary discourse, it has been possible to draw upon elements of these traditions to legitimize current policy directions, implicitly or explicitly. The peculiar requirement that contemporary policy be described as "socialist" leads to complex and selective reference to the Marxist tradition, including its humanistic aspect. If the development of human values is fundamental to socialism, then priority placed upon educating people is a legitimate component of contemporary Chinese policies (see Bao Xinjian 1995). This position could be elaborated in a variety of different directions. The one emphasized in current policy is to see the development of people in an educational sense, especially in science and technology, as a critical element in the development of the forces of production, since the most important force of production is people (see, for example, Yao Zhongda 1984; Jiang Zemin 1989; and Bao Xinjian 1995). The development of the forces of production is a characteristic priority of reform interpretations of socialism in China, in contrast with the earlier, more radical emphasis on transforming the relations of production. By inserting the popular, humanistic aspect of the transformative socialist vision into the reformist strategy of quantitative economic development, the distinction between the two directions is blurred. The resulting national policy on human development retains a strong emphasis on material and specifically economic factors, while capturing the possibility of nurturing quality in other senses as well.

WOMEN'S QUALITY

The policies of the official women's movement for developing women's quality fit neatly into this framework (see Liang Xuguang 1989). Apart from observing that raising women's quality is necessarily part of raising the quality of the nation itself, and that this also makes a contribution through families and child rearing, the Women's Federations have argued that raising women's quality will assist women in pursuing their rights and interests and in achieving gender equality (see Huang Qicao 1993: 17). Indeed, the Women's Federations have pursued a diverse range of policies along these lines. At the more traditional end this has included continuing promotion of harmonious families through the "five-good families" (wuhao jiating) program and training in household management and childcare.

The women's movement has more directly addressed issues of rights and interests and of equality through its efforts to promote women's success in achieving political positions, either through elections or through developing pools of women for recommendation to appointed official positions. Both because the state remains extremely powerful in Chinese society, and because the official women's movement is still more oriented toward and better connected with the state than with the market, the issue of women's political participation has been one of the major priorities of the women's movement in recent years. The intensity with which this issue has been pursued in the women's movement is also a result of the significant erosion of women's political positions in the early years of the reform era, and the determination of women involved in the state sector to reverse that direction. Much of the focus has been upon breakthroughs at higher levels, in an effort to open significant levels of state power to women, but there have been similar efforts at every level down to the administrative village.

Work to promote women's political participation has referred not only to principles of women's rights and interests and of gender equality, but it has also relied upon arguments that women are qualified to hold political or official positions. Women's Federations at various levels have developed "talent pools" (*rencai ku*) of women suitable for recommendation for official position or for promotion within the official hierarchy. The object here has been to increase the numbers of women in official positions, both at entry level (with an eye on the future) and at influential levels (for immediate political support), as soon as possible. Efforts in these directions have emphasized locating and supporting women qualified for such positions and developing programs that give public recognition to successful women—a major purpose of competitions—in order to increase social perceptions of women as well qualified.

There has also been a major effort to improve the qualifications of women targeted for official responsibilities. Staff of the Women's Federations and other women viewed as having potential are provided with short-term professional development sessions. For its own staff, the Women's Federations can facilitate training in a range of programs of varying length, both directly relevant to woman-work or indirectly relevant through professional preparation (for example, in law), and this is now strongly encouraged. The Women's Federations themselves also provide a period of professional opportunity and nurturance, since many of their staff are subsequently transferred to government offices. Their period of work in the Women's Federations helps prepare them for other work—since so much of Women's Federation work is general political work—and introduces them to the women's movement and its ideas in a practical way. As one long-time head of the Ling County Women's Federation, who would herself be transferred to another senior post, has argued, women trained in the Women's Federations have to be very capable since they are called upon to do so much with almost no resources. In addition, they work (especially at the lower administrative levels) in conditions of isolation and limited external support that require women of strong inner resources. Both the work experience and the added consciousness regarding women's issues that derive from this work are included within the framework of increasing women's quality and developing talent. These initiatives together comprise a concerted strategy for improving the inner quality of women already in, or candidates for, official post within and beyond the Women's Federations.

Similar strategies are advocated for women in general, and the various strategies discussed in the following chapters each attempt in one or more specific ways to increase women's inner qualities. This is a considered and explicitly articulated position held by women in senior positions in the Women's Federations who have firsthand familiarity with alternative international approaches focusing on external factors, such as the widely promoted initiatives to provide microcredit for poor women. Although the Women's Federations do attempt to increase funds available to women—by interceding with banks on behalf of larger borrowers and by encouraging successful women entrepreneurs to make small loans to other women—this has not been their chosen focus. One reason for this is a preference for larger projects and for positioning women well in relation to those. Another reason is a decision to pursue organized and collective solutions based on women's organizations, in preference to the individual or household orientation of microcredit. But a major element is a considered preference for using funds for internal factors, principally general and technical education.

This is explicitly a question of locating women more favorably in terms of the development of the forces of production, in which the main driving force is now science and technology. The argument is that women should become more educated or skilled in those areas, and also that women should be encouraged to recognize the importance of science and technology and shift their individual and collective priorities accordingly. As expressed to individual rural women, the priority is practical technical training; as expressed to women staff and those they reach and mobilize as activists (*gugan*), the priority is changing the strategic viewpoint of the women's movement toward promoting women as a force in science and technology, including the basic applied technologies of agriculture and other rural endeavors.

The object is to allocate the scarce resources the Women's Federations can access to provide a large number of women with the types of knowledge that will provide an economic base upon which they can help themselves and change their lives. It seems to be implicitly understood that whatever the women's movement might be able to accomplish in changing external conditions, women will continue to require exceptional internal resources. Here the promotion of quality connects with another initiative, the nurturing of what is called the "four selfs" (sizi): self-respect (zizun), self-confidence (zixin), self-reliance (zili) and self-strength (ziqiang).

Further, the women's movement aims to use the promotion and recognition of women's quality to raise women's social and political status, that is, to intervene in the external world by first changing the internal world. In this case, the object is to change the internal world of others by increasing their recognition of women's quality. The argument is that increasing women's quality will win respect for women and thereby raise women's social status. That proposition can be raised in a general theoretical context (Bai Lijun 1991: 25), or it can appear in practical work in a more concrete manifestation, as I encountered it in Ling County. There the same goal and strategy for attaining it was presented by the county Women's Federation, but it was operationalized in the language of exchange value—women would have higher status where they produced more value (jiazhi), as measured directly through the value of their economic products. Indeed, such measures were used in the "two studies, two competitions" and served as a basis for the selection of winners in competitions and of women models more generally.

The women's movement was responding here to arguments that women were at a disadvantage because they play less of an economic role in the outer domain, and were economically dependent upon men who contributed more in measurable exchange value, both to society at large and to their households. Despite considerable change and the increased visibility and remuneration of women's work in the outer domain since the 1950s, this disadvantage has remained real. Efforts to make women's contribution more visible, as well as to increase value generated by women, may serve to address this rationale for gender differences. The cross-cultural evidence, however, suggests that while economic dependence or lack of visibility and remuneration for women's work are indeed disadvantageous for women's status, it does not necessarily follow that larger or more visible contributions on the part of women result in women's liberation. At this point, the women's movement in China is raising the issue of recognizing the contribution of women's work, and has remained relatively quiet on the subject of the control of the products of women's labor or of other aspects of economic processes.

Nevertheless, a large part of the concrete discussion and action regarding women's quality is directly related to economic matters, especially since the practical work of increasing women's quality in the countryside primarily consists of efforts to provide economically useful education and training. The focus on economic factors in determining women's status is consistent with long-standing orthodoxy in the Marxist tradition. At this point, there is less emphasis than in earlier decades on increasing women's participation in work in the outer domain, since women have for the most part already entered the public workforce. The focus instead is upon the quality of women's labor power, and upon the extent and character of their participation in the market economy.

The quality of women's labor power has become an issue in the countryside, as agricultural labor has been feminized (see Judd 1994). As men leave agriculture for more attractive work, women have been doing as much as 65% of the agricultural work, nationally and in Shandong, and the nation's agricultural productivity has become dependent on women's work. Concern has been expressed within China that women, who were not traditionally responsible for agriculture, may not be capable of doing this work, and that yields may therefore decrease (Davin 1998). Arguments that investing in the improvement of women's quality would contribute to significant national gains in agriculture have been used by the women's movement to mobilize state support and access state resources for women, principally through the "two studies."

Whether women's increasing involvement in agriculture is advantageous for women is a complex issue that will be addressed from several perspectives in the following pages. It is a key element in current debates within China as well as internationally. One point of view, influential within the Chinese women's movement, holds that this is an important new departure for women, which provides rural women with an opportunity to play a major role in the rural economy and, by extension, in rural society. It follows from this perspective that women's roles in agriculture should be supported and that women should be enabled to modernize agriculture. Another point of view, also articulated in China, finds the unremunerative and low-status work in agriculture much less desirable for women, and identifies avenues for departure from agriculture and from the countryside as more liberating for rural women.[1] From either perspective, the future of the majority of women who remain in the countryside is a major concern.

Rural women are still typically at a disadvantage in literacy, education, and training (see Chapter 3). Despite considerable growth in access to education in recent decades, China remains far behind the more rapidly developing Asian countries in its educational infrastructure (Mingat 1998), and women in the countryside have especially limited access to education. While there are programs in effect designed to make nine years of schooling (lower middle school graduation) universal, and while these will have an important long-term impact, there are presently very large numbers of adult women, including young adult women, who have had very much less education. For this reason, the women's movement strategies started with literacy and simple practical training geared toward income-generation. By the mid-1990s, there was increasing emphasis on more sustained technical education for women who already had a lower middle school education but, in either case, the purpose has been to reach women in their economically productive years who have had limited previous access to education and training.

Systematically addressing this issue by organizing rural women for literacy, education, and training has been conceptualized by the Women's Federations as a major component in their effort to raise women's quality. This is a less positive manner of expression than the comparable phrase of "developing women's talent," which is applied to women with more education. Women's Federation staff speak and write about raising the quality of rural women in communications with each other and in addressing policymakers or outsiders such as myself, but they do not speak to the rural women themselves in those terms. The underlying proposition—one that is also spoken explicitly in informal or private

---

[1] Both points of view and some additional material directly relevant to this study have been translated and published in Judd (1999).

contexts—is that the low quality of rural women is a problem that needs to be corrected. It would not be acceptable, or effective, to approach rural women in those terms. Instead, the educational opportunities are offered and rural women are encouraged to avail themselves of them in order to acquire immediately useful practical skills that will increase income. The arguments made are almost entirely economic ones and—in contrast with earlier mobilizational campaigns directed toward meeting specific production or infrastructure targets—are phrased overwhelmingly in terms of cash income.

This is consistent and compatible with the closely connected goal of developing women's participation in the new market economy. In part, this may be viewed as a contemporary variation that has continuities with premodern practices of pursuing national development through use of women's labor, for example, in the High Qing promotion of women's work in spinning and weaving (Mann 1997) or in late Qing cotton textile production (Walker 1993). The utilization of women's labor may well be valuable to national development and significant in the emergence of modern economies (Fox-Genovese and Genovese 1983), but it does not necessarily result in reduction of gender inequities. Contemporary discourse on development does tend to assume that involvement of women in development, as in women-in-development (WID) or gender-and-development (GAD) programs, will be benevolent and result in improvements for women, although this assumption has not received the close critical examination it requires (Walker 1993; Porter and Judd 2000).

The official women's movement is attempting what is, in effect, a domestic Chinese variant of gender-and-development. There is a hopefulness in the approach that indicates that the women's movement envisions market-oriented development as beneficial, or at least potentially beneficial, to women, provided that they can fully participate in it. In the contemporary Chinese context, in which the market is valued as the vehicle through which the Chinese people and nation will be able to realize hopes for prosperity and stature, the women's movement is determined that women not be left outside the sphere of market activity. There are tangible risks attached to the possibility of gender-based exclusion from the now hyper-masculinized sphere of market activity (Rofel 1999: 210). Such an exclusion would leave women structurally disadvantaged in an economy that is not simply material, but is located at the heart of current political culture and its discourse of modernity.

The strategic object is therefore a path of development in which women and the advancement of women's interests are intrinsically connected with the market development process.

QUALITY IN THE MARKETPLACE

The initiative for improving women's quality can be understood when seen within this framework. The perspective encompasses both the specifics of efforts in literacy, education, training, and market activity, and also the shift in consciousness toward market-oriented strategies for change on the part of women, individually and collectively, that the women's movement now advocates as part of improving its own quality and suitability as an agent of change.[2]

This direction involves much more than a slight adaptation of the previous emphasis on economic production to the new circumstances. The women's movement has examined the implications of the shift in political economy and devised a correspondingly reformed program for women. The expression of this vision has been widespread in China, in the official women's movement and beyond it in the unofficial women's movement as well (see Li Xiaojiang 1989), but perhaps would be best expressed here in the local words of a leader of the Dezhou Women's Federation:

> The development of the commodity economy with an individual and dispersed mode of production opens a large-scale and specialized new realm of production, and for women opens a vast area for the development of talent. On the basis of their own particular strengths, women can consciously select production projects that suit themselves—those who can plant will plant, those who can raise animals will raise animals, those who can process materials will process materials. Each will do what she is able to do and each will receive accordingly. This will change the previous pattern of passively doing the work assigned, and only working on the collective land, and will give a deeper recognition

[2]It appears likely that Western and Japanese ideas regarding management have influenced current ideas regarding quality in the Chinese women's movement, although I have not been able to trace the specific lines of transmission. Western management ideas have been widely transmitted in China since the 1980s, and management skills are included in staff training programs run by the Women's Federations. Some indications of probable influences can be found in elements of the English-language literature (Fan 1998; Ng 1998; Jenner et al. 1998; Korabik 1993; Rofel 1999: 202, 263).

of one's own value and one's own ability—labor activism will reach a new high tide. (Yang Yu'e 1988: 5)

In this early statement, the commitment to production is retained, but it is located within a decisively different economic context, one that led the writer directly to her subsequent point that, "The era of reform is the era of competition; the characteristic of the commodity economy is competition" (Yang Yu'e 1988: 6). It is this feature of the reform era that provides a decisive new meaning for quality. Quality becomes those attributes and abilities that enable women to compete in the marketplace, individually or collectively.

The market is the most prominent feature of China's reform era socioeconomic formation. The orthodox position within China is that China remains "socialist" in that its main means of production are still publicly owned. Although this has become less strictly the case over time, it can be argued that the transition away from socialism in China has been characterized less by privatization than by the resurgence of competition (Pei Xiaolin 1998: 85).[3] This is precisely the formulation that appears in the contemporary Chinese women's movement. The state sector remains primary, and the activities in which women are urged to compete are largely connected with the state sector and with state plans. But the recommodification of labor power has placed market-based competition at the heart of the reform era's concept of being human. To the significant extent that the women's movement has accepted and acted upon this concept, recommodification has appeared internally in the gendered construct of women now advocated for success in the market economy.

This is not to suggest that earlier concepts of self-cultivation, either Confucian or Marxist-Leninist, have disappeared. There are strong traces of both in the current synthesis of quality, but they are subsumed within the commodified and competitive vision of quality that is presented as the new goal for personal and collective attainment. This vision is presented most strongly in efforts directed within the women's movement to alter its conception of its own direction. Calls for "each level of the Women's Federation ceaselessly to reform modes of thought and activity unsuited to the market economy" (Zhao Yulan 1994a: 11) have been continually reiterated. The critical element is to remake the

---

[3] The prevalence and intensity of competition in China's variant of capitalism is an important element in the larger context. See Gates (1996).

women's movement itself, since it is through its official organizational network that women in general are to be reached. Messages directed toward ordinary rural women tend to focus on the direct economic benefits of participation in promoted activities, but it is the organizers who are called upon to revise their views. They are no longer to reject involvement in the market or market-linked behaviors as being capitalist, or to adhere only to traditional mobilizational approaches. Instead, the market is to be embraced and quality is to be encouraged and measured through direct quantitative success in market competition.

At this point the concept of quality experiences a fundamental slip: "By reducing any quality to quantity, myth economizes intelligence; it understands reality more cheaply" (Barthes 1973: 153). In the process of constructing quality internally in terms of quantitative exchange value, the possibility of fundamentally different conceptions of what quality might be or what it might be for are erased. At the same time, the market provides a powerfully embracing context that naturalizes quantification and domesticates all thought of quality within its own confining frame (see Taussig 1992: 44–45).

The market is the defining context of the new initiatives of the 1990s, which are strongly marked by the promotion of competition in a variety of modes. It is most obviously prominent in the "two studies, two competitions," but also appears in broader and quite different organizational initiatives designed to give recognition and promote the success of women within and beyond the women's movement (see Chapters 6 and 7). The underlying premise behind these activities is that women's (and men's) value can be assessed quantitatively in the marketplace. This approach has the merit of using a clear standard that is visible and highly valued in contemporary Chinese (and international) society. It also benefits from the magical ability of exchange value to convert qualitatively dissimilar values into comparable units. One of the operations accomplished thereby is comparison between the values of women's and men's work. Despite the relative disadvantage and devaluing of women's work in the economy, the strategy is nevertheless one of using the recognized "gender-blind" mechanisms of economics to reveal the value of women's work. Accomplishing this has required that women increase their participation, not simply in work, but in work that conspicuously produces cash income.

None of the recommended activities has involved direct competition between women and men. Even in the diffuse sense in which everyone is competing in a common marketplace, expectations are geared to an expanding market in which women can add to household and community income without competing directly with men. This works also because the labor and products are somewhat different, and women remain concentrated in the less preferred and less remunerative areas of the economy (agriculture, small-scale craft production, and petty trade), where they do not challenge men.

When competition is actively organized, it is competition among women designed to spur participants in general toward prosperity and to reward the most successful with public recognition and modest prizes. Public recognition may also be provided to the overall competition and to all its participants, and not only to the most successful individuals and groups. The use of specific competitions and awards is a strategic mechanism for generating recognition for women that can then enable women to compete more successfully in the broader marketplace. It is less the organized competitions as activities than the broad, underlying motif of competition in the market that is the significant departure and the keynote of these initiatives.

Even if one accepts the strategic shift toward the market and assesses the strategy within its own terms and context, difficulties emerge with a conceptualization of quality in terms of market competition, despite the efforts that are made to extend rewards and recognition broadly. This is not simply a question of unevenness in people's abilities, successes, and contributions, since even in its most radically egalitarian moments, these differences have been recognized in China and widely used, as in campaigns to emulate models. Most obviously, promotion of competitive conceptualizations of quality accentuates differences and the legitimacy accorded to differentiation. This is problematic for a women's movement that strives to improve life for all women, and especially so for women who are not well placed in the market, as is the case for the majority of rural women.

Even the question of whether promoting the advancement of women through increasing quality is or can be an effective development strategy is open to debate. The following chapters will examine this issue in several concrete dimensions. Here it may suffice to note that there have been cross-cultural indications of reservations about the economic value of increasing education for women when there is a surplus of educated people (Bourque and Warren 1987). While it can easily be argued that China has a need for more education and training, it also has enormous reserves of unemployed and underemployed people, many of whom are well qualified in a variety of ways. As one of the exceptional women entrepreneurs interviewed for Chapter 7 skeptically observed in commenting on this strategy, China does not have a shortage of qualified people. In this respect, China is actually indicative of a more general situation that obtains widely but that is easily obscured by the terms of prevailing discourse about quality. The problem—from the competitive perspective—is not that there is too little quality, but that there is too much. As Wallerstein has observed in another context, "since there is too much talent around, someone must decide who is talented and who is not. And this decision, when it is made among narrow ranges of difference, is a political decision" (Wallerstein 1988: 105). It is also a gendered decision.

3

GAD with Chinese Characteristics

The strategy of raising women's quality in the countryside is embedded in the women's movement program for mainstreaming women in local economic development, the "two studies, two competitions." This strategy is a fusion of initiatives from above to mobilize women to contribute to national economic development, and demands from below for improvement in economic conditions by and for rural women. The local initiatives and their partial incorporation into the mainstream of economic development planning are innovative, but their feasibility is dependent upon the extent to which the national program wins support at the highest levels of the state. Raising women's quality—and thereby increasing production and hastening rates of economic growth—has been key in persuading the state to support this program and its proponents, the official women's movement.

The "two studies" appears as a national program but has its origins in a variety of local experiments, including some in Dezhou Prefecture in the mid-1980s. The program also changed significantly in its early years in response to local developments. This is not simply a question of policy and its implementation, therefore, but a longitudinal process of organized social change manifested at several levels. Although national policy did not generate this strategy, it has been important in shaping local initiatives and in providing a framework within which the strategies of the women's movement have been developed, evaluated, and revised.

In this chapter I will briefly present the underlying economic rationale for the strategy and review the initiative for promoting the courtyard economy (*tingyuan jingji*) that immediately preceded it in some areas, and then became incorporated into the "two studies." This will be followed by a comprehensive review of the national strategy, its central elements, and their development through the period from the beginning of 1989 to the end of 1995 (also see Rai and Zhang 1994). The following chapters will thematically examine various aspects of this program in the particular context of Huaili and its environs.

MEN WORK AND WOMEN PLOUGH

The conventional division of labor between men and women in rural China was formerly expressed in the phrase, "men plough and women weave" (*nangeng nüzhi*). Whether women were as marginal to agricultural labor in the past as this phrase would suggest is questionable, but it is beyond doubt that women now comprise the majority of the agricultural labor force. Men are leaving back-breaking and unremunerative agricultural labor to enter more remunerative areas of the rural economy and to migrate to the cities, leaving an increasing amount of agricultural work to be done by women, who are less mobile in both occupational and geographic terms. This has given rise to a rephrasing of the former description, "men work and women plow" (*nangong nügeng*), using a term for work that designates male labor as non-agricultural.

In the view of Meng Xianfan (1993, 1995), the leading theorist discussing this trend in relation to women's status, the emergence of this new gender division of labor holds encouraging prospects for improvement in rural women's lives. It does so through enabling women who were previously underemployed due to the large amount of surplus labor in the countryside to become income earners. And, in contrast to the situation in which husband and wife are both working together in agriculture or any other household endeavor, in this clearly gendered division of labor women are independent. Women manage the crops and have an income identifiably produced by themselves that is separate from that of their husbands. On this basis Meng welcomes the increased involvement of women in agriculture, even (and perhaps especially) where accompanied by men's movement into other areas of the rural or urban economy. In a later and more theoretical paper, Meng (1995) refers to classical Marxist works and argues that through independently managing agriculture, women enter into more direct relations with the means of production than had been possible under the collective system, where the management was in the hands of a male team leader. They thereby become laborers for themselves as well as in themselves. In other words, release from the constraints of a patriarchal collective system into a small-scale market system is liberating for women, in this iconoclastic reworking of familiar Marxist texts.

There are some difficulties with this approach, especially in that it does not address women's continuing limited access to basic means of production, such as land (Judd 1994; Croll 1994), and in its uncritical embrace of the market. Meng's approach does, however, effectively express the reservations Chinese women have had regarding their disenfranchisement in the collective system. This rejection of collective patriarchy is found among both ordinary rural women and the official women's movement, and it may be a stronger source of their shared enthusiasm for the market than the more obvious pressure to follow the lead of state policy toward a "socialist market economy with Chinese characteristics."

Development of the agricultural sector has become markedly dependent upon women's work. There is some regional variation, because rates of male migration and movement into non-agricultural work are uneven, but estimates that women comprise 60–70% of the agricultural labor force were common by the 1990s, for the country as a whole and also for Shandong. Nationally, women were calculated to provide roughly two-thirds of China's agricultural labor power in 1995 (Han Baozhen 1995: 51), a figure representing 210 million women. On this basis, the Women's Federations have argued that China's agricultural development is dependent upon the effective utilization of women's potential.

The argument is further made that if agriculture is to modernize and to adjust to an increasingly market-oriented economy, women must be provided with the necessary education and skills to enable this transformation. Initially, the focus was upon literacy, and that continues to be a component of the strategy as a value in itself, as well as for economic reasons. But the purpose of education and training in this strategy is more directly related to rural economic development. Even where it includes adult basic education, there is invariably an element of practical or more systematic technical training. The need for providing such training for women has been exacerbated by low levels of state funding for the agricultural sector and the reduction in agricultural extension services that have occurred as part of the government's downsizing.[1] One study (cited in He Yupeng 1995: 110) reported that only 13.6% of rural women surveyed had received any formal agricultural training offered through governmental or non-governmental channels, although

[1] For some details on the lack of extension services and their reduction in the reform era, see Han Baozhen (1995: 53–54).

almost all strongly demanded such training. It also reported that 70.9% of the women attributed their lack of training to not having had the opportunity, and the study found this to be the result of both limited provision of training and the widespread practice of men preferentially accessing the training that was available.

One of the few remaining avenues for increasing agricultural production on China's dwindling supply of arable land is the use of improved agricultural techniques (Smil 1995). The importance of rural women as the people who will have to realize any technical gains in agriculture provides the basis for the Women's Federations' arguments that the state should invest in training and technical support for rural women. This is the straightforward rationale for the "two studies" strategy, and for the claims that the Women's Federations then make on the state for the resources to implement it.

The Women's Federations have not challenged the gendered division of labor that has placed rural women in this position. Indeed, if they did challenge it, they would not likely be able to influence the macroeconomic trends that are responsible for its emergence. In any event, the Women's Federations do not reject a gendered division of labor and their strategy is, instead, to concentrate upon improving conditions for women in those sectors where women predominate. The "two studies" most obviously tries to accomplish this for women involved in agricultural work through training and, less obviously but perhaps more importantly, through improving rural women's access to economic and political resources.

COURTYARD ECONOMY

Formally, the All-China Women's Federation initiated the "two studies" as a national program in January 1989. However, it had actually begun earlier in some localities, and had been preceded by other Women's Federation initiatives in rural economic development for women. One of the conceptually more interesting precedents was the initiative promoting what has been termed the "courtyard economy." This initiative was adopted early in Shandong and was important in Huaili. The courtyard economy initiative is also of national importance as an early approach that has been absorbed into the "two studies" strategy as a continuing component.

Courtyard production continues and supersedes what was earlier known as "sideline production" (fuye). In the collective era, while most of the land was worked in the collectives, small private plots (*ziliudi*) of usually .1 *mu* (1 *mu* equals 1/6 acre) for each person and the small area within each household's walled courtyard could be used for a household's own production. Typically vegetables were grown on the private plots, and domestic animals such as pigs and poultry were raised in the courtyard. The products of both could be consumed by the household or sold, subject to state regulations. It was sometimes also possible to do craft production within the household, provided no labor was hired and crafts were produced only with the labor of household members, but opportunities for this were limited during the collective era. Despite these restrictions, sideline production, especially courtyard pig-raising, was a major source of cash income for rural households.

Sideline production was predominantly the preserve of women, as had been the corresponding forms of household-based production prior to collectivization. Such work was readily compatible with the other domestic demands on women's time and did not violate the cultural norms that declared women's place to be in the home (*nüzhunei nanzhuwai*). Collectivization drew women into the public labor force, but less fully and on less favorable terms than for men. Women could and did compensate for this marginalization through their contributions in the home, where they not only provided unpaid labor in child rearing and domestic labor, but made a substantial and visible contribution to household income (see Wolf 1985: 104–6). In the reform period, when restrictions on production and commerce were rapidly lifted, the former sidelines became still more important in the rural economy, and women remained centrally involved in them.

The concept of courtyard economy refers most simply to household-based economic activities that take place in the inner space within the courtyard walls ubiquitous in rural China. Although hiring labor privately became legal early in the rural reform, courtyard production remains characterized as a form of production that uses a household's own labor. It is a potentially highly rational and efficient optimization of scarce land resources (by 1993 there was a national average of only 1.82 *mu* of arable land per person) and of surplus labor. Although all members of a household may be involved, and all have an interest in and benefit from the courtyard economy, this remains primarily women's sphere, if only because men have privileged access to a wider range of economic options beyond the courtyard walls. The dynamic that places women at the center of courtyard production is therefore similar to the one that places them at the center of reform era agriculture, but the courtyard economy is more diverse and remunerative.

There have been two main foci of interest regarding the courtyard economy in the reform era. Those who emphasize narrowly economic elements have concentrated their attention on the potential of the courtyard economy to use resources efficiently and to generate high rates of income growth for rural households. This literature does not address intrahousehold social relations or labor allocation and makes no mention of gender. This approach is evident in journals of economics and agricultural economics, and may represent a common view among policymakers.[2] Those who emphasize the role of women in the courtyard economy depart from the existing predominance of women in this sphere and discuss strategies for increasing women's activity in the courtyard economy and raising income levels, especially for women in poorer rural households, where the courtyard economy appears as a viable economic choice requiring only modest inputs. This literature is found primarily in general and internal (neibu) publications of the Women's Federations and is oriented toward practical work in the villages.[3]   A central principle of the "two studies" strategy is precisely to bring together approaches such as these, which are viewed as compatible but as having failed to come together. In the case of the courtyard economy, both approaches share a commitment to move from the earlier model of sideline production to a more large-scale, modern, and commoditized form of production that may remain based in a courtyard and may still rely wholly or primarily on familial labor, but that will move the household into the mainstream of the market economy. The result has already been seen in the flourishing of household-based enterprises and their contribution to household and social economic growth. Growth in this sector has been relatively positive for women, because women are often in a stronger position than men within the courtyard economy, and because women are also in a stronger position within their own household enterprises than in the outer domain (including collective enterprises).[4]

---

[2] See such journals as the academic digest in this field, *Nongye jingji*, and also *Zhongguo nongcun jingji* and *Nongye jingji wenti*.

[3] See, especially, the internal publication of the Shandong Women's Federation, *Funü gongzuo*.

[4] Women in Huaili were not enthusiastic about rural industry or about joining together in larger-scale enterprises outside the home. They saw these as inevitably male-dominated, in contrast to the greater autonomy they saw themselves being able

The result has been mushrooming growth in a sphere where women are and perceive themselves to be at a relative advantage, and where even the poorer rural women are not barred from independent entry (see Judd 1994). A strategy that favors the growth of this sector is one that can achieve economic growth on terms that benefit women. Specifically, it does this by generating opportunities to earn a cash income through work processes that women may be substantially able to control, to the extent that these are located within their own households. It is this potential that local organizers drew to my attention in the 1980s, and that contributes to the Women's Federations' continuing inclusion of the courtyard economy in its "two studies" policies.

THE "TWO STUDIES": THE EARLY CONCEPTION

By the time the "two studies" program was announced as a national program to begin in 1989, similar activities had been in place in at least some regions of China for several years. The areas of most extensive early activity were apparently the more agricultural regions, as the early focus had been primarily on agriculture, and leading activists in Shandong have indicated that the "two studies" program seems more appropriate for poorer areas. This is consistent with my own field data, which show the earliest and highest level of activity in the relatively poor area of Dezhou Prefecture (later Municipality). In this area Women's Federation promotion of the courtyard economy had begun by 1984, and Dezhou has consistently been one of the most active administrative areas in both the courtyard economy and the "two studies" since that time.[5] Early initiatives such as these provided the practical activist base upon which the national program could later be based.

As formally presented, however, the "two studies" strategy was a

---

to achieve in household enterprises. This is confirmed by my own observations of male predominance in the management of rural industry, even where the workforce has predominantly consisted of women, as in weaving. My observations in Shandong and elsewhere also confirm the leading role women can play in household enterprises, especially when these are not very large. (When large, husbands may play a larger role in management, especially in the external relations of supply and marketing.) Some comments from Women's Federation staff have also been skeptical about larger-scale organization of crafts even through Women's Federation channels, since these can be vulnerable to the imposition by export corporations of high production quotas and low wages. I am not in a position to comment on whether cooperatives could provide an effective alternative, but this choice did not appear to be available in these areas of Shandong.

[5] Dezhou has been repeatedly cited as a model or advanced unit.

product of national economic development policy as applied to rural women. This aspect of the official discourse is better understood as legitimating the strategy than as explaining it, but the national leadership has elaborated upon local initiatives in a manner that permits their incorporation into the mainstream of national rural development plans and practices (see Huang Qizao 1992; Yang Yanyin 1991). Indeed, my reading of the documents on the "two studies" at the national level is that one of the main purposes at this level is influencing national economic policy and thereby opening doors for local initiatives.

The key element of the argument is that women's work is essential to rural economic development, and that the Women's Federations have the role of mobilizing and enhancing women's economic potential in order to achieve that goal. This meshes seamlessly with current reform policies of using state policy to promote a growth-oriented market economy. At the same time it claims a role for the Women's Federations, which, although the only legal vehicle for organizing women, have historically been very weak in political terms and largely irrelevant to economic policy. The strategy promotes state organization of women's economic contribution, and thereby strengthens the only available political vehicle for a women's movement in China.

The question then immediately arises of precisely what the Women's Federations have to offer and how they propose to contribute to their stated twin goals of promoting economic development and women's liberation. The key element is the proposition that the main problem to be resolved is that of women's overall low quality (suzhi).[6] The "two studies" proposes to raise women's overall quality through comprehensive measures that include general and political education, as well as technical and scientific training. The Women's Federations' offer is that they will provide the organizational vehicle, the staff, and the program for realizing this project.

The concept of quality has been interpreted widely in some of the writing related to this movement, and the first of the "two studies," xue

---

[6] Although the older terminology is not used, the current discourse about quality being the main element is strongly reminiscent of the variant of dialectics found in Mao Zedong's "On Contradiction" (Mao Zedong 1977) and widely popularized throughout China. In this view, the task of the leadership is to identify the main contradiction and to lead in transforming a set of social relations by reversing the terms of that contradiction. This is a process that allows for the tactical concentration of organized action at points in a social field that will have the potential to leverage fundamental change. Raising the quality of women can be read as such an application of dialectics.

wenhua, was apparently intended to provide women with what might be called adult basic education, in order to provide them with tools for improving their lives. This component has included political education, which could be viewed as useful in preparing women to play a larger role in the political life of villages—another current goal—although it remains seen as irrelevant by most rural women.[7] From the perspective of the political leadership, however, political study is a critical component of any program of human development and could not be omitted. In the "two studies," political education in its former narrow sense of the study of the texts of Marxist-Leninist leaders has not been emphasized. The key ideological content the "two studies" conveys is the value of market-oriented economic activity. The general education component of the "two studies" has also included elements related to particular campaigns, such as the one to popularize legal knowledge (*pufa*). The promulgation of the Law to Protect the Rights and Interests of Women in 1992 was followed by efforts to spread information on this law throughout the country, and some additional legal information has also been popularized in the same time period.

As implemented, the first study referred primarily to literacy education and was given particular emphasis in the first few years of the "two studies." This is in line with earlier and continuing national literacy programs and with the Nairobi Forward-looking Strategies on the international level (see Second Report 1994). Literacy education and related programs were intended to be delivered at a variety of levels, depending upon the actual situation in each locality. In Shandong, for example, at the beginning of the "two studies," rural women were estimated to be: 5% upper middle school graduates, 33.6% lower middle school graduates, 50.3% primary school graduates, and 10% illiterate or semi-literate. Only about 10% were thought to have ever received any technical education provided by a professional (Shandongsheng fulian 1989). The general education component was most important for the illiterate and semi-literate women, because it consisted almost wholly of literacy education and did not take women through to further levels of adult education. Indeed, even the literacy goal has been elusive. Activists working at the village and township levels have found it difficult to per-

[7] Political study essentially must be offered by all state-run programs, whether or not it is central to a particular program's goals. It has not been prominent in the "two studies," at least as the "two studies" is delivered to ordinary rural women. It is a necessary part of the cadre development programs discussed in Chapter 5.

suade illiterate women—who are often among the poorest and hardest working in a village—to find time for literacy education. Literacy education has nevertheless remained part of the "two studies," although its importance has varied by location and decreased over time.

The actual practical emphasis of the "two studies" has been upon various aspects of technical and scientific training, *xue jishu*. In the early years of the "two studies" this typically referred to practical technical skills (*shiyong jishu*), that is, skills that were simple, could be taught and learned quickly, and would generate income in the very near future. Instruction for as little as a half day in seed selection, for example, would be offered within this aspect of the program. This training was targeted toward illiterate and semi-literate women, and was ideally combined with literacy training. The prospect of income generation was used to recruit women for both, although the lack of means to address time constraints for these women meant that the practical technical component could be delivered more widely than literacy education.

By 1991, if not earlier, the "two studies" had formulated its educational program in three tiers, of which the early priority of literacy and practical technical training formed the first tier. The second tier targeted women who were literate and had some education for more sustained training in a particular field. It especially aimed to recruit rural women who were engaged in some specialized form of production, and those who were the key figures in specialized household enterprises.[8] The preferred arrangement was to provide training in the field in which each woman was already working, although the diversity of training this required posed a practical problem. The third tier targeted rural women with relatively high levels of education, preferably upper middle school graduates, but also lower middle school graduates. These women were encouraged to enroll in correspondence and broadcast school courses and to become more systematically and comprehensively trained. Women in the second and third tiers were also encouraged to achieve formal recognition of their technical skills through accreditation as rural technician (*nongmin jishuyuan*) or some other type of formal designation. Part of the work of the local level Women's Federation

---

[8] "Specialized households" (*zhuanye hu*) were those that met varying official definitions of rural households that were specialized and economically successful in a particular type of enterprise. In effect, these were the households most successful in the emerging market economy.

cadres became recruiting women for accreditation processes, as well as for training. Numbers of women achieving various designations became one of the standards by which success was measured in the "two studies," along with numbers achieving literacy standards and numbers attending training classes (see Yang Yanyin 1991). Training and associated work at all of these levels was occurring to some degree under Women's Federation initiative even before 1989 (Shandongsheng fulian 1989), but the intensity of activity increased during the "two studies" and became increasingly oriented toward systematic technical training.

Apart from study, the element of the "two studies" most visibly emphasized was competition. The "two competitions" were explicitly to "compete in achievement" (*bi chengji*) and "compete in contribution" (*bi gongxian*). The linking of the two competitions was, in the contemporary Chinese context, a clear statement that women were being asked to achieve economic success and to share the fruits of their success. The most discussed form of sharing was more successful women helping poorer women, often through organized pairings of successful models with poorer women, or through organized sharing of expertise. The local Women's Federation cadres and village women's heads were the organizers of the more formalized sharing, and through this role the women's organizations and the "two studies" gained in social standing. Organized contributions could also take the form of paying taxes, a chronically difficult matter in reform era rural China.

Aid to poorer individuals, households, or villages was not a new feature, but the focus on competition as the mechanism for realizing it was new. On the surface this continued earlier practices of awarding individuals and groups with such titles as "March 8th Red Flag Bearer" or "advanced" unit. The "two studies" has drawn heavily upon longstanding practices of promoting models for ordinary people to emulate, practices with roots in Confucian conceptions of human educability. These have been energetically adopted by the Chinese Communist Party as central to all of its political movements since the Yan'an period.

The models selected in the "two studies" are expected to fill a familiar social role as exemplars in an official campaign. It is standard practice in China for any initiative to be implemented largely through the example of human models. The process is one of first outlining a general policy, applying it concretely in a variety of conditions, identifying successes in these concrete contexts, and then using those successes as models that can be emulated in a wider range of cases. This standard mobilizational technique is designed to avoid blanket application of undifferentiated policy (although that still happens), and to use scarce organizational resources efficiently by concentrating them at a limited number of points. Once the models are generated, they can serve to carry larger numbers of people with them, with modest organizational support. This method has been used so extensively since the 1940s that everyone is thoroughly familiar with it. In the "two studies," the promotion of models was specifically located within the reform era context of encouraging market-oriented competition. Quality, competition, and market forces merged with socialist values of equality, cooperation, and planned development.[9]

Since it was first announced in 1989, the "two studies" included statements that there would be yearly recognition at each administrative level of the individuals and groups most successful in the "two studies." Typically this happens in a public meeting on March 8, International Women's Day. The national standard is to recognize one hundred individual women and thirty groups. Similar numbers are recognized at other levels (provincial, prefectural, and county), with the prestige of the award corresponding to the administrative level. Although a modest prize might be given, the rewards are largely those of public recognition and indirect material benefit. The rewards are balanced by obligations to support the "two studies" and the Women's Federations through helping other women with both funding and expertise, hosting training sessions on-site (xianchanghui) in their own households, and being available for publicity.

In the "two studies," women are encouraged to establish themselves as models through competitive success in the marketplace. In contrast to goals of service and self-sacrifice promoted in earlier movements, the "two studies" calls on women to forge ahead on an individual or household basis. Competitive entrepreneurial success is to be the mark of a "two studies" model. This also applies to village-level women's heads, women who are not part of the Women's Federation staff, but who have responsibility for carrying out its work at the village level. In the past, village cadres were called upon not to have higher incomes

[9] Compare "Competition is arguably the predominant mode of social interaction in modern capitalist society" (Erlmann 1992: 701) and, "Competitive activities train large amounts of female talent and promote the women's liberation movement" (Wu Aiying 1991: 8).

than their neighbors and not to profit by their office. Those who were rich would be suspected of exploitation or corruption. The new demand is for women's heads who will lead in becoming rich through successful entrepreneurial activity. They are, of course, expected to avoid corruption and to devote some of their time to helping other village women to prosper, but they are in the first place to become rich themselves. The same expectation is to be conveyed to all rural women, in line with the reform era goal of prosperity, and is intended to increase the overall level of economic activity and income.

This strategy is entirely consistent with reform era policies of allowing some to get rich first, in the expectation that some of their prosperity will trickle down to others. Campaigns such as these propose to organize and, in effect, to pressure successful women to become part of strategies for "shared prosperity" (*gongtong fuyu*) in the countryside, but the route proposed diverges from earlier approaches, because it is designed to compel women to succeed first on an individual, entrepreneurial basis. The state apparatus has shifted from supporting only communal approaches associated with economic leveling to supporting exactly those approaches it formerly denounced as capitalist.

In promoting this change in direction for rural women, the Women's Federations are endeavoring to make certain that women will not be left behind in subsistence or service work, while the rural economy is being transformed along quite different lines. Placing women at the heart of current development practices, which is the goal of this quintessential gender-and-development (GAD) strategy, requires that rural women accept and excel at market-oriented economic activity. Competition is lauded in the "two studies" as intrinsically necessary to the new forms of economic activity, and as a practical means to unsettle village economies and move them toward market transition. Women are to play a full role in this, and to have their successes publicly validated by the state through promotion of them as models. The models are significant not only in what they have each accomplished, but as a visible statement of what is now prioritized.

The study and competition components are the most obvious parts of the "two studies," and the ones that allow the Women's Federations to make the most direct claims about work accomplished, but they were not the most interesting or innovative components. On the bases provided by increased quality (through training), increased success (through competition), and public recognition (through models) delivered in relatively conventional form through the Women's Federations themselves, the Federations have made claims upon the resources of the key economic development ministries to incorporate women into the mainstream of economic development planning, programs, and resource allocation at every level, from the national to the local. The organizational vehicle for this is the new one of "two studies coordinating groups" (shuangxue shuangbi xietiao zuzhi).

The formation of the national coordinating group was one of the earliest steps taken in the "two studies." It was headed by the chairperson of the All-China Women's Federation, Chen Muhua, and included ranking representatives of the State Council and eleven national ministries (such as Agriculture, Forestry, and Commerce) and other national level units (such as the China Agriculture Bank). The standard structure for coordinating groups, as established since at all levels down to the county, is for the group to be co-chaired by the head of the Women's Federation and one of the ranking leaders of the government or Party at the same administrative level, and for the rest of the group to consist of members of the core leadership of each of the more than ten government departments or parallel organizations targeted for involvement in the "two studies" (see Ye Lin 1989; Wu Aiying 1991). The Women's Federation has a strong preference for the membership to consist of the leaders with actual power in each unit, usually the Party secretary responsible for the work closest to "two studies" concerns, and this applies especially to the co-chair. If these people are successfully recruited, and especially if the co-chair gives effective support, the "two studies" gains access to powerful state structures and their resources. In the hierarchical context of Chinese state organization, recruiting the active support of the leading state figures at each level is critical to receiving effective support—regardless of structure or policy—and much of the organizing work of the Women's Federations is directed toward gaining and maintaining this support. The routine management of the coordinating group is in the hands of the Women's Federation, but the whole point of establishing the coordinating groups is to transcend the boundaries and limitations of the Women's Federations.

It would be difficult to overstate the importance of the coordinating groups for the "two studies." Indeed the "two studies" was announced as a national initiative decided upon by the national level coordinating group, rather than by the Women's Federations on their own (Ye Lin 1989). This committed the State Council and all the ministries and other units involved to work for its success. In Shandong, the first year of the "two studies" was primarily devoted to organizing coordinating groups at various levels throughout the province, devising plans and recruiting women for work that would begin in the second year (Wu Aiying 1991).

In carrying out the "two studies" (or any other initiative), each local Women's Federation requires the support of the state structures at the same level. This is in part a question of the organization of the Chinese state, which locates significant power in the leading bodies (primarily the Party committee, but also the governmental committee) at each level, and subordinates state organs at each level to that leading authority. In the case of the Women's Federations, for example, this means that they receive professional (*yewu*) guidance through the hierarchy of Women's Federations, but that they receive political leadership, financial support, and routine direction from the local Party and government committees.

Furthermore, the Women's Federations have a subordinate status as a mass organization rather than a government department, and are not viewed as central to the more important work of the state (such as economic development and political control). They are understaffed and have minuscule expense allotments that make it difficult for them to do their ordinary work, even without trying to implement a major initiative such as the "two studies." The coordinating groups are in part a channel for accessing funding and other important sources of material support at each level of the state (see Wu Aiying 1991: 10).

In order to organize training effectively for the "two studies," the Women's Federations have argued for systematic measures to provide an infrastructure of space, teachers, expenses, materials, and a plan. Space requirements involve a four-tier organization of one-room Women's Homes (*funü zhi jia*) at the village level, rural technical schools for women at township levels, and science and technology training centers at county and prefectural levels (see [Shandong]sheng fulian xuanchuanbu 1989: 14). The Women's Homes provide an all-purpose organizational locale, while the facilities at all four levels, if only an empty space, can serve as sites for training classes. All of these spaces are provided by local government, often through the coordinating groups.

The teachers are most commonly provided by accessing the technical and extension staffs of the organizations attached to the "two studies" through the coordinating groups. Specialized teachers may also be hired by local governments for specific training tasks, and well-qualified urban professionals often find these short-term rural contracts lucrative. The Women's Federations themselves do not provide expert trainers. Their role is to access trainers from other branches of the state, and to mobilize women to attend the training programs. The programs may be specially designed by the Women's Federations to meet "two studies" goals and to target women as students, but men are not excluded from attending classes.

Effectively running "two studies" initiatives may also require funds and materials in order to give rural women access to costly or modern inputs. Some of these can be arranged through state channels, to the extent that the state controls scarce inputs such as fertilizer, and some require access to credit and purchase in the open market. These resource issues, sometimes combined with training and market information, are a central concern addressed in the "service" (fuwu) sections of the periodic "two studies" reports. A major role for the Women's Federations in the "two studies" is using the coordinating groups to resolve resource issues and serve women's practical needs for capital, materials, knowledge, and market information so that women are better positioned to use their training and to succeed in the market economy. The "two studies" strategy is primarily one of supporting women and households in market activity, rather than directly running enterprises. However, Women's Federations have also been called upon to organize some enterprises (shiti) in order to generate funds for Women's Federation and "two studies" activities.

Making the "two studies" training programs work effectively also requires that the training and this integrated infrastructure become part of state economic development plans. Although the "two studies" is oriented toward the market, the strategy itself is one of directing state resources toward women. State resources are allocated through plans, and the "two studies" are a mechanism through which the Women's Federations make claims on the state for resource allocation, formally through state plans as well as on an ad hoc basis.

THE "TWO STUDIES": FURTHER DEVELOPMENT

The "two studies" initiative was the object of continual internal assessment and public report. Examination of these reports indicates tactical changes in the initiative on the basis of close monitoring of local work.[10] By 1991 leading voices in the Women's Federations at the national level and in Shandong were publicly calling for the further development of the initiative (see Yang Yanyin 1991; Wu Aiying 1991).[11] At this early date in the "two studies," these figures continued to argue that the "two studies" could contribute to agricultural development, to rural stability and overall human development ("spiritual civilization" or *jingshen wenming*), and to the liberation of women. All of these goals were to be accomplished through increasing women's overall quality (through literacy and technical education, and also political and legal education) and incorporating women more fully into economic development in the countryside. This was an argument phrased in classical Marxist terms for the linking of economic development and women's issues, and also open to recent market-oriented revision, and as such was an argument capable of winning support from the highest levels of the post-socialist state. The innovations made on this ideological basis are tactical ones of organizationally making women stronger, first of all in economic terms.

One of the departures was to extend the scope of "two studies" economic activities beyond the focus on grain and cotton typical of the early years of the initiative.[12] From the beginning, the "two studies" had been given a broad mandate, so this might not appear a radical departure. Nevertheless, there was an evident and continuing shift of emphasis toward women's involvement in more skilled and lucrative areas of the private economy. Courtyard economy appears as important in this context, but by now it is no longer primarily an indicator of effective use of courtyard space and household labor, but rather a comprehensive term for household-based enterprises. This was a rapidly growing dimension of the rural production, commerce, and service sectors. There was also an emphasis upon craft production designed for export, another

[10] My sources for these reports consist primarily of the material published in *Funü zuzhi yu huodong, Funü gongzuo, Funü yanjiu luncong,* and occasionally other Chinese publications. I was also allowed to read or was given some local reports in Shandong. The most important of these reports are cited in the text, but there are many others.

[11] This may well have been the case at other provincial and local levels as well, but I have only followed the various levels of the "two studies" initiative in one vertical slice of Shandong province.

[12] Two years after the national beginning of the "two studies," a similar competition-based strategy was adopted for urban women, the "heroine's contributions" (*jinguo jiangong bei*), and the two were often discussed together from 1991. The latter lies beyond the scope of this study. Refer to the journals cited in note 10.

major growth area for the rural economy. All of the production in the "two studies" was to be increasingly specialized, with a greater emphasis on systematic technical education, in contrast with the earlier focus on simple income generation and literacy. The "two studies" was no longer to be a five-year initiative but a long-term, comprehensive, and far-reaching program. In order to realize this, the leading figures proposed a set of adjustments designed to make the "two studies" more effective from the top down. These consisted of adjustments in the three areas of leadership, target management, and service.

Within the area of leadership, the key issues were: the strengthening of the coordinating groups and establishment of a "post responsibility system" (*gangwei mubiao zerenzhi*), that is, a defined system of management responsibility for the "two studies"; the incorporation of the "two studies" into mainstream development plans and increased leadership support for the "two studies"; and further development of a set of policies and systemic support for the "two studies."

The management of formal targets in the two competitions was viewed as a major mechanism through which the "two studies" could be given effective direction. Specific targets were to be set to suit local conditions, but they were also to be set in accordance with goals determined at higher administrative levels. The goals were to be formally recorded and realized at each level, down to that of village and individual, to ensure that the initiative would actually be implemented. The public competition aspect of the initiative was to be strengthened as a means to motivate participation.

"Two studies" organizations were to be established on the basis of providing service to the rural women involved in the initiative. By 1991 Shandong reported having 54,000 service points of one type or another throughout the province (Wu Aiying 1991: 11). The critical issue here is that Women's Federations and the "two studies" were not to rely on purely administrative positions or offices to make the "two studies" work, but were to provide concrete and useful services that would give visible economic results within a short period of time. Such assistance could be comprehensive introduction of a new project, and could include assistance prior to production (as in market information or credit), during the process of production (as in technical training and assistance with supplies), and in the post-production phase (marketing). The goal was a comprehensive system of service provision that would enable women to advance economically. This would establish the

Women's Federations as responsive to the needs of rural women in practical, concrete, and visible ways, while they could at the same time reasonably claim to be helping the state meet its rural production targets.

Initially the "two studies" had been proposed as a five-year program, to run from the beginning of 1989 to the end of 1993. Evaluations were done of the program as it neared the end of this term, and some adjustments can be seen as it entered its second phase. In general, these changes were consistent with the earlier trend toward more systematic training at a higher level and entry into more advanced and remunerative areas of the rural economy. There were also some changes in the presentation of the program, with less emphasis upon political goals than in the hard-line early 1990s, and more emphasis upon furthering women's place in China's "socialist market economy," including a statement from the Shandong Women's Federation leadership that "each level of the Women's Federation should ceaselessly reform all ways of thought and action that are not suitable for the development of the market economy" (Zhao Yulan 1994a: 11; also see Zhao Yulan 1994b, 1994c and Xiao Wen 1995).

This adjustment of emphasis was consistent with the national move toward reaffirming economic reform in the wake of Deng Xiaoping's Southern Tour in 1992, and can be attributed to the Women's Federations' obligation to endorse and formally accommodate itself to current Party policy at any point in time. While making this observation, it should also be noted that none of the policy shifts of the 1990s fundamentally affected the direction of the "two studies," which continued as a strategy designed to improve women's position in the mixed economy of reform era China through involvement with both state and market.

One element in the more recent years of the "two studies" that is more market oriented is the strong advocacy of the use of a type of enterprise entity (shiti) that allows organs of the state to engage in profitable economic activity. The Women's Federations advocate taking full advantage of this opportunity by strongly encouraging staff at all levels to set up enterprises that will earn profits that can be used to fund the expenses of the Women's Federations. Such enterprises might be strictly income-generating propositions as, for example, renting out storefront space in a Women's Federation building, or might take the preferred form of both generating income and providing a useful service, such as child care. In the latter instance, the enterprises would directly provide services for local women and thereby contribute to one of the major goals of the Women's Federations, as well as subsidize other services or activities, such as the "two studies." Especially because of the extreme shortage of funding for the Women's Federations, staff were put under considerable pressure to establish such enterprises and to make them profitable in a short period of time.

Apart from the increased turn toward the market, the "two studies" proceeded in the same direction as before. Improving the overall quality of women remained the key to the strategy (Chen Muhua cited in Xiao Wen 1995: 36), and while this still included political and general education, the focus was increasingly upon higher levels of technical training.[13] In Shandong from 1994, the competition component was revised and renamed to become the "strive to be a woman science and technology champion" (*zheng dang nü keji zhuangyuan*) contest.[14] This was essentially the same as the earlier contest, but with an explicitly higher technical demand; indeed, all the education and training goals have been progressively set at higher levels as the "two studies" has proceeded. The only place remaining for literacy education is in particularly poor and disadvantaged areas that are recognized to be proceeding at a different pace.

Apart from the continuing place for literacy and for poverty alleviation work, the new "two studies" emphasis is on selecting strategic points for breakthrough into significant economic success.[15] This requires targeting the most educated and technically trained women (to become champions), working in the areas where women have established strengths (grain, cotton, and the courtyard economy), and pushing first in the economically strongest municipalities and counties, that is, the areas where initial success will be most readily attainable (Zhao Yulan 1994c: 5; Shandongsheng fulian 1993: 11). Increasingly, the

[13] The usual term used in the Chinese materials would be more literally translated as "scientific and technical" (*keji*) training. This conveys the intention of placing the "two studies" within the overall context of scientific and technical development, but the training delivered was technical and applied. For simplicity, I have generally used the briefer term, "technical" training.

[14] The term translated here as "champion" is actually the title awarded the man who placed first in the imperial palace examinations. It is a traditional term for the top scholar in the most competitive scholarly context in imperial China. Women were entirely excluded from the imperial examination system.

[15] For an indication of the official view of the "two studies" early in its second phase, in English, see Second Report (1994: 17–18) and Program (1995).

Women's Federations are moving to position the "two studies" in the most rapidly developing areas of the rural economy.

The central training issue became the development of a core of rural women with middle school education and some systematic technical training. This was a step beyond the cultivation and promotion of individual models, toward establishing an organized basis for the transmission of technical knowledge in the countryside. Such a core would extend the capacity of the Women's Federation, with its limited organizational and nonexistent technical resources, and it would do so by relying upon rural women themselves. Rural women were to be trained and positioned to participate effectively in the modern sectors of rural development, and some were to be prepared to assist others systematically who had less education and training.[16]

Among several initiatives tried at this time, Dezhou experimented with setting up special classes for women through the Beijing-based Rural Correspondence College. This step, by a much-recognized local coordinating group, was viewed as a highly positive development by the Shandong Women's Federation. The better trained women and more successful models were also recruited into "research associations" (*yanjiu hui*) that were to operate as vehicles for the transmission of technical knowledge and entrepreneurial encouragement to other rural women. By the mid-1990s, the "two studies" was moving toward establishing an organized basis for GAD at the village level.[17]

The "two studies" also took the step, by 1993, of moving into rural industry, through organizing both women workers and women entrepreneurs to join in the competitions and associated activities (Shandongsheng fulian 1993; Zhao Yulan 1994c). This was consistent with other efforts to expand the movement into the most dynamic sectors of the rural economy and to draw the widest possible range of rural women into the "two studies." Successful women were a particular target of recruitment because they were a potential source of added strength for an initiative that was astutely designed but still hampered by lack of personnel and material resources. The Women's Federations were con-

---

[16] The focus of training aimed at the rural public was consistently upon increasing production, rather than upon management or commerce.

[17] Some of the specific training goals in Shandong as of 1994 were: striving to eliminate illiteracy; to have every rural woman acquire two or more practical skills; within five years, to have 400,000 rural women receive the "green certificate" (*lüse zhengshu*) and 200,000 achieve "rural technician" (*nongmin jishuyuan*) accreditation (Zhao Yulan 1994c: 4).

sciously drawing upon private sector resources to construct an effective and broadly constituted base for rural women's organized initiatives under their official leadership.

The resulting comprehensive strategy consisted of three related areas of emphasis: raising the quality of rural women through literacy, education, and training programs; improving the organizational capacity of the rural women's movement; and effectively organizing women to succeed in the marketplace.

4

Literacy, Education, and Training

I s it accurate to speak of women in rural China as lacking in quality—in the senses of literacy, education, and training— either in absolute terms or in comparison with men? Could educational improvements effectively contribute to changes in women's status? China has a long tradition of formal education, and there have been increased efforts to provide various forms of education to young people of both genders for decades. Nevertheless, well-recognized problems have persisted throughout the country, especially in rural areas. Although everyone might readily agree that education is a social good and that improving access to it is desirable, a strategy for change that relies heavily upon changing this factor requires a close consideration of the particular. The village of Huaili provides a detailed case for examination, and this will be the focus here.

NATIONAL CONTEXT

In preface, it should be noted that the larger context suggests that there is reason for concern and for emphasis on education. Despite several decades of improvement in access to education, including literacy training, primary education, and short-term training programs, China has a legacy of educational disadvantage that continues to handicap a large portion of the adult population. This is most dramatically evident in the high rate of illiteracy. China's second official report on the implementation of the Nairobi Forward-looking Strategies for the Advancement of Women stated that there were 127,249,000 illiterate and semi-literate people over the age of 15 in 1990, and that 70.07% of these were women. Indeed, the gender imbalance was actually accentuated among the younger age groups. Women were 72.94% of illiterates and semi-literates aged 15–24, 78.22% of those aged 25–34, 74.37% of those aged 35–44, but only 67.60% of those aged 45 and above (Second Report 1994:

Table 10-1). This is not an indication that women have lost ground, but rather that men formerly had less access to education and that their access appears to have improved slightly earlier than that of women.

The gender disproportion in adult illiteracy and semi-literacy has resulted in substantial proportions of women lacking access to written knowledge. In 1990, 31.93% of women were illiterate or semi-literate. The age breakdown indicates a rapid improvement in the situation: 8.55% of women aged 15–24 were illiterate or semi-literate in 1990, as were 15.03% of those aged 25–34, 28.57% of those aged 35–44, and 71.65% of those aged 45 and above (Second Report 1994: Table 10-2). There was a distinct improvement in these figures from 1982 to 1990, and there were improvements during the 1990s as well. The improvements result in part from literacy training, but also from the effects of increased access to regular formal education working their way through the age pyramid.

Literacy training has been organized as part of the "two studies" activities, especially in its first five-year phase. Women over forty years of age are not included in the campaign, which reduces the scope of the undertaking drastically. The emphasis in literacy training has been placed upon women aged fifteen to forty in remote and poor regions, that is, in areas where illiteracy rates are highest and the benefits of literacy training likely to be greatest. Yearly targets have been set for the reduction of female illiteracy during the 1990s, with a goal of reducing rates to 5% in developed areas, 10% in poor areas, and 15% in poor and remote areas (Second Report 1994: 28; Program 1995: 15). In Ling County, the literacy target was reached and exceeded in 1994 when the county met the higher standard of a female illiteracy rate below 2% and qualified as a "literate county" (wu[wen]meng xian).

The standard criterion used to measure literacy is recognition of 1,500 Chinese characters, which is sufficient for reading simple materials and for some practical purposes, but not sufficient for reading newspapers, for example, without encountering noticeable numbers of new characters. Consequently, while this is a useful level, it is also one with definite limitations. The women's movement is acutely aware of the need to make more education available.

The decisive long-term measure is the extension of effective access to formal schooling throughout the country. The goal in this time period was to achieve the universal extension of nine years of education, that is, education to lower middle school graduation level, and to ensure that girls were fully included. In a narrow sense, this extension of education was not the concern of the women's movement or the responsibility of the Women's Federations. It was to be accomplished through state policy on education, through the state's educational channels, and with public financial support. The task of basically achieving a universal nine-year standard was to be gradually accomplished by 2000, through a series of stages that recognized the unevenness of education throughout the country. By the mid-1990s, the goals were to realize the nine-year standard in areas with 45% of the national population by 1996, in areas with 65% of the population by 1998, and in areas with 85% of the population by 2000 (Quarterly Report 1995: 932). This would, of course, imply slightly lower rates of actual participation, since the goals did not require 100% participation in these areas. By 1993, 97.7% of primary school–age children attended school, but only 81.8% of primary school graduates continued to middle school, although that figure was an improvement on 1992's rate of 79.7% (Statistical Communiqué 1994: 5).

The Women's Federations were concerned about the implementation of education policy, although their only direct involvement was in working to include girls. The policy itself was intended to be gender-inclusive, but there were traditional and continuing pressures to keep girls, especially those of middle school age, out of school in order to care for younger children and, increasingly during the reform era, to work in rural enterprises. Pressures in this direction were especially severe in poorer communities and households, and were exacerbated by some costs associated with education. It has been extremely important to ensure that girls go to school, remain in school, and actually attend class throughout the year (and not drop away while remaining registered), since it is very difficult for young women to obtain the opportunity for education later if this is lost in childhood. Participation rates for girls remain generally lower than for boys, although there is only a relatively small gap at the lower levels. By 1992, girls were 46.6% of primary school students and 43.8% of lower middle school students (Second Report 1994: Table 13).

Education to levels above lower middle school is viewed by the women's movement as highly desirable for girls, and there is a continuing effort to improve the proportions of women at all levels of education above lower middle school (Program 1995: 16). Still, there is less opportunity to encourage girls to proceed further, since there is a serious shortage of positions for all students at higher secondary or tertiary levels. The recent focus has been on expanding wide access to lower middle school education, and not upon comparable expansion at higher levels (see Second Report 1994: Table 12). It is not unusual to come across young people of either gender in the countryside who are spending an extra year in study in order to rewrite entrance examinations for a higher level of school, but competition is tight and not all can succeed, even on the second try.

The practical focus of the women's movement has therefore been upon short-term training. To some extent this has been combined with literacy education, especially in the first phase of the "two studies," although the emphasis has been upon technical training. The women's movement has sought to provide this training through its own resources on a very small scale, as in half-day sessions on practical matters such as seed selection. It has also sought to provide training at a slightly higher level through ties with various branches of local government through "two studies" coordinating groups. The Women's Federations organize sessions and mobilize women to attend them, while government extension workers provide the technical instructors. There is at least nominally a comprehensive rural extension network associated with each of several government departments responsible for rural production (such as agriculture or animal husbandry), although staffing in agricultural science and technology was reduced in the early 1990s (Quarterly Chronicle 1994: 1227). Despite these limitations, there are some human and material resources available, and efforts have been made to increase rural women's access to immediately useful technology. Some Women's Federation staff have a degree of technical competence themselves, since it is not unusual for them to be graduates of agricultural technical secondary schools (nongxiao), and village women's heads have been asked to lead the way in acquiring technical knowledge that they can pass on to other women. During the second phase of the "two studies," the emphasis shifted from literacy (except in poor and remote areas, where literacy was a continuing issue) to higher levels of technical education. An important step in this direction was accomplished through the Women's Federations' use of the Rural Correspondence College (Nonghanda), both in increasing women's access to its regular programs and in creating a program specially for women. The Rural Correspondence College provides a national curriculum in applied agricultural technology, centrally designed by well-qualified staff and delivered locally through printed materials and sessions with local technical extension staff. The minimum educational level considered sufficient for taking notes and following this curriculum is lower middle school graduation, so this is a step designed to build on the expansion of access to lower middle school education. The Dezhou Women's Federation has been active in pursuing this strategy.

DATA AND ANALYSIS

This study will approach the issues of literacy, education, and training in the village of Huaili in some detail, in an effort to go beyond what can be indicated by rates of literacy or school attendance, or by policy initiatives. It will include an examination of literacy, education, and training for women and men in Huaili, based on a sample of 90 households (of the approximately 230 households in the village in 1989) where interviews were conducted in 1989, 1990, 1992, and 1995.

Although the sample was constructed to represent the full range of economic circumstances and household forms, it does have two major biases. It includes all women involved in woman-work and over-represents women who were economically successful and active in household-based enterprises, because I was particularly interested in talking with these women and investigating the variety of channels open to women in the village's political economy. The sample also over-represents the more successful households in the village, in part because local officials preferred to direct me toward the more affluent households, although I also sought and was able to achieve some economic contrast in the sample. The resulting figures should be interpreted as almost certainly showing more education and training than general within the village, and I expect that this bias is greater in the case of women than of men.

In addition to comparisons between women and men based on this sample, I will present an examination of specific sets of cases, traced over time, in order to identify educational trajectories and career paths, and in order to examine the pattern of gender differences present in both education and career. This longitudinal and case-specific approach permits an exploration of the microdynamics of change related to education. This is a methodology appropriate to the concerns here, which are those of strategies for change at the microlevel of villages, households, and individuals.[1]

LITERACY

Table 1 presents the literacy profile of this sample of Huaili residents, broken down by age and gender. Illiteracy or limited literacy is standard for women born prior to 1935.[2] The cohort of women born in the 1950–54 period shows a sharp increase in literacy, but illiteracy becomes rare only among women born since 1960. Men, in comparison, show a much lower rate of unambiguous illiteracy, even in the oldest age cohorts, where almost all the men in the sample attended school at least briefly. Many of these men described themselves as having limited literacy (knowing only some characters, or being able to read but not write), while others said only that they had had one or a few years of schooling decades earlier. The major breakthrough to common, if not universal, literacy for men came with the 1950–54 age cohort, as for women, but represented a much less dramatic change. No men born since 1960 were identified as illiterate or semi-literate. As this table indicates, there are substantially higher rates of illiteracy for women, and illiteracy can still be found among very young women.

Literacy education was raised as a major concern of the "two studies" movement in its initial phase; indeed, literacy education was conceptualized as the main content of the first "study" (xue wenhua). I have been able to locate only one woman[3] in this village who might be considered to have studied literacy in the context of the "two studies."[4] This mother of two teenage children said that she had attended school briefly when young, but had forgotten what she had learned; over a

---

[1] Further discussion of the relation of these educational elements to economic development will be pursued in Chapter 6.

[2] Literacy and illiteracy are recorded as self-reported. I did not detect any indication of falsely reporting higher than actual levels of literacy or education in Huaili, and I consider these data to be roughly reliable.

[3] I will not be identifying individual women by name in this study. Despite the public nature of the research, this seems to add nothing to the study, nor would the use of pseudonyms.

[4] I have found very few cases in this village (or in the others I studied in the 1980s) of either women or men receiving literacy education as adults. Apart from the case discussed at this point in the text, these include two other women and one man in the Huaili samples.

TABLE I

Literacy: Adult Residents of Huaili from
Household Samples, 1989–95

Birthdate	Illiterate		Semi-literate or doubtful literacy		Literate	
	F	M	F	M	F	M
to 1920	0	0	0	0	0	2
1921–29	4	2	1	3	0	0
1930–34	2	0	1	3	0	1
1935–39	3	0	2	3	2	4
1940–44	4	0	2	2	4	6
1945–49	4	1	3	2	4	7
1950–54	7	2	3	2	12	13
1955–59	6	0	3	3	9	17
1960–64	0	0	0	0	15	13
1965–69	1	0	0	0	23	22
1970–74	1	0	0	0	17	8
since 1975	1	0	0	0	5	1
TOTAL	33	5	15	18	91	94

NOTE: This table includes information for all members of households interviewed in 1989, 1990, 1992, and 1995, where these members were no longer in school and information on literacy was available.

three-year period she learned to be literate, through being taught by her children. This is, indeed, the practical method of literacy education currently advocated in this area. However, very little literacy education is done—or contemplated—here, although there were still a substantial number of illiterate women under forty-five years of age when the "two studies" began in Huaili in 1989. (People over forty-five are not targets of literacy campaigns in this area.) Township- and county-level Women's Federation cadres said that it was very difficult to persuade women to attend literacy classes. The "two studies" conception had as one of its core ideas the proposition that women might be attracted to study if literacy education were combined with practical technical training that could contribute to raising their incomes.[5] This may be implemented in some other locations, perhaps ones with higher rates of illiteracy among younger women, but was not attempted in Huaili. The women who might have benefited most from literacy education were among the poorest and hardest working women in the village, and the ones with

[5] Compare with Bourque and Warren's (1987: 187–88) earlier observation, " while women show considerable interest in literacy programs if they are linked to income-producing activities, governments have made little effort to orient programs to these activities."

least time available for anything that did not contribute immediately to the economic support of their households. I do not consider it accidental that the one woman who did take time over three years (1989–92) to learn to be literate was the partner, with her husband, in the village's largest sesame oil operation, and was relatively prosperous. If this village is any indication, and in this respect it does seem to have useful illustrative value, it is difficult to provide literacy education to young married women in poor households, women who are already carrying heavy double burdens and are concerned to use all their time to support their households. Local Women's Federation cadres consequently do not view this as a feasible strategy. As a result, participation in formal education while of school age is of critical importance.

EDUCATION

Table 2 presents the formal education of the same sample of Huaili residents as presented in Table 1. Most of the women born before 1955 who reported having had some primary education also indicated that it had been limited and often not enough to allow them to remain literate as adults, and this also applied to several women in the 1955–59 cohort. Women born during the 1950s were part of the generation in which schooling began to be available to girls in this part of rural China, but primary school education for women did not become general in this area until the cohort born after 1960 reached school age, that is, in the early Cultural Revolution years. Many in this cohort also received lower middle school education. In comparison, the majority of men in this sample, even those in the earliest age cohorts, received at least some primary school education, as did all men born since 1955. The significant transition for men was experienced by the 1950–54 cohort, which was the first that had substantial participation in lower middle school education. Indeed, several men born in all cohorts since 1950 had a formal education that extended beyond lower middle school. Only a few women received an education beyond lower middle school, but this possibility did appear for women born in the 1950s.

The result of this pattern of education in the countryside in recent decades is that there is considerable variation in the educational level of adults in their economically productive years in Huaili. The amount of education varies with age and gender, with women showing a much greater range of possible educational attainment, especially those women born in the 1950s, while the range narrows for cohorts of both

TABLE 2

Education: Adult Residents of Huaili from
Household Samples, 1989–95

	No education or literacy class only		At least some primary education		At least some lower middle school		More than lower middle school	
Birthdate	F	M	F	M	F	M	F	M
to 1920	0	0	0	2	0	0	0	0
1921–29	5	2	0	2	0	1	0	0
1930–34	2	1	1	3	0	0	0	0
1935–39	3	0	4	4	0	1	0	2
1940–44	4	0	4	5	1	1	1	0
1945–49	4	1	8	7	0	1	0	2
1950–54	8	2	9	4	3	7	2	4
1955–59	6	0	6	5	4	8	2	7
1960–64	0	0	2	3	11	7	1	3
1965–69	1	0	5	3	18	15	0	4
1970–74	1	0	4	0	11	8	2	0
since 1975	1	0	1	0	4	1	0	0
TOTAL	35	6	44	38	52	50	8	22

NOTE: This table includes information for all members of households interviewed in 1989, 1990, 1992 and 1995, where these members were no longer in school and information on education was available.

genders born since 1960, when education for women is more general and lower middle school for both women and men becomes relatively common. However, even during the period when research was being conducted, a few school-age girls in some of the poorer households in the village were still missing an education entirely or having it abbreviated.

For both women and men the possibility of an education beyond lower middle school appeared for the cohorts born since 1950, although more men than women were able to access these levels of education, levels only rarely available even to men in the village in earlier years. There has been no breakthrough to general availability of upper middle school or specialized secondary (*zhongzhuan*) education, and this is not likely in the foreseeable future. At the time of the most recent field trip, in late 1995, the county was in the process of convening a major meeting on the popularization of compulsory education through to lower middle school graduation, the current national goal. In the next few years this level of education may become the effective minimum for women as well as men, although it is not now possible to predict when further levels of education will become more generally available.

Table 2 includes only people who had left school at the time of being interviewed between 1989 and 1995, and therefore underrepresents younger age groups. Household interviews conducted during this period identified a few young women and young men proceeding to upper middle school or specialized secondary school, and one young man from the village graduated from the prestigious Shandong University during these years, but villagers seeking further study were also failing the competitive entrance exams. Some studied for an additional year and resat the exams, but the major problem here was not academic success; rather, it was the limited number of openings available. Individual willingness, household resources, and gender issues may be less significant at this level than the lack of a sufficient number of openings for rural students.

With respect to gender, the striking contrast at this level is the difference in long-term utilization of further education on the part of women and men. For men, as will be indicated below, education or training beyond lower middle school was commonly the beginning of a non-agricultural career path that would be sustained. The difference between this and the situation of the few women who acquired an education beyond lower middle school is dramatic. The only woman who had such a higher education among the earlier age cohorts, is a woman who was born in 1942 and graduated from a secondary normal school in the late 1950s. Her career, which should have led to a non-agricultural household registration, was disrupted by her loss of employment as a teacher during the three bad years (1959–61). She later taught as a locally employed (*minban*) teacher in her natal village for a while, but stopped because of a combination of poor health, children, and her husband's absence as a state-employed teacher; she has never worked as a teacher in her marital village of Huaili, where she has long resided.

Another woman, born in 1951, was trained as a village medic after a primary school education. She worked as a barefoot doctor in her natal village and made the rare transition to continuing her profession in her marital village by marrying early, so that she could take the barefoot doctor position of a female relative (*gu*) of her husband's, who was marrying out of Huaili at that time.[6] She continued to practice until the pressure of house calls combined with childcare demands, after her third child, became too onerous for her mother-in-law.

Other women, born in 1942, 1950, and 1954, present cases of women

---

[6] It is unclear whether the marriage was contracted in order to make this transition possible.

without significant further training but who were relatively educated for their generations, and for whom education opened opportunities for being teachers in their natal villages prior to marriage and, in the case of the oldest woman, also a brief period as a village medic in her natal village. One of these women continued teaching in her natal village for a year after her marriage, but none became teachers in Huaili after marriage. The oldest of these women had lower middle school equivalence, and the others each had some secondary education; none of these women had specialized professional training.

The short careers of these women indicate a pattern of opportunity found also for men with relatively high levels of education who are offered non-agricultural career opportunities related to their higher level of general education. Where the experience of women diverges from that of men, however, is that in all these cases the women had their careers terminated upon marriage into another village. This also occurred in the case of slightly younger women with even higher degrees of education, still a scarce resource in rural China, and years of experience in their natal village. One woman born in 1955 who graduated from upper middle school and had some teacher's training taught for five or six years in her natal village, but has never taught in her marital village. Another woman born in 1956 was also an upper middle school graduate who had taught in her natal village but not in her marital village.

These are the only women in the sample born prior to 1960 who had higher levels of education or formal professional training. There is a clear pattern of underutilization of educated women even when they are trained and experienced within areas traditionally considered suitable for women, such as primary school teaching.

Younger women have been somewhat less dependent upon formal village structures for their career opportunities after graduation. One upper middle school graduate born in 1962 also learned her father's trade (crafting false teeth) through a full apprenticeship and developed a successful business in local rural markets. A much younger upper middle school graduate, born in 1970, was living in apparent leisure in a complicated domestic environment. And one young graduate of the county's specialized secondary school that trains graduates to return to the countryside with a skill is an independent medic in a clinic managed by her mother in Huaili.

While this may appear to be a lengthy list of examples, it is actually a complete list of all women in the sample (of a total of 143 women no longer in school) who have an education beyond lower middle school. Apart from their small number, the significant conclusion that emerges is that these women have not had the opportunity to use their education, or the prior experience many had in their natal villages, for the communities of their adult lives. None have taught in Huaili and, although this may be related to the practice this village has of preferring men as teachers, it is apparently common for a woman to terminate her teaching career upon or shortly after her marriage, because she will not have the opportunity to continue her career in her marital village.[7] Many of these women have become successful in the private sector during the reform era, but this has been the result of individual or household initiative rather than of officially nurtured careers.

It is also the case that some of the most educated rural women (including at least one of the women cited here) benefit from their education to leave the countryside. My data do not enable me to assess the quantitative importance of education as an avenue for young women's exit from the countryside, although interview data indicate that parents and young people do commonly consider and work toward this goal.[8] The data presented here do, however, very clearly show that it is difficult for a rural young woman's education to lead to a career in the public sector of her marital community. And it is essential to note that the concern of the official women's movement is precisely with women's contribution to the communities of their adult lives and to the economic development of these communities. The policies being examined here are not concerned with increasing opportunities for individual women as a goal in itself (which could be criticized as promoting bourgeois individualism), or with aiding women to make an exit from the countryside. The concern, rather, is with the lives and contributions of adult women who remain in the countryside and have become its economic backbone.

EDUCATION FOR MEN

The disadvantage women experience in using their education in the public sphere may become clearer when contrasted with some of the

---

[7] I have been able to identify only one young woman in Huaili who was working as a teacher. This young woman, born in 1977, studied for a further year after lower middle school graduation without being able to pass the entrance exams to the next level, and then obtained a position teaching in an adjacent village.

[8] Also see Parish et al. 1995.

TABLE 3
Training: Adult Residents of Huaili from Household Samples, 1989–95

Birthdate	Female	Male
1930–34		army training class
1935–39		army training class
		learned to raise mushrooms informally from specialized household
1940–44	medic training	
	self-taught noodle-maker	
1945–49	learned to raise chickens from Prof. Hu and informally at *Nonghanda*	
1950–54	learned to raise chickens from Prof. Hu and informally at *Nonghanda*	self-taught photographer
	learned to make sesame oil from husband's family	army-trained electrician
		army training class
	illiterate woman learned to be restaurant cook	collective and army medic; on-job training as collective accountant
	tree nursery skills	self-taught teacher
1955–59	self-taught seamstress	apprentice carpenter
	learned to make saleable snacks as temporary contract worker	army training; on-job commercial training in collective enterprises
	trained 20+ days to be village women's head	trained as collective tractor driver
		trained as collective tractor driver
	informal study of chicken raising at *Nonghanda*	trained by collective to be veterinarian, then driver, then electrician
		tractor driver in collective
1960–64	learned mirror making from husband	learned to drive tractor as temporary contract worker
	apprentice maker of false teeth	carpentry training
		on-job training in collective as electrician
1965–69	on-job training as women's head	apprentice
		on-job training in collective mirror factory; army art training
		commercial training as temporary contract worker
		meat processing training as temporary contract worker
		correspondence school while teacher in township
1970–74	apprentice seamstress	
	apprentice seamstress	
	learned noodle making in natal family	
	apprentice seamstress	
since 1975	illiterate learning mushroom raising as temporary contract worker	

NOTE: This table includes information for all members of households interviewed in 1989, 1990, 1992, and 1995, where these members were no longer in school and where information on training was available. Only training (*peixun*) reported as such is included here; training and skill acquisition is considerably underreported for both women and men, especially where it occurred in a relatively informal context. There were no reported cases of training received by either women or men born before 1930.

comparable patterns for men, who experience not only a wider range of options, but commonly also an integration of education, training, and career opportunities. Here I will not present all the cases in the same detail, but will summarize the further education situation for men (also see Tables 2 and 3) and give examples selected to indicate the salient contrasts with women, as well as the range of opportunities available to some men. It is important to note that it was also a minority of men—if not quite so small a minority as in the case of women—who have enjoyed what are still relatively privileged opportunities.

The most direct contrast is observable in the case of teachers, as this is a role that is acceptable for both women and men in rural China, although only men can have continuous careers in the field. In Huaili an even more extreme situation obtains, as all the teachers in the village of which I have any record have been men. The principal of Huaili's primary school is a man born in 1957 who graduated from upper middle school and served in the army for three years; upon demobilization he became a local (*minban*) teacher and later the school principal. A younger man in the village graduated at the top of his English class in upper middle school, and this earned him the opportunity to become a local teacher of English in the township lower middle school. There he enrolled in correspondence school in the field of politics and, at the time of being interviewed, he had just sat an exam for admission to normal school, which, if he succeeds in entering, will allow him to become a teacher on the state payroll. A third man in the village, born in 1955, graduated from upper middle school and taught in the village for five years. Then he was given one year of medic's training in the township clinic and became a brigade-employed medic in 1982. He has had a one-half month upgrading course since then and remains on the village payroll, although private medics now also practice in the village.

In each of these cases, high levels of formal education (upper middle school) provided non-agricultural career opportunities that were enabled and fostered by the local collective system, while it existed, and by local government since 1984. Similarly striking patterns obtain for other fields, including ones where formal education (*wenhua*) is combined with, supplemented by, or effectively substituted with some form of training (*peixun*).

TRAINING

The concept of training is a difficult one, as its boundaries are quite blurred. In some cases training seems to merge with specialized education, as in some less formal types of teacher's training, while at the other end of the continuum it merges with on-the-job training and may not be considered or reported as training at all, even by those who received it. Some of the training is indicated in Table 3, but this includes only cases where those interviewed considered themselves to have been trained. In my judgment, this includes most of the more formal training (*peixun*) received by village residents, but little of the less formal training. This table is therefore much less comprehensive than Table 1 or Table 2. The material contained in Table 3 will be presented together with more inclusive interview and work history data to provide a more complete and contextualized view of training opportunities differentially available to residents of Huaili.

In this discussion, I will interpret training broadly, to include formal and informal training that resulted in the acquisition of a skill that could lead to either employment or remunerative self-employment. This does seem to be the culturally relevant significance of any form of training in rural China. Training is less formally recognized than education and is valued for its practical consequences. The only form of training that I am excluding from this discussion is the occasional very short (often half-day) sessions in practical (often agricultural) skills offered widely in the village. To the extent that these targeted women in the "two studies" activities, they will be discussed in Chapter 6.

Many of the opportunities available in the countryside have been provided through various levels of the collective structure (team, brigade, and commune), or through the governmental structures that replaced these (village and township).[9] During the collective era, entry to any type of work that was not purely agricultural involved some level of the state in labor allocation, and this naturally extended to providing the training essential for someone to undertake such work. In effect, all such opportunities fell within the realm of the state monopoly on the

[9] In Huaili the production team was replaced by the agricultural group, but with much reduced scope and significance (see Judd 1994). Most of the opportunities described here seem to have been more associated with the brigade/village level, in any event, as that was the lowest collective/administrative level with major responsibility for areas beyond the purely agricultural.

allocation of labor. Women were sometimes employed in areas considered suitable for women, such as primary education, health work, and work as village women's heads, and some training might be provided, although teachers were often selected primarily on the basis of a higher educational level and did not always receive teacher's training. Women's heads are usually trained on the job, if at all, although one woman in my sample did report twenty days of training in her natal village, where she subsequently served as women's head. As seen earlier, women are not able to move their teaching profession from their natal to their marital villages. Neither of the two women in the sample who had been women's heads in their natal villages had been able to move this position to their marital village, and they and local Women's Federation cadres were firm in their assertion that this could not be done. Women can be given opportunities in their marital villages, and many women are recruited to serve as women's heads after they are in their marital villages. But the break early in women's adult lives anticipated through the predominant practice of patrilocal postmarital residence renders it less likely that local leaders will select young women for training or that, if they receive it, they will be able to use it later in their lives.

In addition, there are patterns of customary gender division of labor that effectively exclude women from many areas of work and training. And while it is possible to locate cases of daughters being given preferential opportunities in their natal village, as in the case of the trained women's head cited above, who was the daughter of the village Party branch secretary, similar ties that can nurture a man's career through several shifts and turns work for a woman only as long as she is in her natal village.

SYSTEMIC NURTURANCE

The opportunities women miss can be made clear by citing a few cases of men who were positioned to receive a sustained period of education, training, and career opportunity through collective or government channels. It should be noted that decollectivization has not disrupted these channels, which operate in much the same way as in the past, but with a smaller number of official positions available. The rural economic reform has altered this situation only by adding additional channels of advancement in the private sector. It has therefore been possible for some men to receive sustained nurturing of their career across the threshold of decollectivization, while others chose to use training received in the collective era to establish private enterprises in the reform period. Opportunities for village-level structures to nurture careers may be reduced, in the reform era, unless a village has significant enterprises and resources, but this transition is sufficiently recent that there are still numerous men in their economically active prime who have benefited in this way. To the extent that the public sphere remains an important area of economic activity in rural China, access to its channels of training and career development—and gender differences in access to those channels—will continue to have long-term importance.

For example, one man born in 1958, who was the son of a team head, graduated from upper middle school during the Cultural Revolution[10] and was sent to the county seat for two years of training and certification as a veterinarian for large animals.[11] He worked as a veterinarian in the brigade for one year, but did not like the work. He was then trained by the brigade for a year to be a driver and drove for the brigade for half a year. Subsequently, he received the opportunity for short-term training as an electrician. He worked for the next ten years in the brigade/village and in nearby public service during the time this area of the countryside was initially electrified. He was not trained to a level at which he was qualified to do electrical work in urban construction, however, and at the time of being interviewed, was self-employed in rural transport as a driver. This case should not be dismissed as exceptional because the man had a cadre connection; many men have such connections, and so do women. The difference is that although fathers and daughters strive to use familial connections in the interests of daughters, there are structural obstacles to their being able to do so effectively on a long-term basis. There are several men (and no women) in Huaili who have been trained as electricians by the collective or while in the army, and who have had relatively attractive opportunities in the rural electrification process.

[10] He spontaneously described this as being a lower level of upper middle school, because of the conditions prevailing in education at that time. During the Cultural Revolution, lower middle school education usually meant a total of seven years of schooling.

[11] Rural veterinary work is not presently done by women in China. Although women are trained as veterinarians in small numbers, they work as teachers or in other urban roles.

More common instances of collective training for young men lay in the area of tractor driving. As one younger man born in 1959 openly indicated, he had the opportunity to learn to drive a tractor following lower middle school graduation because many of his classmates were disqualified by being women. He drove a tractor in the brigade for five years and bought the tractor upon decollectivization, becoming one of the first men in the village to enter the private motorized transport field, a particularly remunerative area of the rural economy.[12] At one time all tractor drivers had learned this skill within the collectives, and were then able to move into private transport. This skill remains advantageous, although it is now more dispersed among the rural male population, if at an often lower level of skill.

In some instances men could also be viewed as acquiring some accounting or managerial skills while serving as team or brigade cadres. Apart from the minor role of women's head, all such positions were held by men in Huaili, and either exclusively (as was most common) or predominantly by men in other villages of north China. For example, one younger man, born in 1959, worked as a storeman (*baoguanyuan*) for one of Huaili's production teams before decollectivization, and later moved successfully into running a garage and oil store. Another former storeman in the collective era became both head of one of Huaili's three agricultural groups (*nongye zu*) after decollectivization, and the owner, with his wife, of a successful shop. Theirs was one of the conspicuously affluent households in the village in 1995. Yet another man served in the army for six years, and after demobilization learned business in the brigade-run shop and through doing sales work in the township paper factory, skills which he has put to use in the private sector.

There are also some types of training that are transmitted outside the state sector, primarily informally within the family, but sometimes also through formal apprenticeships, within or beyond the family, a practice that has revived during the reform era. Truly formal apprenticeships are relatively rare in Huaili, although one man considered himself to have apprenticed with his father as a carpenter; and one woman gave details of an apprenticeship contract with her father in the art of making false teeth, a skill customarily taught in the male line but

[12] I have seen women drive in rural China, but rarely and not within this village. The usual reason cited for disqualifying women as drivers is that driving distances alone in transport work places a woman's safety and reputation at risk.

that this man had transmitted to a daughter as well as to a son. More recently, in the reform era, one especially successful seamstress in the village took on several apprentices, two of whom later set up their own small enterprises and had apprentices of their own. All the seamstresses are women, and this is evidently a less attractive skill than the others, for women leave its hard work and tight market schedule when they are affluent enough to do so, as the original leading seamstress did while still in her early thirties.

Some other skills are transmitted through the family line. Making sesame oil is a traditional skill in the area that has been transmitted through the male line in several Huaili households. Women commonly learn to do this work when they marry into a household with the skill, but I am not aware of any households where the skill was transmitted through a daughter from such a household to her subsequent marital family. The customary expectation is that this skill is a familial asset, but at least one woman cited as a success in the "two studies" movement in 1992 indicated that she was teaching the skill to another household, apparently under the encouragement of the women's head.

One other skill transmitted within families during the research period was the making of dried noodles (*guamian*). This was work largely done by women, and the skill was being effectively passed to daughters-in-law who could carry the skill as well as some capital into a new production unit upon household division. Daughters also learned the skill, although I am less certain that they would have been able to carry it into their marital households since the production standard, by the 1990s, required significant investment in machinery. At least two of the more successful households in Huaili reported teaching this skill to other households, and the women's organization actively encouraged this.

It is important to note, in reading Table 3, that there is a difference in time frame not apparent from the table itself. The training men received through collective structures was primarily acquired during the collective era and, although many managed to carry the benefits through into the reform era, Huaili is a village with a weak public sector and hence one no longer able to train and promote the careers of large numbers of men. In contrast, the training reported for women of similar ages was almost entirely received in the reform era, either through private channels (such as apprenticeships in sewing) or through the emerging training programs promoted by the Women's Federation (as in raising chickens).

MILITARY SERVICE

One of the most important channels of advancement in rural China is through military service. One of the two oldest men in the village with education beyond lower middle school was born in 1938 and had completed part of lower middle school before joining the air force. There he attended a school at the specialized secondary level where he was trained as an airplane mechanic, and was kept on staff at the school after his graduation. After demobilization, he returned to Huaili as head of its militia, but soon his technical training (and presumably also his political training) led to his being transferred to a commune enterprise where he became factory head and Party branch secretary. He was responsible for running a large and profitable enterprise for more than twenty years and, although he helped more than twenty other people obtain non-agricultural registration, he did not do this for himself. When ill health forced him to retire with only a small stipend, he returned to Huaili and eventually started a small store. This man is somewhat unusual because of the importance of the position he held earlier, but a result of China's household registration system and its tight control over rural-urban migration has been a return of qualified and experienced people to the countryside upon retirement, or upon loss of position for economic or political reasons. He is, however, quite indicative of an important line of training and opportunity available to men in all but the oldest living generations, that is, through the military.

The oldest man in the sample to have served in the military, born in 1934, attended literacy class while in the military, although all the others who have served in the military entered with a good level of education for their generation (usually some middle school education). Virtually all men who serve in the military receive significant additional training or experience, or acquire political qualifications, such as Party membership, that provide them with opportunities for leadership positions in the countryside, should they return. Indeed, entry into military service is a privileged opportunity that commonly marks a man as someone with the potential to leave the countryside, or to return to a leading position in his community. In my sample of a total of 121 men no longer attending school, there are seventeen men who have had army service. Not all of them show signs of having had their future substantially improved by this service, but many do. One important dimension of quality is the political dimension, and both selection for army service in the first place and any demonstrated success while in the army, such as being admitted to Party membership, is a qualification for political advancement.

The village head at the time of one of the field trips was a man born in 1954 who had served in the army, where he had entered the Party and had been designated for officer training, but his unit was demobilized during a period of reduction in the size of the army. He returned to the village and occupied a series of positions as cadre, while juggling this with entry into the restaurant business during the reform era. He was a priority target of political training on the part of the village leadership, with the goal of making him the future Party branch secretary.

Another man, born in 1950, learned to be an electrician during his seven years of military service, and then worked as an electrician for the brigade from the time of his return from the army until decollectivization. Since that time he has been a partner with his brothers in a small mill, where he looks after the machinery.

A younger man, born in 1965, was good at art in lower middle school, worked in the brigade decorative mirror factory for a year, and then spent three years in the army where he learned more art. He now has his own decorative mirror enterprise in the village, and has trained his wife to work with him.

Although women are eligible to serve in the armed forces they do so in very small numbers, and I have yet to encounter any rural woman with a past of military service. This is an important avenue of political and technical advancement that is effectively, if not formally, closed to rural women. Although this portion of the argument has been focused upon technical training, since that is the centerpiece of the "two studies" strategy, the political importance of military service and of cadre training must also be mentioned. The effort to improve women's quality explicitly and significantly includes improving their political quality, and preparing women to take on roles in the outer domain in rural China is dependent on initiatives in this area. Political study and measures to provide women with opportunities to enter the village outer domain through membership in either the village committee or the more powerful village Party branch is a concurrent major policy of the Women's Federations.

STRUCTURES OF OPPORTUNITY

In summary, women presently in their economically productive adult years in Huaili have higher rates of illiteracy, lower levels of formal education, and more restricted access to training than do their male counterparts. Perhaps more important, even when they do have relatively high levels of education, they may be unable to use this education in their adult years. Women do not enjoy access to a continuous structure of education, training, and career development facilitated through the public sphere as do some rural men. Consequently, women's abilities are systemically underutilized in the countryside, even when they have received some early educational or non-agricultural career opportunities.

A development strategy focusing on training as the key point of intervention in the interests of women must therefore address structures of opportunity and the question of whether women will effectively be able to utilize any training that is provided.

As the strategy has unfolded, it has involved a diversity of measures to train and position women in both state and market sectors of the rural economy (see Chapter 6). In order to achieve this, a stronger rural women's movement has been needed, and this has been emphasized concurrently with the women's movement initiative for economic development. Strengthening the women's movement organizationally has been critical and is itself conceptualized and presented as raising women's quality.

5

Grassroots Organization

In order to accomplish any of the changes advocated by the women's movement, an organizational vehicle for change was required. This was not entirely a new problem, but rather a familiar issue for the state and the Women's Federations, since the connection between policy and organization is a fundamental tenet of Marxist-Leninist political organization. Building a national organization reaching into every village had been a long-term and central task of the Women's Federations from their beginning. In the reform era this organization was under examination, and there were initiatives to draw wider numbers of women into a revised form of "woman-work." This new form would emphasize voluntary participation in activities oriented toward seeking prosperity through the market. This required a degree of organizational innovation and adjustment, although the direction from above remained consistent with classical policies and practices of organization building.

The blending of statist and market approaches is also evident in the emphasis upon organizational "quality." The classical approach was one that recognized the importance of the people implementing policy through the standard proposition that, once the political line is set, cadres are the determining factor.[1] From this perspective, building an organization of strong cadres is essential to achieving political goals. The Chinese Communist Party has arguably placed exceptional emphasis

---

[1] The classical position, very familiar in China, is: "After a correct political line has been worked out and tested in practice, the Party cadres become the decisive force in the work of guiding the Party and the state. A correct political line is, of course, the primary and most important thing. But that in itself is not enough. A correct political line is not needed as a declaration, but as something to be carried into effect. But in order to carry a correct political line into effect, we must have cadres, people who understand the political line of the Party, who accept it as their own line, who are prepared to carry it into effect, who are able to put it into practice and are capable of answering for it, defending it and fighting for it. Failing this, a correct political line runs the risk of being purely nominal." (Stalin 1947 [1939]: 626.)

upon the cultivation of its cadres, in association with a Confucian heritage of nurturing leaders. The emphasis on this approach may also have been a product of the Party's early history in scattered bases and underground units where cadres had to be capable of effective concerted action even when scarce and dispersed. This approach has been embedded in every subsequent rectification and political study initiative. At the same time, emphasis upon human resource development and quality, in both organizational and individual terms, is characteristic of contemporary market-oriented conceptions and strategies, albeit for quite different reasons.

The organizational resources available to the Women's Federations to carry out their strategy of raising women's quality are critical for the possibility of realizing this strategy. Indeed, a major and increasingly important element of the strategy has been the raising of organizational quality within the women's movement. In this chapter I will examine these issues, starting with the grassroots situation in Huaili from 1988 to 1995, and proceeding to township and county levels. The chapter will conclude with an indication of organizational changes being made in rural woman-work.

HUAILI

Foreign researchers do not ordinarily do field research in villages the authorities consider to be bad examples. I am no exception to this, although Huaili is a village I reached as the result of protracted efforts to avoid model villages and to find a somewhat representative agricultural village in an area of modest economic success. When I first entered the village, in January 1988, it was one well connected with county officials and evidently regarded as fairly successful. I was then doing research focused on decollectivization and household social organization and, while I was taking a gender-inclusive approach to my research and investigating the women's movement as part of the general context, neither women's issues nor the Women's Federations were initially central to my research. I do not think, therefore, that I was invited to Huaili (among a number of other potential sites) specifically because it had a more active women's organization than most other communities, although that is the case. Rather, I think that this was part of a more general sense in which this village was in tune with current policies being promoted by the county. I suspect that Huaili may have received more support for its woman-work in following years, as I returned repeatedly and appeared to be making Huaili the site of long-term field research centered on women. However, when I returned in 1995 after an absence of three years, I found Huaili's women's organization to have lapsed into relative inactivity and the township's priority to have shifted to an adjacent village. While one village cannot represent a comprehensive range of possibilities in the rural women's movement, the diversity of circumstances obtaining through the field period may indicate some part of the range—as well as the problems—of sustaining a women's movement over a period of years.

In January 1988, the village was receiving more than usual attention from the county Women's Federation. In 1987 Huaili had been one of a handful of villages in the county that had been the site of a large-scale visit to its Women's Home (*funü zhi jia*, a space in the village dedicated to woman-work) and to several of its households successful in the courtyard economy (*tingyuan jingji*) initiative. Huaili had long been one of several villages in the county where the county Women's Federation made an effort to maintain contact. These village contact points (*lianxi dian*) were one of the structural channels through which the county Women's Federation sought to lead developments in the countryside by keeping in touch with the grass roots and promoting successful examples that might then be emulated by other villages. This is a long-term variant of the standard Chinese policy of developing model points through which to instigate similar developments in a larger area (*yidiandaipian*). During the period of preparation for the on-site meeting, an energetic and capable vice-head of the county Women's Federation made roughly weekly visits to the village, and personally organized the women's group and its activities in the village. This represented a level of effort that the county Women's Federation, with a total staff of nine at that time—and 986 villages in the county—could not sustain even for selected contact villages. Huaili in the 1980s was, therefore, not representative of the general situation in China's villages, but rather indicative of what could happen where substantial inputs were available. The research I reported later (Judd 1994) was based upon this early situation, primarily as represented in 1989, when I did a systematic series of household visits in the village, and when the vice-head in question was still present.

I made a brief visit in 1990, when Huaili's women's organization was in transition after two women's heads in succession had left the village, and consideration of who might be the next one was underway. By 1992, one of these candidates had been appointed. Together with a new Women's Federation cadre at the township level, there were major initiatives underway in Huaili to implement the package of changes associated with the "two studies," including economic development, competition, and organizational strengthening. For about two years, this energetic team led Huaili in an active promotion of the village women's organization and in economic development for village women, along the same lines as those advocated earlier, but with a more locally grounded organizational basis.

It is, however, extraordinarily difficult to retain any effective team under current conditions. By 1995, Huaili had again lost a women's head to migration out of the village, and the township cadre who had worked with her had been promoted to the post of vice-head of another township. "Two studies" work had stalled while the village waited and hoped that the former women's head might return. When she had not done so after a year, a replacement was found, within a context in which demands upon village women's organizations had shifted toward birth-planning work. Huaili was no longer leading the way in the "two studies," although it was a minor participant in the newer study and organizational initiatives of the second phase of the "two studies."

The discussion that follows will therefore utilize material from three distinct periods in Huaili—the precursors to and early steps in the "two studies" during the late 1980s, the organized effort to implement the "two studies" as observed in 1992, and the retreat to a lower level of activity evident in 1995.

VILLAGE WOMEN AND WOMEN'S COMMITTEES

Although the countryside has traditionally been the primary focus for the Women's Federations, they have always been sparsely staffed and have never had any staff below the level of the township. In this respect, the situation of the Women's Federations is similar to that of government departments. They are concerned with work in the villages, but rely upon village residents themselves to conduct the work.

The village institutions for woman-work consist formally of women's representatives, a women's committee, and the women's head. I have had the situation described to me, by staff of the county Women's Federation, as one that provides for one woman representative to be selected for every thirty women active in the labor force, that is, women between sixteen and forty-five years of age. These women comprise the women's representative committee (*fudaihui*), and they elect three to five women to form a women's committee, the number depending on the size of the village. These committee members indirectly elect a head for the women's representative committee (*fudaihui zhuren*), or "women's head." It is possible that such formal structures and processes are now to be found in practice, as local government moves toward more formal governmental structures and grassroots elections. However, I have never been able to observe these in operation, and the descriptions provided by women at the village level are somewhat different.

I have not encountered the women's representative committee as an actual body of representatives in any village I have visited. I understand the usual practice to be the convening of meetings of village women in general rather than of representatives, although not all women are actually expected to attend. The term used, "women's representative committee," should be interpreted broadly as referring to the general structures of organized woman-work at the village level, rather than as referring to a particular formal institution.

The smaller women's committee can be found, and it varies in its level of activity. In practical terms, however, virtually all of the work associated with the women's organization in villages is the responsibility of the women's head. Consequently, women's heads are the critical link between village women and communities and the larger scope of woman-work and the Women's Federations. The women's heads are expected to accomplish the work through organizational vehicles within the villages that draw village women into meetings and other activities.

In part because of the public discourse about woman-work and women's committees, and in part because I was interested in tracing gender differences in lines of interhousehold and suprahousehold social organization, I systematically asked women in households I visited about their connection with the village women's organization. I used the term *fudaihui*, but expanded upon it to include any form of associated activity. Tables 4, 5, and 6 provide a summary of the responses from inquiries in formal household visits in 1989, 1992, and 1995. Since I had initially been told that all women participated, and this was a village with a strong record in woman-work, it seemed appropriate to make this inquiry regarding every woman in my household sample. It immediately became apparent that the number of women involved was

TABLE 4

Participation in Women's Committee Work, Huaili, 1989

	Participation in Women's Committee				
Age	No involvement	Attends meetings only	Meetings and some further involvement	Committee member	No data
Young, unmarried	4	4			7
Up to 29, married	5	3	1	1	3
30–39	3	11	1	3	0
40–49	3	5	0	1	2
50 and over	8	1	0	0	0
TOTAL	23	24	2	5	12

TABLE 5

Participation in Women's Committee Work, Huaili, 1992

	Participation in Women's Committee					
Age	No involvement	Attends meetings only	Meetings and some further involvement	Committee member	Involved and a model	No data
Young, unmarried	2	1	1	0	0	1
Up to 29, married	2	1	6	2	2	3
30–39	1	2	13	1	3	1
40–49	4	0	1	1	1	4
50 and over	2	0	1	0	0	3
Age not known	0	0	1	0	0	1
TOTAL	11	4	23	4	6	13

TABLE 6

Participation in Women's Committee Work, Huaili, 1995

	Participation in Women's Committee						
Age	No involvement	Birth planning only	Attends meetings only	Meetings and some further involvement	Committee member	Involved and a model	No data
Young, unmarried	11	0	1	1	0	0	0
Up to 29, married	1	1	2	2	1	0	0
30–39	3	1	2	5	1	3	3
40–49	3	2	2	3	2	1	4
50 and over	8	0	0	1	0	0	3
TOTAL	26	4	7	12	4	4	10

quite limited, although this was not a formal matter of including one woman in thirty.

Several categories of women were systematically excluded. Older women were exempt, from some time after their sons married and brought in daughters-in-law, unless they or their households had a particular contribution to make to woman-work in the village. One elderly cadre's wife, who had a daughter who had been a women's head, indicated that there were also informal pressures keeping older women away. She said that if they attended, they would be laughed at by other women. Young, unmarried women were also generally exempt, perhaps because of their youth and probable imminent departure from the village, but presumably also because some of the work of the women's organization and of the content of the meetings included birth-planning policies. Young married women did not initially become a target of recruitment for the women's organization. The category of women most actively pursued was that of slightly older married women, well established in their new households, and often running their own nuclear family households. These women already had one or two children who were attending school; indeed, a standard method of notifying women of a meeting was to send a message home through announcements in the village school. Married women of this age group were central to the economic well-being of their households (and hence targets for the "two studies"), and were also of primary concern for birth-planning policies, which were partially promoted and implemented through the women's organization.

The Women's Federation would have preferred a higher rate of participation in meetings at the village level, and where the Women's Federation cadres accompanied me on these household visits, the limited participation provoked discussion and explanation. The customary exemption of various categories of women, as outlined above, was presented in the course of these discussions and was confirmed by the way in which village women spoke of their relation to the women's committee. These discussions were revealing in several senses.

It was clear, from the official side, that women were being called to attend meetings, and sometimes also to participate in additional activities (such as the courtyard economy) as part of state-initiated political activities. Although all my information is from the reform era, this had clear continuities with long-standing practices of required attendance at political study meetings. It was explicitly the case that each household was ideally expected to send (only) one woman to represent it. Participation was largely a matter of compliance with official requests, and my impression is that it was often no more than this. But even this degree of compliance was by no means universal; it had to be sought and given. One village woman described simple attendance at meetings as "very active" (*ting jiji*) participation, indicating the difficulty of drawing women into more active involvement.

As for the women themselves, many were completely blank on the subject of their relation to the *fudaihui*, or did not recognize this standard official term. Indeed, none of the cadres accompanying me even attempted to explain that concept, with the notable exception of the 1992 women's head, who was presumably attempting to educate me in the actual working of the village women's organization. She would elaborate upon the question by telling women that I was referring to her and the activities she did together with the village women (*zanmen*). It was very much the case that personal networks and personal connections drew women into meetings and activities more than formal meetings and organizations. The particularly high rate of activity in 1992 (see Table 5) was the result of this women's head's tirelessly working with individual women to draw them into the "two studies" activities at that time. Similar although less extensive informal ties centered around some women's heads were also evident in other years.

The majority of village women either did not attend meetings or only attended meetings. The material in Tables 4, 5, and 6 should be read with the understanding that my sample included all of the most active women in the village, and that the "no data" cases can confidently be classed as minimal involvement. While many women were simply not targets for involvement in any case, many other women were uninterested or resistant to being involved. Some women indicated that they were too busy with household economic activities, and this was accepted as a quite legitimate reason for not being involved, although the women's organization did try to get the most economically successful women involved in helping poorer women and in training.

The women who did report being involved on a level beyond just attending meetings reported a range of activities. Many, especially in the earlier years, reported attending some classes or participating in courtyard production in the 1980s, or similar training and productive work related to the "two studies" in 1992. In 1992, there was occasionally a mention of legal education, and the women's head at that time had been cited as a model (at the relatively high level of the prefecture) in popularizing law. However, the legal education did not necessarily or only refer to the Women's Law of 1992. It also referred to legal provisions regarding paying taxes, a difficult matter in the countryside following the dissolution of collectives.[2] In 1995, at a time when the courtyard economy had retreated and the "two studies" was less emphasized in Huaili's woman-work, many of the specific mentions village women made of their connection with the village women's organization concerned taxation and birth-planning policies.

It is impossible to assess the impact of the women's organization on women's actions in a precise sense, since it is difficult to disentangle the variety of motivations that might have been involved in any of the encouraged activities. This will be discussed in more detail in the following chapter. Here I would only note that my impression, based upon observation, is that activities that were being actively promoted at any particular time were carried out by a noticeable number of women, but that their participation remained dependent upon active mobilization and did not sink deep roots. Even the comparatively welcome activity of courtyard economy production was very much more in evidence when that was a mobilizational priority than in later years, despite its potential for raising household income. Women and their households might prefer other uses for their courtyards, or other avenues for generating income, or even more leisure. Choices were varied, and not necessarily in accord with state policy in general, or the goals of the Women's Federations in particular. Policies such as paying taxes and limiting family size had much less prospect of active support.

While it should also be noted that there were village women who did see benefit in particular policies, primarily the economic ones, and willingly and actively participated, the disinterest or even quiet resistance of the majority posed an organizational challenge. The established formal mechanism for reaching village women was through a women's committee. Each village was expected to have one, and these could of-

---

[2] During the collective era, taxes could be levied on the collectives. After collectives were dissolved and the market economy invigorated, taxes were largely collected from households. The local government organs that replaced the collectives were a channel for collecting taxes, and may have worked more or less effectively for agricultural taxes. It was more difficult to assess income and tax liability for households with their own enterprises, especially those in commerce. This area of activity was a major area of growth in Huaili, and the importance of persuading people to voluntarily pay taxes may have been especially great in this village. It was also a major concern throughout the township.

TABLE 7

Members of Women's Committees, Huaili,
1988, 1989, 1990, 1992, 1995

Description	Year				
	1988	1989	1990	1992	1995
women's head, 1982–88; older woman with cadre background and history of work in county seat; recovered urban registration and left Huaili in 1988	X				
young married woman who had successfully run village business with husband; when husband left village for managerial position in larger enterprise, she became a wealthy housewife; considered for women's head by WF, but left village	X	X	X		
committee member in 1988 and women's head in 1989; daughter of retired village cadre; in natal village following divorce, until left for work in county seat	X	X			
the only woman Party member in the village, having joined in her natal village; in poor health, and not very active	X	X	X	X	
independent entrepreneur; active in women's organization, and once considered for women's head and Party membership	X	X	X	X	
one of the first women entrepreneurs in the village, running successful restaurant		X	X		
women's head, 1991–93; young woman who broke into a traditional men's branch of commerce; active entrepreneur; model; married into retired village cadre family; considered for Party membership; left village to pursue business in city				X	
self-taught seamstress who later became shop-keeper; member of League when young				X	X
in residence in natal village for better commercial site (not uxorilocal); successful seamstress who taught sewing voluntarily for village women's committee and ran successful business with several apprentices; later ran shop				X	X
women's head and village birth-planning worker, 1994–95					X
successful entrepreneur in chicken and pig raising from 1988; model					X
cook running restaurant together with her husband; wife of village cadre					X
entrepreneur in grain business					X

ten be identified actually, although they were not always very active. Huaili did have a women's committee throughout the period of my visits to the village, and the membership is indicated in Table 7.

Members of the women's committee were asked to serve by the village leadership, in effect, by the Party branch secretary. The demands of committee membership were not onerous, but involved a willingness to attend meetings and promote official policy. This may explain the predominance of women with official connections among the membership, although personal contact with the village leadership was also important. There were some indications that there were more women in the village willing to be involved in woman-work than were actually serving on the committee at any time. I was sometimes given an impression of frustrated aspirations on the part of individual women who were involved in the official programs but either not on the committee or not invited to serve as women's head. The women's committee itself was largely a body that was expected to hold and attend meetings, which, at the most active points, were reported to occur once a month or more. Committee members were also expected to be active in the various official campaigns or local initiatives of the women's organization, and this was generally so.

There was also a considerable number of models, especially in the courtyard economy and the "two studies" activities, who were not recruited into the women's committee, but were frequently called upon to support official initiatives. These women were especially requested to help with policies involving market activity intended to help women out of poverty and toward prosperity, or where examples of success were required for public purposes, including reporting to higher official levels. Indeed, much of the work of the women's organization depended upon recruiting these women beyond the formal structure of the women's committee to become involved in village woman-work.

While it is important that Huaili had a women's committee that met from time to time, both the committee and the wider circle of women upon whom woman-work depended were reliant upon leadership and mobilization by the village women's head. In this reliance, Huaili was consistent with the general situation in the countryside. The pivotal role of the women's head made women in these roles critical for realizing Women's Federation strategies in the countryside.

WOMEN'S HEADS

When the Women's Federations or any other branch of the state wants to reach rural women, it does so through the institution of village women's heads. In principle, each administrative village in China has a person occupying this role, and the position usually is filled. In common with all other occupants of leadership roles within villages, the women's head holds rural household registration and is dependent upon rural sources of income. Her rural registration means that she is not on the staff of the Women's Federations and never will be. However, to the extent that the work of the Women's Federations enters villages, it does so through the women's heads. In Shandong alone there were 87,475 administrative villages in 1995, and all but about two hundred of these had a women's head in place (there are always a few vacancies). This is a very sizable body of people upon which the state is able to draw, but the work in any particular village is completely dependent upon this one woman, since she provides the only gender-specific channel between the state (including the Women's Federations) and village women. This is a formidable number of women strategically located at the community-state interface, and it is hardly surprising that the women's heads—their recruitment, training, and mobilization—are the primary focus of Women's Federation work in the countryside.

A brief review of the series of women's heads in Huaili from 1988 to 1995 may serve to indicate some of the issues. The first women's head I encountered there was an energetic woman then forty-six years old. The daughter of a production team head, she had moved to a town for work available there in the early 1960s, and acquired urban registration. Her work unit was disbanded in 1966, and the women without education were sent back to the countryside. At this point, she and her children had to go to live with her mother-in-law in Huaili, although her husband, a former soldier with urban registration, remained at his job in a city elsewhere in the province, and visited when possible. By the time I met her, she had successfully reclaimed urban registration for herself and her children and was soon to leave for the city to join her husband. Perhaps her wider experience, as well as her family political background, made her suitable as a women's head. She was certainly capable, energetic, and enthusiastic about woman-work. However, her atypical background contributed to the difficulty in retaining her, and she had herself replaced a woman who had left the village in 1982. As a member of an older cohort, she had relatively little education, and would eventually have found herself less favored by the Women's Federations, which by the 1990s were advocating retirement of the older women's heads and their replacement by younger, educated women who could acquire and lead in the technical training being promoted in the "two studies."

In 1989, the women's head was a woman in her twenties who had graduated from upper middle school. This woman had previously been a member of the women's committee and, in addition to her education, enjoyed the advantage of being the daughter of a particularly esteemed former production team head in the village. She was temporarily in the village, together with her son, benefiting from a supportive natal family during a divorce, and was preparing to leave the village again. Both work in a town or city and remarriage were in her plans, and by 1990 she had relocated to the county seat. Whether because of the temporary and stressful nature of her return to the village, or because of her quiet and rather shy disposition, she was not as active a women's head as had been her predecessor.

In 1990, the position was vacant and the village Party committee was actively considering at least two prospects for the position. The woman ultimately appointed was already a notable success by 1992 and demonstrated many of the qualities then advocated. She was in her mid-twenties, had married into the household of a former village head, had a lower middle school education, and was strongly oriented toward the market. She had initially made her mark by moving into an area of petty commerce that had until that time been exclusively male. Largely on this basis the village Party branch secretary selected her to be women's head and, in support of the current policy that asked for women's heads each to have an economic project, allowed her to rent a small plot of un-allocated land from the village upon which to grow tree seedlings. This woman was extremely hard working and ambitious, and made the necessary effort to succeed both in her new post and in her own economic activity. Indeed, she was a model of the quality—and qualities—sought in women's heads in the 1990s. She received some useful help from a well-matched township Women's Federation cadre in preparing reports and other written material, the only women's head in Huaili to do so of whom I am aware. This woman's active work in promoting the "two studies" through individual recruitment and work with many village women made her an exceptionally successful women's head. Huaili probably reached its peak of activity during her brief term. Although cited as a model at the prefectural level (in popularizing law) and put forward as a candidate for Party membership, she left Huaili in 1993 to pursue independent commerce in Tianjin together with her husband. The village kept her position open for a year, in case she decided to return. Although her children remain with their paternal grandparents in Huaili, her business appears to be doing well and she has not returned to the village to live. Her situation is indicative of a common one affecting recruitment of women's heads. The goal is to find women who are capable of economic success in the market themselves and who can lead others in the same direction. But they must not be so successful and busy that they do not have time for official work, or that they have the opportunity to leave the village. Women who are already successful businesswomen (as in specialized households, *zhuanye hu*) are rarely recruited as women's heads, although they are commonly asked to help in woman-work and are cited as models.

The woman who became Huaili's women's head in late 1994 and was still in office in 1995 represents another line of possibility in the 1990s. Although the same criteria applied as in the previous few years, the county was in the mid-1990s very actively encouraging women's heads to serve at the same time as village birth-planning workers, largely as means of providing them with remuneration, because township governments would pay for this work, while women's heads had to be funded by villages. This may have restricted the choice of women available. The woman who accepted this position was in her late twenties—with a six-year-old daughter and five-year-old son—and seemed willing and able to conduct the birth-planning work then required. Most of the work she did in the village in 1995 involved either birth planning or encouragement of women in commerce (in this village of small merchants) to pay taxes. She had some involvement with the local Rural Correspondence College classes for women in raising chickens, but was not primarily involved in "two studies" work. She was capable and responsible in her work, but the work had shifted in this village toward a more administrative direction.

A very considerable difficulty facing woman-work at the village level is the recruitment and retention of suitable women. As the recent history of Huaili indicates, those women who are most capable and suitable may well be those with other opportunities as well, including opportunities for leaving the countryside. Locating women who will perform well in this position, who are not already too busy with other work (as is commonly the case for those running household enterprises), and who will not soon leave is a formidable challenge. The Women's Federations are concerned about this as a critical issue in developing its organizational base, but is not in a position to directly control the recruitment or the conditions of recruitment of women's heads.

Despite the occasional formal description of the women's head as being elected by the women's committee (and the possibility that this may happen in practice at some times and places), she is in practice selected by the village leadership, that is, the village Party branch secretary and Party branch. In cases where the Women's Federation is directly involved with a particular village, it might offer an opinion or consult with the village leaders, but they are under no obligation to defer to the Women's Federations. It is the village political leadership that is responsible for selecting women's heads and for supervising and supporting their work. Women selected for these positions are those in whom the village leadership has confidence, and they are women who are willing to take on the burden of additional meetings and work as directed by the village leadership. There has usually been little compensation for the women's heads; they have not really been incorporated into the androcentric leadership structures of village communities, and have received little or no material remuneration. These conditions have left women's heads marginalized and doing woman-work in their spare time. As a result, the human resource of women's heads is much stronger in appearance than in reality.

The Women's Federations have been seeking to alter these conditions and to influence the selection of new cohorts of women's heads. They have been doing so in large part by working through the political leadership at their own levels (each Women's Federation is under the authority of the Party committee at its own level), and persuading the Party to make strengthening the network of women's heads part of its program for basic level development. In Ling County, this was accomplished by 1994 (Lingxian fulian n.d. [1995]) and lies behind the changes that have been made in the ranks of the women's heads.

One of the long-term concerns has been to incorporate women into the village political leadership. During the 1990s, this has taken the form of a demand to have women enter the "two committees" (liang wei). In practice, this translates into a demand that the women's head enter the village Party branch, where she is a Party member, and otherwise enter the less powerful village committee. During the early 1990s, the proportion of women's heads in the two committees increased sharply in Ling County, and by 1995 the county Women's Federation reported that this had occurred in 807 of the 986 villages in the county. This had not been a priority in Huaili, and the earlier women's heads had not entered either committee; I was told in 1995 that the women's head had entered the village committee, but the village leadership was at the time in an interregnum while lacking a Party branch secretary, and this entry may not have been meaningful.

The issue of remuneration for women's heads was given much more attention in Ling County in these years, and this was viewed as having a more immediate impact upon woman-work. In some cases (166 in the county by 1995), pensions had been arranged for long-serving women's heads who had retired. This was in line with a recent movement toward pensions for other village officials, but was also viewed in the Women's Federations as an important element enabling renewal in the ranks of women's heads. The larger question was one of persuading villages to provide remuneration to serving women's heads. Since any such remuneration would have to come directly from village sources and constituted an additional charge upon the village taxpayer, this was not easily demanded by the Women's Federations. By 1995, nevertheless, most villages had been persuaded to make some payment to the village women's head, and for 749 of the villages in Ling County, this was reported to be at a level of 50% or more of the remuneration for the village Party branch secretary. Huaili participated in this trend, and moved from an occasional daily payment in lieu of lost income in 1989 to a regular yearly salary in the 1990s.

Village salaries were not a complete solution to the problem, however. The Women's Federations sought to recruit a new generation of relatively educated and entrepreneurial young women who would have the ability to lead the "two studies" by example and through training and expertise that they could offer to others. Ideally, each women's head was to be in the process of acquiring further training, increasingly through the Rural Correspondence College, and also to have an economic project of her own. Women such as this were often very busy, and the more successful ones were earning incomes with which public office could not compete. Indeed, the same problem was also posed in recruiting men into village leadership posts. The Women's Federations hoped, nevertheless, to provide enough funding to make the position a form of part-time employment, especially when combined with an in-come-generating project at the same time. The village land rented to Huaili's women's head in 1992 provided a basis for one such project.

By the mid-1990s, the Women's Federations, at least in Shandong, had moved still further toward creating a professional body of staff at the village level. This was accomplished through an arrangement whereby women's heads served simultaneously as village birth-planning workers and received additional remuneration from the township governments for doing this work. This arrangement had administrative advantages for the state in taking birth-planning work directly to the women who were the main targets and, at least in Huaili and Ling County, coincided with a increased emphasis on birth planning and demands for intensive work with village women. Birth-planning work had not been given particular emphasis in Huaili prior to 1995, but there was a noticeable shift in that year, in line with a broader shift in the county. Almost all of the women's heads in Ling County were also birth-planning workers—as many as 889 out of 966 serving women's heads—in 1995.

In addition to making the post more attractive, the Women's Fed-erations asked that women's heads be younger and more educated than in the past. This was a move to improve the basic quality of the women in these positions in a direction that would make the women's heads suitable leaders for the "two studies." Lower middle school graduation was considered the minimum that would allow people to participate ef-fectively in the technical training being advocated, especially at the level provided through the Rural Correspondence College. The wom-en's heads were expected to take the lead in enrolling in the women's classes being run by the Rural Correspondence College and to achieve the standards for rural technicians (nongmin jishuyuan).[3] Each women's head was also expected to have an economic project for her own pros-perity, so that she would be leading other women by example.

Ling County had moved a considerable direction toward meeting these goals by 1995. By that time, 787 of the women's heads were under forty-five years of age, 794 had at least lower middle school education, 628 qualified as peasant technicians, and 787 were enrolled in the Rural

[3] The nongmin jishuyuan designation is achieved through examination in a spe-cific area of agricultural technique (such as animal husbandry). It is divided into sev-eral levels (basic, first, second, and third), and can be acquired through independent study without attending a formal program. In 1992 I was told there were one to three people with this designation in each village. Increasing the number of women who met this standard was one of the quantitative goals of the "two studies."

TABLE 8

Women's Heads in One Township, 1992: Age, Education,
Political Status, and Years of Service

Age	Education	Political status (League or Party member)	Years of service	Comment
21	lower middle school (lms)	League	2	kindergarten teacher
30	lms		2	kindergarten teacher
41	lms		3	teacher
34	lms		1	
29	lms		1	Huaili
55	primary school	Party	27	
37	lms	Party	5	
50	primary school	Party	23	
26	lms		1	
38	primary school		3	
21	lms		1	
36	lms		1	
22	lms		2	
32	lms		2	
39	lms		1	
56	primary school	Party	30	
20	lms		1	
35	lms		1	
26	lms		1	
30	lms		1	
22	lms		3	
26	lms		1	
63	illiterate	Party	32	
51	primary school	Party	6	
53	primary school	Party	27	
20	lms		1	
20	lms		1	
33	lms		2	
21	lms		1	
27	lms		2	
28	lms		1	
30	lms		1	
44	primary school		5	
37	primary school		1	
42	primary school		1	
21	lms		1	
41	primary school		1	
37	lms	Party	5	
36	lms	Party	3	
35	lms		1	teacher
41	primary school		3	
54	illiterate	Party	27	
27	lms		1	
21	lms		1	
23	lms		1	
30	primary school		1	
22	lms		1	

Age	Education	Political status (League or Party member)	Years of service	Comment
36	lms		2	
24	lms		1	
33	upper middle school		2	
30	lms		1	
51	illiterate		3	
48	primary school	Party	1	
21	lms		1	
38	lms	Party	3	
21	lms		1	
34	primary school		2	
37	lms		1	
36	lms		2	
21	lms		1	
27	lms		2	
40	lms	Party	2	township culture and education office
28	lms	Party	2	bank
38	lms	Party	2	supply and purchase co-op

NOTE: This table includes all women's heads in the township in which Huaili is located, as of 1992, based on township Women's Federation records.

Correspondence College. In addition to these more technical qualifications, the women's heads were also expected to be politically reliable and to have potential for political advancement; 533 were members of the Party or of the Youth League (Lingxian fulian n.d. [1995]). As the instance of Huaili demonstrates, however, movement in these directions was not necessarily smooth. Women's heads could be selected who met these criteria, and they could be encouraged to join in training and economic activity, but the need for constant replacement of departing women's heads was disruptive. As indicated in Table 8, which presents the situation of all women's heads in the township in which Huaili is located, the overwhelming majority were relatively new to their positions in the early 1990s.

The actual work that the women's heads were called upon to do was in the first instance official. They were expected, in a manner analogous to the Women's Federations, to serve as the Party's conduit to women in the village. They could be called upon to work with women to accomplish whatever the current political goals and priorities might be. The women's heads were expected to maintain the organizational framework of committee and meetings that provided official access to women as a defined group within each village. This was a visible feature clearly identifying their role as official. They would then use the meetings and any other activities to pursue the official policy. This was often a matter of supporting general policy (such as collecting taxes) and could be the promotion of a policy specifically targeting women (such as the various birth-planning policies). They were also expected to maintain the less formal channel of local women "models" and other successful women, who were drawn upon to help in economic work, including poverty alleviation and the "two studies."

In addition to their mainstream political role, women's heads were also charged with implementing the full range of woman-work at the village level. This could include continuing tasks such as promoting healthy families (as in the "five-good family" programs) or serving as a mediator, especially in disputes involving women. Indeed, any particular task that the Women's Federations—as well as the political leadership—wish to carry to village women has required the work of the network of women's heads.

In some cases, women's heads have been provided with employment paid by the village for performing concrete duties connected with their responsibilities as women's heads, but going beyond the expectations for women's heads. In other villages in Shandong, I have encountered women's heads who concurrently worked for the village as the paramedic responsible for women's health (including birth-planning work) or as a kindergarten teacher.[4] Huaili had never provided such employment for its women's heads, although the province-wide move to have women's heads take on birth-planning work for remuneration through township governments was similar in some respects. This was apparent in Huaili only during my 1995 field trip. Previous to that time, I had not been aware of the women's heads doing birth-planning work in Huaili (although this was not unusual elsewhere), and it appears to have previously been a responsibility of the political leadership in the village, principally of the Party branch secretary.[5] It should also be noted that birth-planning work in Huaili was not a high priority and not strictly consistent with the one-child policy, although it was not seriously in breach of it. The norm in Huaili for younger families prior to the mid-1990s had been two children, which was reasonably close to the national goal.

[4] Preschool education was a responsibility of the Women's Federations in Shandong, but not in all provinces.

[5] In 1992 the Party branch secretary introduced me to a woman who was then being considered for appointment as Huaili's birth-planning worker. I was later told that she had decided that her shop kept her too busy to take on this role.

However, this changed in Huaili from about 1994, with the introduction of more systematic methods for implementing the one-child
policy. These methods had been tried earlier in other locations, but
seem only to have reached Huaili at that time. The work this approach
required of the village birth-planning worker (and women's head) was
one of constant monitoring of all married women in the village of childbearing age, including even those who had been sterilized. The birth-
planning worker was required to maintain a monthly record of each
woman's menstruation, in order to identify any pregnancy at an early
stage. The birth-planning worker had to report any woman who was late
to the township birth-planning worker, and also to make a report of all
births to the township at the end of each month. This required constant
visiting of women in this age group, and the women's head did, indeed,
know this set of women well and was able to assure me that there had
been no unauthorized births since her term had begun. The large number of household visits and revisits I conducted that year confirmed that
this did appear to be the actual situation.[6]

In addition, the village birth-planning worker was responsible for
ensuring that village women turned up for the physical examination required by the township every three months. This resulted in early de-
tection of pregnancies, and unauthorized pregnancies were required to
be aborted; ensuring that this occurred was the responsibility of township authorities and not of the village birth-planning worker or the
women's head. This set of practices resulted in increased effectiveness
of the one-child policy and reduced the frequency of late abortions.
However, this was accomplished at the cost of close, intimate surveillance of women's bodies.

I was somewhat surprised to discover the 1995 women's head de-

---

[6] Given the sensitivity of the subject, I did not inquire about birth-planning practices in Huaili at any time, apart from some discussions initiated by others, most of
which took place in connection with this change in activity in 1995. However, my attention to households meant that I became aware of childbirth patterns and have detailed records on children in all households I visited. I believe that my nonintrusive
approach meant that I was getting accurate accounts of household composition, and
that this was also the case in 1995. Of course, strict compliance with the one-child
policy had at that point been brief (only one year), and I have no way of knowing
whether some births might simply have been delayed. Second children were permitted under certain conditions even at that time. The 1995 variant of the policy permitted a woman to have a second child if her first child was a daughter, and if the mother
was at least thirty years old and had obtained permission for the pregnancy in advance. There was no quota for the number of births a village could have.

scribing this work to me. I had come to expect the women's heads to be involved primarily in economic work in this area, and the Women's Federation staff with whom I was working had been strongly emphasizing to me the merits of their new policy direction in the "two studies," that of relying upon women's voluntary participation in woman-work and responding actively to rural women's expressed priority of moving toward prosperity.

I inquired of the Women's Federation staff whether asking women's heads to act concurrently as birth-planning workers posed problems in their work—in view of the voluntary, market-oriented character of the "two studies" and the administrative character of the birth-planning work. None of the women with whom I discussed this issue denied that there was a different character to the two kinds of work, but all argued that they could be and were compatible components of woman-work. To some extent, this must be understood within a context in which woman-work, as well as many other aspects of life, are enmeshed in official policy constraints from which women (and men) in China do not expect to be relieved. It is inconceivable that woman-work would not be a matter of following state policy. However, it may well be the case that these divergent strands of policy are more easily resolved at a higher administrative level within the Women's Federations, where staff are transmitting and monitoring numerous policies rather than working directly with rural women. I have not personally encountered a case where a women's head was actively and effectively pursuing both the "two studies" and the birth-planning policies, although I cannot exclude that possibility.[7]

The mandate of the women's heads was so large that performance was necessarily partial and selective, although it was not the women's head herself who would select which part of her mandate would receive attention. This decision would be made by the village political leadership, in consideration of the local political priorities. This might include attention to the Women's Federations' current initiatives in woman-work, although this would not necessarily be the case. For this reason, it has been essential for the Women's Federations to find ways to insert themselves more firmly into the mainstream of local political processes and policy formation. The "two studies" is one of the primary strategies currently employed for this purpose. It is also a key element

---

[7] There are also practical limits, of course, in terms of how many policies a single person can implement energetically at one time.

in the contemporary form in which the Women's Federations are pursuing one of their continuing core responsibilities, the participation of women in the market and the mobilization of women to contribute to national economic goals.

The "two studies" has been an initiative that has required a very large commitment of work on the part of the women's heads. They have been called upon to play a major role in training and in economic activity, with numerous concrete tasks and goals being specified and monitored. In addition to all the problems this has posed for recruiting and retaining women's heads, it has also raised the question of developing women's heads' quality. The nurturing (*peiyang*) of people with leadership potential has long been an established organizational activity of both Party and Women's Federations. In the "two studies," women's heads have acquired heightened importance as a target for nurturing, and the qualities being instilled are new, including skills to succeed in the market. The responsibility for this work has largely been shared by the lowest two levels of the Women's Federations in the countryside, the township and the county.

THE TOWNSHIP WOMEN'S FEDERATION

In the formal administrative structure of the Women's Federations, which parallels that of the government, the township (*xiang*) level is the lowest level provided with Women's Federation staff (see Table 9). The township roughly coincides with the former commune in Shandong and is the most basic level of administration covered by official personnel with urban registration. Women's Federation staff located at this level often come from rural backgrounds, but hold the registration status that allows them to move into government positions at township or higher levels. They are never recruited from the ranks of women's heads (who hold rural registration), and often enter their positions as young women newly graduated from secondary technical school.[8] Since townships typically have one or at most two women assigned to the Women's Federation, such a person may well find herself the head of the township Women's Federation without having any relevant experience, training, or even interest.

[8] Entry into secondary technical school is highly competitive in rural China and a very considerable achievement. Part of the attraction is that graduation may confer urban registration status.

TABLE 9

Ling County Women's Federation Staff, 1992

Unit	Age	Education	Political status (League or Party member)	Post
county	45	college (*dazhuan*)	Party	head
county	36	secondary technical (*zhongzhuan*): agriculture (*nongxiao*)	Party	vice-head
county	30	sec. tech.: agr.	Party	vice-head
county	26	sec. tech.: textiles	Party	organization and propaganda section head
county	29	college: correspondence	Party	youth and children section head
county	36	sec. tech.: normal	Party	staff
county	31	upper middle school (ums)		staff
county	21	sec. tech.: agr.	League	staff
township (tp) 1	48	lower middle school (lms)	Party	head
tp 1	40	sec. tech.: normal	Party	vice-head
tp 1	29	college: WF cadre college		staff
tp 2	39	sec. tech.: Party school	Party	head
tp 2	22	sec. tech.: normal	League	staff
tp 3	39	ums	Party	head
tp 3	22	sec. tech.: forestry	League	staff
tp 4	25	sec. tech.: normal	Party	head
tp 4	23	college: electrical	League	staff
tp 5	38	sec. tech.	Party	head; Party vice-secretary
tp 5	25	college: petroleum	League	vice-head
tp 6	34	sec. tech.: normal	Party	head; Party committee
tp 6	27	sec. tech.: normal		vice-head
tp 7	30	sec. tech.: normal	Party	head
tp 8	43	lms	Party	head; Party committee
tp 8	23	sec. tech.: preschool ed.	League	staff
tp 9	29	sec. tech.: normal	Party	head; Party committee
tp 9	25	sec. tech.: preschool ed.	League	vice-head
tp 10 (including Huaili)	40	sec. tech.: normal	Party	head
tp 11	25	sec. tech.: preschool ed.	Party	head
tp 11	22	sec. tech.: preschool ed.	League	staff
tp 12	25	sec. tech.: preschool ed.	League	vice-head
tp 12	25	college: agr.	League	staff
tp 13	38	ums	Party	head; Party committee
tp 14	38	sec. tech.: WF cadre college	Party	head; Party committee
tp 14	25	college: normal		vice-head
tp 15	44	sec. tech.: WF cadre college	Party	head; tp vice-head
tp 15	24	sec. tech.: preschool ed.	Party	vice-head
tp 16	38	sec. tech.: normal	Party	head
tp 17	38	sec. tech.: normal		head

Unit	Age	Education	Political status (League or Party member)	Post
tp 17	23	college: construction	League	staff
tp 18	34	sec. tech.: agr.	Party	head; Party committee
tp 18	24	college: normal	League	staff
tp 19	43	sec. tech.: agr.	Party	head; tp vice-head
tp 19	25	sec. tech.: preschool ed.	Party	vice-head
tp 20	44	sec. tech.: normal	Party	head
tp 20	22	sec. tech.: normal	League	staff
tp 21	38	sec. tech.: agr.	Party	head; Party committee
tp 21	23	sec. tech.: normal	League	vice-head
tp 22	47	sec. tech.	Party	head
tp 22	24	sec. tech.: preschool ed.	League	vice-head
tp 23	50	sec. tech.	Party	head; Party committee
tp 23	28	college: normal	Party	vice-head
tp 24	51	lms	Party	head
tp 24	25	sec. tech.: agr.	Party	vice-head

While in these positions, the township Women's Federation staff may actually have very little time for woman-work. In 1992, the head of the Ling County Women's Federation presented the findings of a survey indicating that basic-level Women's Federation staff, that is, staff at the county and township levels (among whom the greatest number were at the township level), reported that more than two hundred workdays a year of each person's time were spent on general political and administrative work, such as tax collection and birth planning, and that these were considered "hard" (required) tasks, in contrast to the "soft" (flexible) tasks of woman-work that had to be done in the less than three months of time remaining (Yan Guirong 1992: 16). This meant that, in addition to their lack of preparation, the staff had little opportunity to learn on the job, or even to do the work at all.

In addition to these obstacles there has also been a practice of frequent transfer of township staff, including Women's Federation staff. Frequent movement of official staff is a long-standing practice of the Chinese state and presumably has a number of advantages in keeping official personnel more tied to the state than to local networks. It has disadvantages in terms of stable implementation of policy, although it might also be noted that policy itself has by no means been stable since 1949. I have located some cases of individuals serving in the township Women's Federation for extended periods at earlier dates (1958–74 and 1982–89), although by the 1990s there appeared to be a marked shift toward serving a single three-year term. In the ideal arrangement, favored by the Women's Federations, experience at this level would prepare women for more responsible positions in the mainstream of local government. I was told in 1992 that seven to ten such promotions would be made each year in Ling County, and this seemed to be the usual career path. Higher levels of the Women's Federation are too sparsely staffed to provide many openings, and one of the central concerns of the Women's Federations at this time was the preparation of more women for mainstream official position. Township Women's Federation work was identified as a prime training ground for women who might be able to enter other positions in township government. Three years of participation in the general work of the state at the township level, combined with some woman-work and related training, was considered effective preparation for such a next step for women who showed promise. And, as a senior Women's Federation cadre pointed out to me, it would not be desirable only to promote the stronger personnel; the weaker ones had at least to be moved. Continuity of staffing at this level was not a concern or goal of the Women's Federations in the 1990s.

Training Women's Federation staff at the township level was considered desirable, and as much as forty-five days a year of training has been recommended by the head of the Ling County Women's Federation (Yan Guirong 1992: 17). A more realistic goal has been to gather the township staff for two or three days of training in the winter, when work is less busy, but even this was not always achieved. I am not aware of any such training having been systematically provided in the township with which I am most familiar, although Women's Federation staff did become knowledgeable over time.

In any event, the township Women's Federation was not the critical level for conducting woman-work in general, or the "two studies" in particular. This township has sixty-one villages and (in 1992) approximately 9,800 women between the ages of eighteen and sixty. There was no expectation that the sparse, novice staff of the Women's Federation in the township would work directly with such a large and dispersed number of women. Rather, the township Women's Federation provided a conduit through which the policies of higher levels were transmitted in a face-to-face way to the village women who would do the actual work—the women's heads and, as appropriate, other models of local success. The main responsibility of the township Women's Federation was to provide this channel. Where training was involved, the events would be organized by the Women's Federation, and the teaching would be done by township technical personnel (for productive work related to the "two studies") or by county Women's Federation staff (for policy and woman-work issues). The venue would commonly be provided by the township Party school.

Township Women's Federation staff would ideally also provide further supervision and training for village women's heads. Ling County, for example, had twenty-four township-level units, and this work would normally have to be done at this level if it were to be done at all. In practical terms, it could only be done by the more experienced and capable staff, and even then would usually only reach the stronger women's heads located in villages with relatively strong political leadership.[9]

Township Women's Federation staff were expected to keep written records on the women's heads and on work on the various current initiatives of the Women's Federations, such as the "two studies," and provide these to the county Women's Federations. There were also efforts made to introduce specific work standards for both women's heads (implemented through the township Women's Federation) and the township Women's Federation staff (implemented through the county Women's Federation). The "1994 Town and Township Women's Federation Post Objectives and Responsibility System Assessment Standards" (see Appendix) is illustrative of the detailed demands placed upon basic-level staff in the women's movement, and of the mechanisms proposed to induce them to meet these demands. Documents such as this, although referring to a range and volume of work that could rarely if ever be fully undertaken, provided a basis for assessing staff, identifying which should be replaced, and selecting the best for designation as "excellent woman cadre" (youxiu funü ganbu) (Lingxian fulian 1994: 10). Mechanisms such as these were intended to institutionalize a degree of surveillance, and motivate those doing woman-work at each level to apply pressure on those one level down to produce reportable results.

[9] Without strong political leadership in a village it was difficult to accomplish any official political task, and this would not usually be attempted. At any point in time there were always villages experiencing a temporary lack of leadership. Addressing this issue would precede any other initiative. Women's Federations would also have an interest in promoting the selection of strong women's heads, but the selection was not in their hands.

THE COUNTY WOMEN'S FEDERATION

The county is the key local level of the Women's Federations. In part this is because the county level of the state is a decisive one for local political processes; neither the township below nor the prefecture above occupy quite so important a role in local affairs. Much of the work of the Women's Federation consists of efforts to influence local authorities at the county level to support woman-work. Critical measures, such as the renewal of the ranks of women's heads, the entry of women into political office in townships and villages, and resources for "two studies" training, have depended upon political support, personnel, and material resources from the county political leadership.

The county level is also important because this is the lowest level that has a sufficient concentration of Women's Federation staff to be able to undertake woman-work. When I first went to Ling County in 1988, there were ten or eleven staff in the county Women's Federation, although several were very young, and most of the work and responsibility rested with only three or four women (the head and vice-heads). In 1992, the number of staff had been reduced slightly to eight, and by 1995 it had been further reduced to six. As with the lower levels discussed below, there is considerable fluidity in staffing, and the numbers present at any point in time do not necessarily match authorized staffing levels (*bianzhi*). These were also declining, in line with general policies to reduce the size of official staffs: in 1992 the official staffing level was nine, and in 1995 it was five (then with an additional two positions allocated to the office for children's work). This is not a large number of staff, but it was officially considered minimally sufficient to direct woman-work within the county.

The yearly reports on work accomplished and work plans for the coming year consistently indicate attention to all of the regular tasks of woman-work, as well as any current official initiatives. Obviously, not everything could receive significant attention. In the case of Ling County during these years, there was routine work in responding to individual women's requests for help (with either official problems or domestic ones); increased attention to women's legal rights, following the proclamation of the Women's Law (Law to Protect the Rights and Interests of Women, *Funü quanyi baozhang fa*) in 1992, especially with respect to women's access to housing following divorce[10] and to the buying and selling of women in marriage; popularization of the law to women, including but not limited to the Women's Law; increasing the representation of women in elected and nonelected official positions; work with women in the county seat and towns, including efforts to extend the birth-planning policy to the unofficial migrant population; and work involving children of preschool age.

The main concerns of the Ling County Women's Federation, as indicated in documents, interviews, and observations of work, were in the two areas of economic development and organizational strengthening. Ling County is an interior, primarily agricultural county located in the relatively poor prefecture of Dezhou along the border with Hebei. Although Shandong is a coastal province, areas such Dezhou have not fully shared in the prosperity one associates with the coastal provinces and, indeed, that prosperity is invariably uneven. Agriculture is not an avenue to prosperity, and improving economic conditions has been difficult in the Dezhou area. During the years of this project, Ling County enjoyed some improvement to the agricultural infrastructure through a World Bank water control project, although this cost several communities (including Huaili) significant loss of arable land. In the late 1980s, there was heavy reliance upon grain and cotton farming, and limited diversification. Ling County's county-level and other rural enterprises were not strong enough to withstand the massive closing of rural enterprises in the early 1990s, and this placed grave pressure on local governments and households.[11] However, by 1995, moves toward economic diversification and increasing economic ties with Tianjin were bringing opportunities to the area. In this context, both immediate local needs and national priorities focused upon growth made economic develop-

[10] This problem arises in urban contexts, here including the county seat, because state-allocated housing is commonly allocated through the husband's work unit.

[11] One of the more drastic results of the "cooling out" of the Chinese economy in the wake of the economic and political crises of the late 1980s was the closure of perhaps as many as a million rural enterprises. During a 1992 revisit to the three widely separated Shandong communities I had studied in the 1980s, I found that the two situated in wealthier areas with thriving rural enterprises had weathered this period quite well. Ling County, in contrast, with a much weaker base, had its rural industry almost completely destroyed. This apparently precipitated the reassessment and change in strategy toward building upon the county's agricultural strengths that was evident in 1995. See Judd (1994, 1997).

ment the top official priority in Ling County. Given the agricultural character of the county, this required attention to increasing agricultural productivity, and diversifying production beyond grain and cotton to a range of cash crops, especially vegetables. In addition, Ling County shared in the national pattern by which men were increasingly moving into non-agricultural work and the less preferred and less remunerative agricultural work was becoming feminized, with 60% or more of the agricultural work being done by women (see Judd 1994, 1999). Consequently, the county Women's Federation had pressing reasons—related both to women's own lives and to county economic development goals—for making rural economic work its priority.

In practical terms, this meant promotion of the courtyard economy initiative and then of the "two studies," along the lines required by national policy. Within the county government itself, the county Women's Federation established a "coordinating committee" (xietiao xiaozu) in 1989. The head of the coordinating committee was a vice-secretary of the county Party committee (to give the committee authority); the vice-heads were the head of the county Agriculture Committee (who was also a member of the county Standing Committee) and the head of the county Women's Federation. Seventeen other county level official bodies were represented on the committee by vice-heads (of various ranks): the Agriculture Bureau, the Forestry Bureau, the Irrigation Bureau, the Township Enterprise Bureau, the Commerce Bureau, the Grain Bureau, the Foreign Trade Bureau, the Finance Bureau, the Supply and Marketing Bureau, the Education Bureau, the Animal Husbandry Company, the Broadcast and Television Bureau, the Civil Administration Bureau, the Science Committee, the Science Association, the Agriculture Bank, and the Diversification Office. The coordinating committee was administered from the office of the county Women's Federation and provided the channel through which the Women's Federation could and did seek support in personnel (technical trainers) and material resources (seeds, services, funds) to carry out the "two studies." Although it is impossible to record the details of resources granted through this channel, it is certain that they were provided, since the "two studies" was actively promoted in Ling County, and there were no other resources available.

It is, indeed, one of the distinctive features of both woman-work in general and the "two studies" in particular that the magnitude of the tasks is not matched by the allocation of funding. This situation, common for women's organizations globally, has its particular Chinese features. The Ling County Women's Federation has never had significant funds to disburse. In 1992, for example, its total annual expense budget was RMB 1,000. This amount excluded salaries and costs associated with meetings, but it also effectively excluded spending for the "two studies" or any other major initiative. In those cases, the Women's Federation would invariably have to seek additional funding. This left the Women's Federations constantly in the position of having to ask for funding and never being directly able to control its own finances. The arrangements for the implementation of the "two studies" through coordinating committees continued and further institutionalized this budgetary arrangement. Funds and other resources could be accessed, subject to local political approval and cooperation of the various bureaux involved, but the Women's Federations would not be able to deploy these funds or resources independently.

During the 1990s an additional avenue became available for funding the state sector, and the Women's Federations availed themselves of the opportunity. State units became permitted to operate income-generating economic entities (*jingji shiti*). In some cases such activity provided income to members of the unit, although I am not aware of this having been the case for the Women's Federations. The Women's Federations asked their units to run economic entities that would contribute a useful service and that would generate income that could be used in the work of the Women's Federations. The Ling County Women's Federation had two such entities. One was a day care center that had been established in 1986, had been converted to an economic entity in 1991, and then immediately generated a yearly income of RMB 2,000. The second was the construction in 1992 of a one-story eight-room building that the Women's Federation planned to rent out as office or commercial space. The building had cost RMB 16,000 to build. This amount had come partly from the income of the day care center, and each person on the county Women's Federation staff had contributed RMB 1,000 (an amount equivalent to several months income). While these contributions were expected to be reimbursed in the future, this was a major financial commitment for the staff to make for the organization.

In principle, this type of self-funding, or perhaps cultivating some vacant land, was also an option open to township Women's Federations and village women's committees. However, the funds and work required did not necessarily make this attractive, and I did not encounter this in Ling County except at the county level.

The very limited and conditional access of the Women's Federations to funding and material resources meant that they had to rely especially heavily upon their human resources. Attention to organization and to cadre development is standard in China, in any situation, and these were highly emphasized concerns in the Women's Federations. I am unable to identify a time when these were not concerns for the Women's Federations, but the intensity of attention may have increased during the "two studies."

Because the Women's Federations had to rely primarily upon a small number of people dispersed through the county, attention to organization and personnel were critical. Efforts to rectify problems in townships or villages with weak, disorganized, or missing (*ruan, san, lan*) staff or women's heads were constantly undertaken in one locality or another, and were standard elements in work plans. County staff also sometimes played a direct role in selected localities. These localities, designated "contact points" (*lianxi dian*), were intended to serve as examples that other localities could emulate, and they also served to keep county staff in touch with local conditions and to train local women in woman-work. Such points could be either general purpose points or ones that were associated with some particular initiative. The township in which Huaili was located had been a general purpose contact point for the county for some years prior to this study and throughout its duration, although another township became the county's contact point for the "two studies" during the 1990s. Townships similarly had their own contact points (typically villages with strong women's heads and supportive political leadership, or ones conveniently close to the township center), and women's heads had contact households (*lianxi hu*). In effect, organizing strategies experienced at one level could be replicated at the next level below. Still, direct involvement of the county staff was the exception rather than the rule, and most work depended upon increasing the capacity of township staff and women's heads. This task was concurrently pursued in several different ways: general education and training, managerial supervision and evaluation, and political development.

The county Women's Federation staff were themselves all reasonably well educated by 1995: the head was a college graduate, one junior staff member was an upper middle school graduate, and all the remainder were technical secondary school graduates. Some members of the staff had previously or were at that time working on acquiring further educational qualifications, either part-time or on the job. In addition, there is an institutionalized system of short-term training for Women's Federation cadres at each level. At the provincial level, the Shandong Women's Federation runs a major training center that is a branch of the All-China Women's Federation Cadre Management Training College. Women's Federation staff at both county and township levels have the opportunity to be sent to attend short-term courses at this college, and a few are selected for this training each year. The training consists of a mix of general education (writing skills), work skills (management), and knowledge related to woman-work.

The county Women's Federation is responsible for training township Women's Federation staff and women's heads. Since the late 1980s, there has been a one-week training session for women staff with official potential at the township level, that is, for all township Women's Federation staff, as well as other women being prepared for responsible official position. The course is run jointly by the Party Organization Department and the Women's Federation and consists of political education, leadership training, and background related to woman-work (the Chinese Marxist view on women and the history of the women's movement).

I was also told that the county organizes one-day training sessions for women's heads twice a year. In each case, the women's heads of four or five townships will be brought together in a township, and someone from the county Women's Federation will address them. Half the day will consist of information on the current woman-work initiatives (such as the "two studies" or organizational strengthening) and the current year's work plan for woman-work. The other half day will consist of some form of simple technical training. These two elements are always combined for training sessions for women's heads. In order to ensure that women's heads would have the necessary educational basis to enable them to participate in training and education, and to be able to take notes and keep records, the Women's Federations sought to have lower middle school graduation set as a minimum educational expectation for women's heads.

While some of this activity described as "training" may have contributed to increasing the ability of the grassroots staff to conduct woman-work effectively, it was not extensive, and much of it consisted of conveying basic information (background for woman-work, current policy, and work plans). It was therefore not the only, and perhaps not the most important, measure for improving organizational quality.

The Women's Federations also relied heavily upon new measures to instruct township staff and women's heads in their duties and to motivate them to fulfill them energetically. Structurally, this was no doubt necessary, since virtually all of the work the county Women's Federation sought to accomplish had to be done by township staff and women's heads. The new element was the use of specific management guidelines in the form of "post responsibility standards" (see Appendix).[12] Similar management practices came into wide use in China in the reform era, and the Women's Federations were here acting in the mainstream of contemporary official practice. These instruments were highly detailed evaluative tools. In addition to their other uses, they embodied the competitive approach the same women were being asked to promote and encourage in the "two studies."

Quality also had a political dimension, since it was necessary to have women doing woman-work who supported and understood current policy. Willingness to undertake the work was the most immediate test of this standard, since not everyone showed enthusiasm for becoming a women's head, and the staff assigned to Women's Federations had so many general tasks assigned that their energy in pursuing woman-work could not be assumed. The training sessions described above addressed the political knowledge component of this issue. The Women's Federations also made an organizational effort to foster the political advancement and incorporation of the women upon whom it depended at the grassroots. The decisive issue was membership in the Party or, for younger women, in its preparatory body, the Young Communist League. Party membership is not widespread in China, but it is normally required for participation in a leading political role and for many kinds of official work, including woman-work at county level or above.[13]

---

[12] The example provided in the appendix is the document used in Ling County to manage township Women's Federation staff. There was a similar document at the township level devised for managing village women's heads, and I have consulted this document as well. I expect that the surveillance and management of the township staff was more effective than that of women's heads, but similar principles were used and a comparable point system was itemized.

[13] In urban and intellectual centers it is sometimes possible for individuals to hold

One of the measures adopted has been to identify women's heads as priorities for consideration for membership in the Party. Ordinarily, very few women are Party members in rural China—there was only one in Huaili during the entire time I visited the village—and entry to the Party would, under current policy guidelines, also provide the women's head with entry to the Party branch committee, the leading political body in the village. The Women's Federations at higher levels were actively intervening to open these channels of political advancement to women in the 1980s and 1990s. Village Party branches were asked to give special attention to identifying and preparing suitable women candidates for Party membership. The exceptionally effective women's head in Huaili in the early 1990s became such a candidate, but she left the village before the process (which ordinarily takes a year or more) was completed.[14]

For staff of township Women's Federations, Party or League membership would also provide a degree of entry to the political inner circles, although not automatically to political leadership. In order to function effectively in the thoroughly political work of the Women's Federations at the county level and above, Party membership was essential and standard (see Table 9).

Paradoxically, a central aspect of the political preparation of women for woman-work in these years came to be the inculcation of an orientation toward the market, a view that would previously have been anathema to the Party or the Women's Federations. In the reform era, the market was seen as a means of achieving prosperity, for households and for the nation. The turn toward the market was to be led by the state and its policies, and the state's personnel were called upon to revise their past political assessment of market activity, previously denounced as capitalist. Arriving at this revised understanding was part of political education in the reform era. A corollary for the Women's Fed-

---

important posts on the basis of expertise and without Party membership, but this would not normally obtain in the countryside. Conspicuously successful people are also often targets of recruitment efforts.

[14] These special efforts have been required in order to increase access to Party membership for women because of the barrier indirectly but formidably created by the norm of patrilocal post-marital residence. Women have rarely had time to go through the preparation for Party membership and be accepted before they marry out of their natal villages where they are known and perhaps well connected. When newly arrived in their marital villages, they are expected to remain primarily within the inner domain and they have to start virtually from the beginning in creating networks and building prestige.

erations is that they also sought to foster an expertise in market-oriented activity among their staff, since they interpreted their political role as being one of leading women to success in the market. One of the qualities now conspicuously sought was therefore demonstrated ability to succeed in the market by generating significant income, usually through entrepreneurship.

RESEARCH ASSOCIATIONS

In order to make this move toward the market, the Women's Federations were working toward new modes of organization in the countryside. A prime goal was to draw in women who were conspicuously successful in market-oriented activities, and involve them in supporting woman-work, specifically the "two studies." Where these women had used some particular technical skill in their successful enterprise, there was the opportunity to ask them to share this skill with others in their communities (especially the least advantaged). But even where technical skill was not at issue (as in much of commerce, where capital or connections were more decisive), these women constituted a resource of energetic people and positive example.

Such women were often identified as models in a variety of formal and informal ways. Model status was a widely used honor in China, and was adopted in the "two studies" as well. In addition, the "two studies" specifically identified and honored women who had met targets in either technical training or income generation. Part of the Women's Federation program of organizational strengthening consisted of mechanisms for incorporating these examples of success in the market more closely into the work of the official women's movement.

One of the newer means for doing this was the creation of technical research associations (*jishu yanjiu hui*). The Dezhou Women's Federation called for the formation of these associations in 1993, Ling County began organizing them in 1994, and there were reported to be ninety-eight of these, based in villages and townships, by 1995. These associations were described as being non-governmental (*minjian*), but they were Women's Federation creations. They were a more formalized version of a strategy that had already existed for some years. The associations brought together local women who were models of success and women who had achieved some of the technical training goals in the "two studies" under the leadership of the women's head (more commonly) or the township Women's Federation staff (where at the township level). The associations would meet to exchange technical information and encourage further technical study, although I have not been independently able to confirm how active these new bodies were.

They could also play a role in local economic development initiatives. In the case of the township examined in this study, where chickens became the focus, the Women's Federation developed a research association on this topic. It was headed by the township Women's Federation head who, despite no previous background in this field (she was a former teacher), had led the way in the recommended manner by becoming involved in chicken production. She had bought two thousand chicks and hired someone to help her raise them, and so made herself a participant in this economic development initiative as an entrepreneur. The research association also prominently included a woman in Huaili who had been engaged in large-scale chicken production since the 1980s, as well as others actively involved. The association worked with a Tianjin animal husbandry professor brought in by the township to provide technical expertise, although her presence had been arranged by the township and was not dependent upon the existence of the association (also see Chapter 6).

In addition to their manifest technical purposes, the research associations were indirectly a channel to tie women and their economic activities more closely to the Women's Federations and their economic development strategies. The Women's Federations acknowledged that at least some of the contacts pursued and information exchanged did not require formal organization. The move toward formal organization may have given more access to some women who would have been bypassed by the informal networks of the more successful—and this was one goal of the formal research associations. Perhaps more importantly, the research associations were intended to signal and organizationally embody the new departure of the Women's Federations toward the market.

OBSERVATIONS

The Women's Federations have a formal presence that reaches into every village in China, but it is a thin and fragile network at best. The preoccupation of the Women's Federations with organizational rebuilding in the 1990s has gone beyond routine concerns to address a critical practical issue in making their strategies effective. While working to consolidate the formal administrative structure at each level, the

Women's Federations have also been seeking to reach beyond administrative mechanisms or, as they put it, to move from "push" to "pull." Rather than push people to participate through administrative means or through a more or less compulsory political campaign, the goal has become to pull rural women into activity by providing them with inducements. As one local document (Lingxian fulian n.d. [1995]) indicated, this new approach would consist of three elements: 1) technical training and the raising of women's quality, 2) the use of models to lead women forward, and 3) providing useful services (such as access to expertise in chicken raising). The Women's Federations sought—in the "two studies"—to demonstrate that they could deliver this type of new organization and, in the process, consolidate their place in the mainstream of rural economic development and policymaking. Making the "two studies" work is the decisive challenge of this strategy.

6

Mobilization and Competition

The "two studies" was consistently described in terms intended to set it apart from earlier mobilizational efforts; it was not a movement (*yundong*), but a set of activities (*huodong*). The state recognized the weariness of the people with mobilizational campaigns, and also the difficulty of mobilizing rural people after the collectives had been dissolved in the early 1980s. Women now had to be persuaded to participate in activities the state chose to propose, and competition was viewed as a tool for motivation.

The relation between mobilization and competition provides the central tension in the "two studies." Insofar as it is an organized set of activities, the "two studies" starts as a state-initiated strategy for changing the situation of rural women. The distinctive element here is not alone the emphasis on education and, through education, strengthening of women's independent abilities. This might also have been promoted through more administrative means. The distinctive feature in this strategy is rather the element of competition. In effect, women are being *mobilized for competition*. On the most visible level this refers to registering women for the specific contests in the program. These could spur women to increased economic activity or, alternatively, incorporate independently successful women into the program through the process of registration. While these contests were important for the program, the truly significant aspect of competition was women's participation in the market.

Women were actively mobilized to register for the "two studies" activities, and this directly consisted of their formal undertaking to achieve production goals in agriculture. A fundamental tenet of the entire program remained the classical Marxist proposition that women would improve their social status through their participation in public labor. To this extent the "two studies" was very similar to the movements of previous decades. It departed from the past in its reform focus on pushing women into the market and measuring economic success, not by production or use value created, but by cash income or exchange value. While part of the classical Marxist argument for the liberation of women through labor was preserved, it was now encapsulated in market-based economic processes and standards of calculation.

According to the Women's Federations themselves, which organized the mobilizational aspects of the "two studies," the formal administrative elements, including the various contests that were organized, were secondary. The key element was to achieve demonstrable economic results in the mainstream of the commodity economy. Economic contributions made by women in any other way might remain hidden or marginal to the new forces in the Chinese rural economy. Rural women were to be motivated to enter the market by both mobilizational measures and by the prospect of economic benefit.

This initiative was completely in tune with the larger trend in Chinese society toward seeking prosperity through the market and highly valuing monetary success. Through this initiative, the Women's Federations strove to hasten women's entry into the marketplace and to provide women making this transition with respectability. They sought to increase the visibility and prestige of women who were successful in the marketplace by the standards currently accepted in Chinese culture—cash income. Such success was clearly understood to be a highly competitive process, in which success and failure could be clearly and precisely measured. Increased incomes would mark the importance of women's contributions, draw more women into the activities, and demonstrate the value of the Women's Federations' work. Through these reform means, the Women's Federations argued, preexisting goals of raising women's status in society and in the household could be promoted.

Participation in the market thereby becomes a defining feature of the state program for women. More importantly, women's competitive success validates the state's policies regarding women and women's role in economic development. The tension between state and market is not a conflict between incompatible opposites, but is rather a relation internal to the operations of the reform political economy. Just as the imperial Chinese state had accommodated commerce, the reform Chinese state was internalizing the global market.

The "two studies" proposed and embodied a fusion of state impetus and control with reform mechanisms of market activity and competition. By using market-oriented systems of competition, organized through regular administrative channels and through the "two studies," market approaches were integrated with mobilizational strategies. Competition also worked indirectly through the market itself, and there it worked its strongest influence. The ultimate test of the initiative was its ability to improve the tangible economic conditions (measured primarily through income) of the women registered in the "two studies" and of their communities. This informal dimension of competition drove the "two studies" more profoundly and pervasively than the formal mechanisms. In the fusion of state and market approaches at the ground level of implementation of the "two studies," the subtlety of the reach of the reform state becomes apparent.

This chapter will review the microstrategies of mobilization and competition realized in the "two studies" in Huaili and the larger context of Ling County. The specifics of the policies and the implementation strategies changed over time, and will be presented historically.

THE COURTYARD ECONOMY IN PRACTICE

The courtyard economy (*tingyuan jingji*) concept referred both to an earlier, more limited initiative, and to a later component within the "two studies." In both senses it was based on the productive use of the inner realm of enclosed courtyards. Land was scarce in densely populated Shandong, and especially in Huaili, which had found itself located in the path of a World Bank water control project constructed in the 1980s. Huaili had lost more land to this project than had many other villages and, by 1989, the standard per capita land allocation was .67 *mu* of grain land (corresponding to the previously collectivized farmland) and .1 *mu* of vegetable land (corresponding to the private plots of the collective era) (see Judd 1994). Even where land was a little more plentiful, supplementary production of what was earlier termed "sidelines" (*fuye*) in courtyards had provided a major component of household income, and women had been the main producers of that courtyard income (also see Wolf 1985).

In promoting women's productive labor within courtyards for cash income, the Women's Federations were implicitly building upon an established and culturally accepted base, although they did not choose to emphasize this point. Instead, emphasis was placed upon using an underutilized resource to produce significantly increased household income. Since land was so scarce, even the small amount of land within courtyards could have noticeable economic value.

Houses in Huaili were built in the usual courtyard manner. The house itself—all one story in this village—faced south for warmth and had a front courtyard, comparable in size to a North American front yard, entirely surrounded by a high wall with a single gate (solid and equipped with a lock) opposite the house. Lots were restricted in size as part of the government's efforts to minimize the non-agricultural use of arable land, but the use of the land was not standardized. Houses varied in the amount of living space, and whether or not there were buildings along one or both sides of the courtyard. Where there were such additional rooms, these were usually used for economic undertakings, such as battery production of chickens or rooms for making noodles, but this applied only to a minority of Huaili households.

Using some area within the courtyard for domestic animals was much more common, and virtually universal except in the busiest specialized households. Most households had a pigsty, although some might have an ox tethered in the yard, or a number of chickens and ducks, either penned in or running loose. Raising animals was a staple courtyard enterprise for women and appears widely in reports of courtyard economy initiatives and competitions.

In the Dezhou area and in Ling County, the Women's Federation began working on developing the courtyard economy in 1984–85. The county Women's Federation's experienced head said that the courtyard economy was chosen as a focus because this appeared to be an untouched area with potential. She observed that agriculture had shown increases in production in the early 1980s following the initiation of the reform program, and that rural industry then had leadership and initiative. This left the courtyard economy as a politically vacant area into which the Women's Federations could move. That is, in addition to the previously discussed economic and gender-related reasons for focusing upon the courtyard economy, this was also a tactical move through which the Women's Federations sought to establish themselves in the reform era political economy.

A major effort was made in Huaili from 1987, when it became targeted for development as a model. One of the vice-heads of the county Women's Federation, an able and energetic leader, made almost daily visits by bicycle (about one hour each way) to organize this village's courtyard production. Since the county Women's Federation had only nine full-time staff at the time, and there were hundreds of villages in the county, this is an atypical allocation of resources. It is also the usual way in which models are developed, through an approach that recognizes that change is uneven, and that therefore resources may have to be concentrated at particular strategic points in order to make breakthroughs.[1] Two villages were developed as models in the county at this stage, Huaili in vegetable and *xiangchun* (a tree with edible leaves) cultivation, and another village in edible fungus cultivation. Later in 1987 a delegation from Dezhou Prefecture visited these two villages and four or five other sites in the county for on-site meetings to examine the work done at each place and to visit a few model households. Anticipation of this tour lay behind the intensity of work in cultivating the models.

Vegetables were a suitable focus for work in Huaili, because the village had made a success of vegetable cultivation on private plots during the collective era, which had ended for Huaili only in 1984. There was no need for training or for significant resource inputs in order to grow vegetables more or less intensively in courtyards, although the Women's Federation did provide some help in accessing seedlings and obtaining market information. A similar practical knowledge base existed for *xiangchun*, and Huaili had an even greater advantage with this crop. The edible leaves are a delicacy, and Huaili had the reputation of being the village that produced the only *xiangchun* leaves that the exacting Empress Dowager Cixi had considered good enough for herself at the turn of the twentieth century. Expanding production of *xiangchun* in Huaili therefore held particular promise, and many new trees were planted following decollectivization. The women's organization in the village claimed credit for instigating the planting of 2,000 of the 11,000 *xiangchun* trees in the village as of 1989. These trees were commonly planted in courtyards, although there were also households that chose to plant them densely on private plots. The care of these trees was not difficult, but their presence in courtyards could be incompatible with vegetable cultivation.

Both vegetables and *xiangchun* were cultivated on a significant scale during the period of emphasis on courtyard production. This extended into 1989 in Huaili, where the "two studies" began to be applied by the

[1] Courtyard economy has been repeatedly targeted as a breakthrough point, including in Dezhou in 1988 (Dezhou diqu 1989) and in Ling County in 1994.

end of the year, although the continuities between the courtyard economy and "two studies" initiatives were explicit and strong. In the early summer of 1989, Huaili's women's head indicated that increases were still occurring in rates of vegetable and *xiangchun* cultivation, and that perhaps 60% of the households had vegetables in their courtyards, depending on courtyard conditions, and that virtually every household had *xiangchun* trees.

My own sample at that time showed lower rates of participation in the courtyard economy, but the difference is to be expected given the ubiquitous pressures on reporting processes in China, and it is also possible that more households had participated at some time in the courtyard economy than did so exactly at the time of my household study. Excluding specialized households, which were less oriented toward courtyard production and did not need it, twenty-one out of twenty-eight households (75%) reported and were seen to have *xiangchun* trees, and nine out of twenty-one (40%) reported and were seen to have vegetables growing in their courtyards (Judd 1994: 133).

Courtyard production had the potential for generating substantial income, although this was not always easy to realize or necessarily a net gain. *Xiangchun* do not produce marketable leaves until their second year, but can provide an average annual income of RMB 30–40 for each mature tree with little effort. In summer 1989 a maximum annual income of RMB 1,000 was cited as possible from the intensive cultivation of three crops of vegetables in an optimal courtyard area. These figures should be seen in the context of an average per capita annual income of RMB 700 in Huaili at that time. Courtyards, however, are not large. A typical size would be 15 by 18 meters, or 270 square meters, and not all of this space would be available, as it would also have to include a walkway, storage spaces, and space for farm animals. A few households did choose to put a large part of their courtyard into vegetable production—and the chief vegetable cultivators were usually but not always women—but this was a minority choice.

There were several clear reasons for choosing not to grow courtyard vegetables. None of the specialized households did so, either because their courtyards were fully occupied by their household enterprise (drying noodles, for example) or because the household members were busy with more profitable activities. Some others indicated that their houses were not well located, and that this strategy worked better for houses newly built on agricultural land than for those that had long been house sites. Vegetable cultivation was also not ideally compatible with the shade of *xiangchun* trees or the feeding of such domestic animals as goats or oxen. In effect, substantial amounts could be made from courtyard vegetables only if the courtyard was almost wholly given over to this purpose and worked very intensively. This was a more attractive proposition for households that had fewer alternatives, but even they often preferred other uses for their courtyards.

Raising farm animals, either for work (oxen, donkeys) or for consumption (pigs, oxen, goats, fowl), was a major economic alternative for households, and one in which women have had a continuing predominant role. The courtyard production initiative in Huaili paid almost no attention to animal husbandry, and it continued virtually unaffected throughout this period. This is not, however, to suggest that it was unimportant or inactive. Virtually every household raised animals, most commonly pigs, to contribute to the household income. In Huaili there was at one early point an effort to promote the raising of goats as an extra initiative in this area. However, this reached its maximum at no more than ten households, because the limited riverbank and other public grazing area made it uneconomical for a larger number of households to undertake. Apart from this small effort, although households in Huaili did uniformly raise animals in their courtyards for income, this was not organized by the Women's Federation. Women already had the skills, and they watched the market prices for animals and fodder closely. There were noticeable shifts in animals raised and increased diversification over the time I visited the village. Indeed, in 1995, the popular choice was the new one of a single head of beef cattle tethered by the road outside the courtyard. Women responded to market conditions and opportunities without special assistance or encouragement. The Women's Federations focused instead on extra initiatives that they thought would not otherwise have been undertaken, or not undertaken on the same scale. The probable reason the courtyard economy did not emphasize animal husbandry more is that it was an area that already had a high level of activity. Households commonly raised as many animals as they could through use of feed produced from their own land (feed costs tended to be too high to permit profitable expansion beyond this limit), and were well informed about and sensitive to market conditions. There was limited room for additional growth in this area, and therefore no reason to promote it.

Some households at this time were using their courtyard area for

household-based enterprises, and a few of these were already so successful in 1987 that they were included in the itinerary of the prefectural
site visit that year. These included a household making large quantities
of dried noodles, using machinery in a side room and the courtyard itself
for sun-drying the products; and a household that used one room at the
side of the courtyard to raise chickens in factory-type conditions. These
were not the core activities of the early courtyard economy initiative in
Huaili, but they were central both to Huaili's chosen direction for economic development, household-based enterprises or "projects" (*xiang-
mu*), and to the "two studies" initiative as it later developed here.

The courtyard economy established in these years did not continue
in quite the same manner. By 1995, indeed, there was remarkably little
sign of courtyard vegetable production, and *xiangchun* trees, while still
growing, were no longer a local priority. In my revisit that year, I found
no households with noticeable courtyard vegetable production among
the thirty-eight visited (twenty-five first-time visits and thirteen repeat
visits). The "two studies" had developed in Huaili during the intervening years, but had moved away from the specifics of vegetable and
xiangchun production.

But despite local vicissitudes in level of activity, the general concepts the Women's Federation worked with showed some marked continuity. Many of the elements summarized above as characteristic of
the "two studies" at both earlier and later stages can be found in the local presentation mounted on a wall in Huaili's Women's Home (*funü
zhi jia*) in 1988. The very existence of this location, a room in an underutilized public building belonging to the village, is itself an unusually early instance of public provision of space for women's activities.
Its presence in 1988 Huaili was presumably related to the recent prefectural tour, and the space quickly fell into disuse, as activity returned to
the standard rural style of being located in the homes and personal networks of village leaders, including the women's head. Nevertheless, the
Huaili Women's Home does express some of the core values of this and
later initiatives. It is worth presenting the full text of the "Women's
Place Activity Plan," dated May 1, 1987, and still found mounted on its
wall in January 1988:

> In the first quarter: run two sessions of training in sewing, and two
> sessions of training in vegetable and *xiangchun* technique, by inviting
> representatives of specialized households and technicians to provide
> classes; also provide information on how to prosper to rural women at
> large and quickly raise women's ability to prosper. Implement the sys-

tem of committee members taking responsibility for [specific] households and helping households in difficulty to escape poverty and prosper.

In the second quarter: Organize all the women of the village to attend one ideological and political study class on the "four selfs" [*sizi*]. Provide instruction on child psychology to the household heads of kindergarten and prmary school students; and organize a cultural evening.

In the third quarter: Mobilize the masses of women to do a good job of field managemnt.

In the fourth quarter: Run one or two training classes on legal knowledge, with the emphasis on the Marriage Law and the Inheritance Law. Select "five-good" families, March 8 Red Flag Bearers, and Women Prosperity Champions (*zhifu nü zhuangyuan*). Organize relief activities.

The document was identified as the product of the Huaili Brigade Women's Committee, villages then still commonly being referred to by the term for the collective equivalent, brigade, but was certainly prepared in association with Women's Federation staff from outside the village. The prominence of the linked themes of training and rural prosperity are strikingly close to the themes of the "two studies" promulgated nationally one and a half years later.

It is difficult to ascertain after the fact exactly how much of this plan was implemented, but repeated visits to some households affected by this and later initiatives, as well as discussions with the organizers, indicate that key elements of it were put into practice, including the training classes. If it was not fully implemented, it is nevertheless important to note that this type of program was being tried in the countryside well before the launch of the "two studies." This demonstrates that the "two studies" was not simply a top-down imposition, but was based upon some practical efforts and experiments at the grassroots level.

A Dezhou Prefecture Women's Federation work summary for 1988 and plan for 1989 (Dezhou diqu 1989) discusses quality prominently, and indicates the potential of courtyard economy for promoting commercialization and the development of a more complex rural economy. This was the direction next taken in the "two studies," but it was one the organizers found very difficult. For county Women's Federation leaders the problem was one of implementing a very ambitious program with minuscule human and material resources. Township Women's Federation cadres, as well as women's heads and women's committee members in Huaili, expressed still more concrete concerns about the difficulty they were finding in identifying fields in which women could

be practically helped or the concrete means by which they could provide
such help. The Women's Federation had some mobilizational capacity,
but not the economic or technical resources to help women effectively.
The subsequent course of the "two studies" is a process of trying to resolve these blockages on a practical level.

THE "TWO STUDIES"

The "two studies" was reported to have begun in Huaili only toward the
end of 1989. This is consistent with the Shandong plan to spend the first
year establishing coordinating groups and making plans, and then to
start the study and competition activities in the second year. Within
Ling County, the "two studies" was identified as the county Women's
Federation's central work (zhongxin gongzuo) for 1990, that is, the highest priority around which all other work should revolve (Lingxian fulian
1990). Huaili might have had an advantage compared with some other
communities, because of the active promotion of the courtyard economy in this village, and because the "two studies" was explicitly
viewed as its further development. However, the loss of the local organizing personnel associated with that initiative actually meant that
Huaili did not move quickly into the "two studies." The county Wom-
en's Federation was never again directly active in the village of Huaili,
although the township in which it is located remained a contact point
(lianxi dian) through 1995. The township Women's Federation head
who had been present through the earlier initiative was promoted to a
leading position in the township unconnected with woman-work, and
was replaced with a teacher new to woman-work, but very energetic in
its conduct. Within the village of Huaili, the "two studies" was hampered by the lack of a women's head. The woman who had briefly filled
this role in 1989 had left for a factory job in the county seat, and her
imminent departure had hung over her entire tenure. Several candidates
for the position were under consideration by the summer of 1990, but it
was not considered essential to fill the position continuously.

The township level reported the establishment of a "two studies"
coordinating group, with the township Party vice-secretary in charge of
political work as its head, the new township Women's Federation cadre
as its vice-head, and technical and teaching personnel from the agriculture, forestry, education, and supply and marketing offices as members.
Both before and after the change in personnel at the township level, the
Women's Federation had organized one-day technical training classes in

cotton and grain production, with the emphasis upon seed selection. One or two women were brought in from each of the smaller villages and three or four from each of the larger villages in the township (which has a total of sixty-one villages) for these classes, and the women trained were then expected to pass their new knowledge on to other women in their communities. The object was to spread information about seed varieties that were both high yielding and disease resistant, with the modest goals of increasing production and income. Women in the township had also been organized to register for the competition element of the "two studies," although only sixty-six women were reported as registered in the summer of 1990. The "two studies" was in its very early stage at this point, and was not greatly different from the courtyard economy effort, except in that its training and productive focus was now on the main local crops of grain and cotton.

In theory there was also supposed to be a "two studies" coordinating group at the village level, with the village women's head being the active member and the village Party branch secretary and other village leaders also participating. This did not exist in Huaili in 1990 and, in fact, there were no "two studies" activities underway or even expected in the village in the absence of a women's head. Although the "two studies" did become very active in Huaili soon, when a women's head was appointed, a "two studies" coordinating group never materialized at the village level (except in name), and would actually have been meaningless. It would simply have replicated the small group of village leaders who had general responsibility for village affairs—the members of the Party branch and of the village committee—with the addition of the women's head, if she did not already belong to one of the two committees.

The situation in Huaili and at the township level in 1990 indicates one of the major problems affecting the development of the "two studies" or any other local initiative for women in rural China, the difficulty of recruiting and maintaining a stable organizational base of women leaders to carry out the practical work required. Huaili effectively illustrates the extremes of the organizational continuum. Although effective women's heads have been recruited, they have been difficult to retain, and the village has repeatedly encountered periods during which there was no women's head. At such times, all woman-work comes to a halt. When an effective women's head is in place, a high level of activity can be achieved, and this was the case in Huaili by 1992. At that time,

TABLE 10

Women's Basic Situation and Statistics on Participating in the Competition, Huaili, 1992

Name:	Age:	Educational level:		Party/League member:		No. people:	
Unit:	Area of competition:			Yearly income:			
Scale of pro-duction:	Crops			Orchard area	Domestic livestock	Investment in processing projects	Commercial area	Yearly income in each project
	Grain area	Cotton area	Vegetable area				
Competition measures:							
Goal-achieving situation:	Grain/cotton production and yearly income						
	Contribution to the state						
	Education and technical study						
	Aid to the poor and help to those in difficulty						

the particular focus was the "two studies," and Huaili exemplifies what was expected, attempted, and realized under favorable organizational (and typically modest economic) circumstances, in the first phase of this initiative.

The "two studies" in Huaili in 1992 can be viewed from at least two distinct perspectives: as meeting the requirements of the national program of the Women's Federations, and as arising from and remaining rooted in the recent local history of the women of Huaili. Both perspectives may be used in a manner that is accurate and meaningful, each within its own frame of reference. Huaili was in a relatively high degree of compliance with the formal features of the "two studies." It was part of this compliance that Huaili's "two studies" activities in 1991 and 1992 had been recorded in the extensive files kept under the direction of the township Women's Federation head.

Huaili moved rapidly to register women for the "two studies" competition, along the lines required by the Women's Federations, which were pushing for high and rising rates of registration. Ling County claimed participation rates of 10% for 1990 (the first year of the "two studies" in this area), 60% for 1991, and 78% for 1992. Registration was officially encouraged by linking it with favored access to fertilizer, pesticides, kerosene, loans for investment, and superior seeds, a measure reminiscent of earlier mobilizational campaigns. Registration itself was done in writing according to a standard form along the lines presented in Table 10. In mid-1992 I was able to examine the individual forms for ninety-nine women in Huaili, as solicited by the village women's head. This represents a high participation rate, since Huaili had only 230 women in their productive years at this time, and young unmarried women were not included. The target for the initiative was married women who were in their key productive years and who were responsible for households.

The forms consistently provide basic information on the education and economic situation of the registered women. All the women reported education ranging from primary school to various levels of secondary school, most commonly lower middle school, and none were indicated to be illiterate or semi-literate. This relatively high level of education, somewhat higher than that found in my household sample (see Table 2), may in part be due to the relatively young ages of the registered women, who were mostly in their twenties or thirties with only a few in their early or mid-forties. Since I did encounter women in my household visits who readily reported being illiterate or having limited schooling in the presence of the village women's head, it seems less likely that these records represented misreporting than that less educated women had not registered. This registration process should have assisted in identifying appropriate women for the various levels of training in the "two studies," and it may have done so in Huaili. Certainly the training program in Huaili assumed that literacy was no longer the issue and that the emphasis should be on short-term training in the early 1990s, followed by 1995 with more selective enrollment in the Rural Correspondence College.

Each woman also registered in a specific area of competition, consistent with the range of economic activities in Huaili: sixty-two in crop cultivation (*zhongzhi*), twenty-three in commerce (*jingshang*), ten in processing *(jiagong)* of goods such as sesame oil and clothing, two in crafts (*gongyi*), and two in animal husbandry (*yangzhi*). Regardless of the area of competition in which women registered, almost all reported cultivated land (the amounts were household and not individual figures) and reported a commitment, under "Contribution to the State," to provide 100 *jin* (or 150 *jin* in a few cases) for each person in the household, essentially an agreement to pay agricultural tax, which has been a persistently problematic matter in the countryside since decollectivization made this a household-based collection problem. In fifteen cases, there was a separate commitment to pay tax in cash on the part of women whose households had commercial or other productive projects; for four who were so specialized that they had no land at all, the amounts were substantial ones of RMB 1,000–5,000, although the amounts in all other cases were much smaller ones of RMB 100–500. Here the official face of woman-work is apparent, meeting demands to deal with standard political work, in this case tax collection.[2]

[2] The tax collection issue in Huaili was entirely an issue of collecting taxes for higher levels of the state. The administrative village of Huaili met its modest financial needs by renting out buildings it had inherited from the production brigade of Huaili. It made no attempt to collect taxes or expand its level of economic activity, and preferred to foster independent business rather than try to establish village enterprises (apart from an abortive attempt at a small weaving workshop in the late 1980s). Land-holding households were subject to an agricultural tax of 70–100 *jin* per person per year, to be paid in wheat or a cash equivalent to wheat. During this period, Huaili households reported total grain yields of about 1500 *jin* per *mu*, of which slightly less than half would be wheat; the land allocation per person was .67 *mu* of grain land. Yields were considered chronically underreported, and the village accountant was able to describe detailed procedures then in use for calculating yields

In the "Education and technical study" category, where women could report their interest and participation in the training component of the "two studies," the majority of the forms were blank, although twenty-nine did include a variety of general statements to "participate in study" (*canjia xuexi [ban]*) and "advance in technology" (*jishu xianjin*). Only a few made somewhat more specific comments: "processing study class" (*jiagong xuexi ban*), "already registered in study class" (*yi jiaru xuexi ban*), or "participate in technical training" (*canjia jishu peixun*). Indeed, while training was provided in Huaili as advocated in the "two studies," the focus here was proportionately more on economic activity and income-generation than on training.

The final category, "Aid to the poor and help to those in difficulty," was used by only five women, all of whom were relatively successful. One storekeeper offered to take initiative in helping those in need, two others made similar offers of accommodating those in need, and a fourth simply offered all-around service. The leading seamstress in the village, who had long been a key resource for the local women's organization, offered to make clothes for Children's Day (June 1) celebrations and to help the elderly who were alone and in need (presumably with clothing). Assistance by the successful for the needy was an explicit goal of the movement, and many of the more economically successful women were called upon to assist, either with cash (usually loans) or often with training and expertise to help poorer women initiate small projects.

All the items on the registration form were directly connected to the formal competition element of the "two studies" and allowed assessment according to the criteria set by the county for the selection of "advanced experts" (*xianjin nengshou*), as the models in the "two studies" were termed. Briefly, there were four types of criteria: meeting

---

and values of crops based on the assumption that reporting would be low. Officially, the land in the area was thought capable of producing 2500 *jin* per *mu*. There were also handbooks available for assisting in these calculations for agriculture. It was not difficult to arrive at a rough calculation of tax owing on agricultural land, which made evasion of agricultural tax more difficult than evasion of other taxes (although not necessarily easy to collect). Businesses were subject to business taxes, and this was a very much more complicated matter since it was impossible for a tax collector ever to know the actual financial situation of a household business. Consequently, the emphasis was upon exhorting businesses to be compliant and exemplary in paying taxes. This was the main issue in Huaili since there were so many household businesses. There were also a variety of other levies of less significance. Tax evasion, here as everywhere, was understood to be rampant.

specified levels in education (minimum of lower middle school) and technique; meeting specified production goals using advanced techniques; being capable of managing relations between state, collective, and individual; and being active in helping the poor and having a good reputation.[3]

Registered women could be assessed as meeting "two studies" standards or as excelling as advanced experts at each level beginning with the township. The successful women would be eligible for consideration at each higher administrative level through to the national level. While meeting the basic standard of the "two studies" competition was accessible to most women, there were fixed numerical limits for the advanced experts at each level, which kept the honors and awards restricted to relatively few. Huaili, as one of the early sites of success in the "two studies," had thirty women meet township-level standards in 1991, of whom twelve also met county-level standards. Eight of these were township-level advanced experts, of whom two were county-level advanced experts. One of the two, Huaili's women's head, was also a designated model at the prefectural level in the popularization of the law (pufa).

The designation of models was just one familiar administrative

---

[3] The specific guidelines for "advanced experts" (xianjin nengshou) set by the Ling County Committee Office in its Document 20 of 1989 (October 13, 1989) were: 1) Education and technology: a minimum of lower middle school graduation and knowledge of one or more practical technique(s) (shiyong jishu), the use of both shown in production with outstanding results that qualified the woman to be either a rural technical key member (nong jishu gugan) or a rural technician (nongmin jishuyuan). (The former term referred generally to women who did well in training offered through the township and county Women's Federation channels in the "two studies," but was not a formal designation. The latter term refers to someone qualifying through examination as having a degree of expertise in one area of agriculture. There are four levels within this designation, and the rural technicians may be remunerated in the village for leading in agricultural work, but they remain rural residents and not state employees.) 2) Specific production targets using advanced techniques: these were producing 2,500 jin per mu of grain; producing 250 jin per mu of ginned cotton; earning RMB 2,000 for other crops; advanced management, larger scale and earning RMB 3,000 per year for animal husbandry; using scientific methods and earning RMB 5,000 per year for processing; using science and earning RMB 10,000 per year in forestry and orchards; or following state policy on prices and taxes, using scientific management and paying tax of RMB 2,000 per year in commerce. 3) Capable of managing relations between state, collective, and individual: the person follows laws and policies, is a model in constructing the two forms of civilization, and meets state plans and tasks. (Note that this criterion would exclude any woman not complying with the state's birth-planning policy.) 4) Energetically help the poor and aid those in difficulty, and have a good reputation among the masses.

mechanism used in the "two studies." Several other numerical measures were used to direct and assess the work of village women's heads
and local level Women's Federation staff, including numbers of women
registered, numbers of women reaching specified educational and technical levels, and numbers of training courses delivered. From this administrative perspective, Huaili was compliant and successful in 1991–
92.

However, formal mechanisms give limited insight into the actual
work of implementing an initiative such as the "two studies," which
was intended to go beyond standard administrative measures and connect itself with emergent social and economic development in the
countryside. As can be seen from the preceding description, traditional
methods of mobilization had not been abandoned, but something more
was being sought. The new generation of women's heads, recruited and
trained according to new criteria of education (as well as political suitability) and orientation toward the market (as well as compliance with
laws and plans) provided the key to realizing this departure.

In the case of Huaili, the new women's head recruited in 1991 had
previously drawn attention by being entrepreneurial in moving into a
previously all-male area of small-scale commerce. And later, in 1991,
she went to Beijing to learn new techniques of raising tree seedlings, a
potentially lucrative cash crop not previously cultivated in Huaili. She
needed extra land for this purpose and was able to rent some good agricultural land publicly held in the village (see Judd 1994: 31–32). She paid
more than the standard rent—land was a scarce and valued commodity
in Huaili—but received the additional amount she needed. Her access
to it appears to have been an instance of village support for the strategy
of having each women's head be active in running an income-generating
project of her own. This particular initiative on her part was not very
successful—she lost much of the crop in 1992—but she did energetically pursue other activities, including her work as women's head. She
was highly oriented toward the market, and left the village (together
with her husband, while the children remained with his mother in
Huaili) to pursue commerce in Tianjin in 1993, with enough success
that the couple was considered to be there on a long-term basis by 1995.
While serving as women's head, she was a suitable choice to assist
women in setting up their own projects, and was making a success of
this position for herself.

The most visible work of this women's head consisted of the ap-

proved activities of holding meetings, organizing training, and mobilizing women to register for the "two competitions." She reported extremely high rates of participation in these activities—to the point of
claiming that all women under forty years of age had joined in study and
competition—although this may more closely represent the number of
women formally registered in the "two studies" than those actively
participating. The discrepancy is best interpreted not as individual
overreporting, but as compliance with customary levels of hyperbole.
As indicated by the results of my household surveys and reported in Tables 4, 5, and 6, this woman did raise the level of participation to a dis-
tinctly higher level during her term. Some elements are relatively constant: the calling of meetings and the formal presence of a women's
committee and of some women models in the community. The distinctive difference lay in the wider active participation under the inclusive
category, "meetings and some further involvement," which peaks
strongly in 1992.

Despite the end of the collective era and the move away from campaigns, it remains the case that meetings are held in rural China to
which people come with more or less reluctance, in a relatively empty
and formalistic way. Mere attendance at meetings is something that
can be generated to a degree, but meaningful involvement requires
more. The changed approach advocated for the "two studies" implicitly
recognizes this in advocating linking its mobilization with practical
training and economic activity. The concrete problem is that of providing meaningful substance to either the training or the economic activity. As most readers will realize from comparable educational experiences of their own, it is difficult to design and deliver appropriate training to a large number of people. Some will already be familiar with the
material and complain that it is a waste of time, while others may find
even the topic irrelevant to their needs. It is hardly surprising that many
women chose not to participate in the organized activities.

Discussions in households indicated that much of the effective work
took place in individual encounters with the women's head, apart from
meetings, and through a relationship with her (or with other models)
that was not necessarily viewed as official. This is typical of the informal way in which women's movements commonly operate, although it
is a departure from the more formal characteristics of the mobilizational approach. Mobilization also requires personal ties, and these
were especially fostered between leaders and led, but they were subor-

dinated to the formal organizational structure. The practical significance of the approach of the "two studies," in an organizational sense,
was the more open recognition of informal and decentralized networking, which was phrased in the newly legitimating terms of discourse
about the market.

The concrete actions the women's head took consisted of helping
poorer women, those without household economic projects, to initiate
a project. This could include urging a woman to participate in training,
although this seems—rather conspicuously—not to have been decisive.
The key element was more often helping a woman to make contact
with one of the women models in the village, who would provide some
combination of advice, on-the-job training through employment or apprenticeship, and access to specialized technical inputs. The models
would be willing, in part because they were urged to provide this service
by the women's head and (in more prominent cases) by the Women's
Federations, and also because they could benefit through the work of
the employee or apprentice or through selling materials to the new entry to the field. In the cases where there was successful expansion of activity in a particular area, the models retained a leadership position in
each field that was not compromised by the entry of smaller-scale or
less skilled women as producers. Later in this chapter, this development will be traced in the diverse cases of sewing, mushroom cultivation and chicken raising.

In other cases, the contribution appears to have been access to small
amounts of start-up capital. The women's head herself or, through her,
the village Party branch would make a small loan directly or guarantee a
larger loan from a bank, although this formal assistance did not occur
often in Huaili. The wealthier women in the village were occasionally
called upon to help in the same way, in part as an official part of the
movement, but also in response to more diffuse social pressures to
share their wealth. Measures such as these extended access to loans, but
most loans appeared to come through informal channels, especially
from relatives.

While any type of income-generating activity was encouraged
within the "two studies," the emphasis in Huaili was described as
"courtyard economy," although the specific content of this term had
changed compared with the late 1980s. While courtyard cultivation of
vegetables did continue to be advocated, it was no longer the primary
goal. In the 1990s, any household-based activity of a commercial or pro-

ductive nature fit this description in a literal sense, since some part of it would take place in the courtyard or in a side building constructed in the same area. And all the activities did actually get included, even if they might take place elsewhere (a plot of land or the marketplace), since all the non-agricultural activities in Huaili were very small-scale household-based enterprises. This was consistent both with the larger meaning of the Women's Federations' discourse on the courtyard economy and with Huaili's own path of promoting household projects.

The demands on the women's movement in Huaili were now more complex than in the earlier stage of mobilizing women to grow vegetables and *xiangchun* in their courtyards. While the individualized approach described here would surely have had advantages even with the more uniform strategy, it was essential to the diverse initiatives. In 1992, the women I spoke with in Huaili were running projects that included: restaurants, mushroom cultivation, recycling bottles and other used materials, sewing, small- and larger-scale shops of various types, dried noodle manufacture and sale, inns, beekeeping and honey production, selling clothing in periodic markets, manufacturing snack foods, chicken raising, pig raising, clinics, and sesame oil production. In a few cases there had been considerable investment in buildings (inns) or machinery (noodles), or some particular skill might be essential (as for seamstresses), but in many cases people moved readily from one project to another as opportunity and market conditions changed. This was especially the case in small-scale commerce, but also applied to animal husbandry and vegetable cultivation. Here the key was flexible adaptation to changing market conditions, and I found that the mix of small projects had changed every time I visited Huaili. Assisting women to prosper in this environment required an entrepreneurial ability to promote a diversity of projects. Unless Huaili were to supply some larger area with one or more specialized goods, the women of Huaili had to move diversely into a variety of local market opportunities. This was not something that could readily be directed by an official plan. Indeed, much of the revitalization of rural China in the reform era derives precisely from a move away from cumbersome planning and toward decentralized market activity.

Despite the women's movement's embrace of the market, it did not choose to focus primarily upon commerce. This was evident even in Huaili, with its strong emphasis on shop keeping, although there was an occasional indication of the Women's Federations providing useful market information to commercial households. There was, however, no training offered in business development or management in any form or at any time. There were presumably also some practical problems—the local Women's Federation staff would want business to thrive in their communities but, with numerous households competing in a small market, would face problems in deciding whom to provide with a business advantage. Cooperation among women in development was easier to promote in areas where many women could thrive (such as vegetable production) than in areas where competition between women (as in petty commerce) was an unavoidable aspect of the market. The larger issue, however, was probably an underlying set of values on the part of the women's movement that privileged production over commerce, and preferred to support production for the market over purely commercial activity.

In whichever manner women chose to become involved in the market, they required new knowledge about how to do so successfully. From the production perspective, the knowledge provided through education and training could be valuable, as could information on emergent opportunities for the production of new goods for local or distant markets. As the market became more complex and diversified, so also did channels of economic knowledge. The women's movement can here can be viewed as flexibly responding to this new environment by generating women's heads who could provide microsupport for household projects and for links between women across household boundaries in spreading knowledge that was both technical and business-oriented.

An important element here is the incipient emergence of a women's network for the transmission of economic knowledge parallel to the existing androcentric networks in rural communities to which women have little or no direct access. Androcentric ties were effectively supported by official structures within villages as well as by kinship and residence patterns (Judd 1994). I would argue that here one can see the women's movement attempting to foster a women's network working across the household boundaries that so deeply divide women in rural China (Judd 1994: 202–11). The contribution of the official women's movement largely takes the form of brokering and promoting women's access to either public resources (in the hands of government departments or village committees) or private resources (in the hands of local models). It is surely the case that some access to these resources would still have circulated, mediated through male household heads and through the limited informal ties between women, but the "two studies" and the broader shift in organizational style that it represents marks a determined effort to support and expand a women's economic network. While the official channel of the women's heads was used and strengthened in this process, the object was not necessarily to draw women into meetings and the women's committees, but to increase their participation in the local economy. In the case of Huaili in 1992, this meant enabling women to be more effective independent actors in small-scale market activity, and this may well be a major aspect of the courtyard economy component of the "two studies" in general.

In communities such as Huaili, which was relatively well located (on a paved highway) for a village remote from an urban center, there were opportunities for the very small scale projects that were at the heart of its economic development prospects. Even so, the work of assisting women to prosper through numerous individual projects was enormously labor intensive and would not necessarily place women in the forefront of local economic development once that moved to larger-scale initiatives.

Three years later, in 1995, the first year of the second phase of the "two studies," Huaili and its residents were still committed to a development strategy based on small-scale household-based projects. However, the county and township development focus had shifted toward favoring large-scale endeavors. The second phase of the "two studies" matched this approach with an altered emphasis upon higher levels of training appropriate for larger and more technically demanding projects.

Huaili and its encompassing area had earlier been primarily agricultural but, in the 1980s, had attempted moves toward rural industry, the route that had brought prosperity to much of rural China, especially in areas favored by good location. Unfortunately, this area was a relatively late and weak arrival to rural industry and suffered a near-total collapse of its rural industry in the crisis of 1990. As the area recovered in the 1990s, it altered its development strategy from rural industry to commercial agriculture. A key element here was a growing economic integration with the Tianjin economic region, and corresponding growth in market opportunities. Ling County determined that its best opportunities lay in its comparative advantages in agriculture and in producing commercial crops for sale primarily in Tianjin, although more distant markets were also sought. The county pursued an integrated development strategy in which each township focused primarily upon one particular specialty and endeavored to provide it with public support. For most of the townships, the chosen specialty was vegetable cultivation, although for the township in which Huaili was located, the choice was large-scale production of chickens. The lack of emphasis on vegetable cultivation in this township, compared with its neighbors, may have contributed to the decline in intensive vegetable cultivation in courtyards in Huaili, although vegetable and other crop production continued to be prominently encouraged by the Women's Federation elsewhere in Ling County (Liu Peiying and Huang Jiansong 1995).

Large-scale chicken production in Huaili and its environs was primarily an initiative of the county and township governments, although the Women's Federations claimed credit as well and did have some involvement in line with its mainstreaming GAD approach to development. In preparation for this undertaking, the township brought in an animal husbandry specialist, a professor from Tianjin, together with two of her students. They stayed in the township from March 1994 to June 1995, during which time they gave classes on raising chickens and provided chicks and equipment for township households, all on a commercial basis that was profitable for the Tianjin experts and valuable to the township. In 1995 a program in chicken raising began to be offered through the Rural Correspondence College, aimed at women in the villages selected as the loci of the chicken-raising project. In late 1995, the township Party secretary was finally able to announce the signing of a major joint venture contract for the export of frozen chickens to Malaysia and Hong Kong.

In association with this development, there was a shift in emphasis in the training offered by the Women's Federations. They began to work closely with the Rural Correspondence College, a relatively new institution that aimed to deliver a more advanced and systematic practical technical education in the countryside than previously available. It was formally rated at the college (*dazhuan*) level, but was not strictly the equivalent of regular colleges. Students entered by examination, and lower middle school was the effective entrance standard; students also faced examinations upon leaving in order to qualify for a designation such as "rural technician" (*nongmin jishuyuan*). The course of study lasted one year and included one day of expert instruction every three months, tutorials once or twice a month by local technical personnel, and the study of a substantial textbook.

Dezhou Prefecture was very interested in the opportunities offered by the Rural Correspondence College, as was Ling County, and branch schools were established in the county from 1992. The number of locations, classes, and students steadily increased although, even with Women's Federation endorsement by 1993, there were relatively few women registered. The response the Women's Federations made to this was to establish special classes that targeted women. Men could also attend these, and a few did, but the object was to connect the classes offered with the local development being promoted for women. By 1994, the goal was to have one such class of thirty women in each township. In Huaili's township, this was then achieved with thirty women coming from numerous villages in the township. In 1995, there were sixty women, twenty from each of the three villages specially targeted for the township chicken project. In addition, five women from Huaili were reported as attending, although not all may have been formally registered (auditing was permitted). These were women in the village who were raising at least a few hundred chickens, and also Huaili's women's head, who did not raise chickens but was expected to attend and play an organizing role because of her position.

While not all women or even all villages had access to Rural Correspondence College training, it was nevertheless expected to develop a core of more technically trained women who would work in significant mainstream projects. The women's head was intended always to be one of these women, to organize them to attend classes, and also to lead them subsequently through the vehicle of "research associations" (yanjiu hui). These associations began in Ling County in late 1994, and were intended to bring together the rural women newly trained and accredited through channels such as the "two studies" and the Rural Correspondence College. They were described as mass organizations, that is, not part of the government, but connected closely with it. There were 1,080 of these in Ling County by the end of 1995, and one of these was in Huaili's township.

Huaili itself was no longer central to local development plans. These had shifted toward three other (of the sixty-one) villages in the township. Huaili was still able to make some use of the support given to the chicken-exporting project; it provided local expertise and resources that could be used for Huaili's complementary efforts in commercial egg production, and these expanded at just this time. However, Huaili was no longer a priority for the economic development work for women being conducted by the Women's Federations. At this time it also lacked a Party branch secretary, as a result of a disagreement between village and township levels, and was coasting in the interim with little formal leadership. In addition, the township Women's Federation head who had been so supportive of Huaili in recent years had been promoted to vice-head of a different township (one of the promotions of women that took place near the time of the 1995 World Conference on Women), and her successor was not yet familiar with Women's Federation work. Huaili was now in an almost classic situation of a women's organization at the weak end of the organizational continuum. The few positions that required people to support the women's organization were vacant or only newly filled, and Huaili was not a priority for any external support.

Despite these limiting factors, Huaili did have an active women's head at this time, one appointed in the autumn of 1994. She was less entrepreneurial than her immediate predecessor, although she was a young women with a lower middle school education, and consequently met these key criteria for the post. She did not have a project in her household in the sense in which that term had been used in previous years, although she did keep one or two head of cattle, and this was described in 1995 as being her household economic project. Cattle had become a newly popular choice for Huaili households, so she was in line with local households in this respect. However, her primary activity was not economic development work. She described that aspect of her work as "seeing whose income was higher." This was a succinct expression of the competition criteria of the "two studies" as applied in practice, and the basis on which models could be designated. The other concrete element of her "two studies" work was encouraging women to pay taxes. Tax payment was part of the social contribution component of the "two studies," as well as of the general political work women's movement personnel were called upon to do. Tax collection had been a vexatious issue in the countryside since the dissolution of collectives, and was especially difficult where so many households were engaged in commerce; hence its importance in Huaili in 1995.

Rather than concentrate on "two studies" work, however, she was concurrently birth-planning worker for her village, and it was this that consumed most of her effort. Since village birth-planning work was remunerated by the township government, she was, in effect, doing this part-time job as her income-generating contribution to her household. The work consists largely of ensuring that each woman of childbearing age goes to the township for a physical examination every three months. If a woman does not go as scheduled it is the birth-planning worker's responsibility to ensure that she does so. This measure is intended not only to reduce births, but also to reduce the frequency of abortions, especially late abortions, and probably does so. As is usually the case, the birth-planning worker was also responsible for education regarding reproduction, and she held meetings for this purpose. In the course of household visits we did together, this women's head appeared very knowledgeable about the situation of women in the target age range for birth planning, which is the same age that is targeted for economic development work. I was told that both tasks could be conducted together, and presume that this may have happened, primarily through her helping women make contact and receive help from the models in the village. Still, it was clear that economic development work was conducted less actively than in the recent past. This is very likely the situation that obtains in many villages with less favorable political or economic conditions than those once enjoyed by Huaili. In those cases other priorities (tax collection, birth planning) come to the fore, and support for development is selectively directed to other villages.

Huaili continued to have some activity in development for and by women. In late 1995, fifty-six women in the village had projects sufficiently successful to have been noticed and recorded at the township level. These included continuations of earlier projects as well as new departures: raising chickens, processing dried noodles, processing sesame oil, running grain shops (when private grain shops became permitted), making clothing, selling clothing, running inns, running restaurants, shop keeping (foodstuffs and various other goods), growing mushrooms, selling vegetables, running a clinic, and recycling. The initiative and knowledge to establish these enterprises came from examples in the village and from opportunities created both formally through the women's movement and informally through women's networks.

PROJECTS

The development of the "two studies" over time and its relation to literacy, education, and training for women can be traced concretely through an examination of how women developed household projects in Huaili. A diversity of situations can be explored by systematically reviewing all the households in four different sets of cases. In order to establish that improving women's quality through education or training is the key to improving women's place in rural economic development, it is necessary to demonstrate that education or training does actually make a difference for women. This can be tested using data from Huaili, both synchronic data from the relatively large and differentiated 1989 sample, and diachronic data that traces the acquisition and transmission of economically useful skills among women over the period from 1989 to 1995.

In my earlier work (Judd 1994), using the 1989 Huaili sample of forty economically differentiated households, I distinguished between categories of: 1) specialized households, as officially recognized in Huaili at the time and characterized by having such successful household projects that they had forgone access to village agricultural land; 2) self-identified specialized households that had significant household projects, but were not recognized officially as specialized and had not given up their land allocation; and 3) ordinary agricultural households. In Table 4-3 in Judd (1994), reproduced here as Table 11, I indicated the highest level of education attained by members of the core couple in each of the forty households in the 1989 sample. This table supports an argument that there is an association between higher levels of education and the ability of a household to achieve specialized household status in the early years of decollectivization. There is also a suggestion that differences between women across the three categories are sharper than those for men, a finding that is consistent with the wider range of educational attainment for women in Huaili than for men. As I argued then, a successful conjugal partnership was at the economic core of most of these specialized households, and a woman's capacity to make a major contribution to her household's projects could be of decisive importance to the household's overall economic success.[4]

---

[4] I have considered and have rejected the possibility of recalculating the contrasts based on the total sample of ninety households, although I will use the additional household data from 1990, 1992, and 1995 in discussing patterns of formal and informal transmission of economically useful skills. Huaili no longer identifies a category of "specialized households," and all the households formerly in this category now receive the same per capita allocation of land as do other households, although they may allow a closely related household within the village to farm the land. There is therefore no clear marker between the truly specialized households and those with medium- or smaller-scale projects. While there were a few changes both upward and downward in household fortunes, the original group of specialized households did include the entire set of specialized households recognized at that time. In the revisits at intervals of only a few years, I did not aim to recreate a similar cross-section of village households, but focused upon households with significant recent changes and extended my interest toward households with newer and usually smaller-scale proj-

TABLE 11

Highest Level of Education Attained by Members of the Core Mature Couple in 40 Households, Huaili, 1989

	Household category					
	Non-specialized		"Specialized"[b]		Specialized	
Education[a]	F (n = 18)	M (n = 18)	F (n = 13)	M (n = 12)	F (n = 9)	M (n = 9)
None	10	2	3	0	1	0
Primary	6	8[d]	8	11[c]	0	2
Lower middle school	2	5[b]	2	1[d]	4	3
Upper middle school	0	2	0	0	2[d]	3[c]
Higher	0	1	0	0	2	1

NOTE: The one exception to a core mature couple is that of one household where the economic figure is the eldest (unmarried) daughter of the household. She is included in these figures in place of her mother and stepfather.

[a]In each case these levels should be read as "at least some education at this level." The tertiary education is teacher's training in three cases and paramedical training in one case.

[b]Some households identified themselves as "specialized" although they did not meet the official criteria for specialized households and still worked agricultural land. They were more involved than ordinary rural households in nonagricultural projects and are in an intermediate category.

[c]One person in this category has also received further education during army service.

[d]One person in this category has also completed an apprenticeship.

When examined more closely, the situation of the conspicuously successful specialized households has a rather more complex relation to the question of the validity of the strategy based on quality and the "two studies" activities in particular. Table 12 presents more detailed information on the nine specialized households in the previous table, and also on one of the self-defined specialized households that, on the basis of its economic activity when visited in 1988, 1992, and 1995, is more appropriately classed with those households (1989 had been an atypical year for that household). It is apparent from this table that all of these households moved rapidly into the private sector as soon as decollectivization occurred, demonstrating considerable entrepreneurial initiative, and that in several cases the enterprises are wholly commercial (wholesalers), while in other cases commercial aspects have played an

---

ects. The 1989 sample therefore serves well as a synchronic base, and the later additions allow tracing how training has been accessed or skills transmitted to households starting projects later, either on their own or in association with such official initiatives as the "two studies." It is also preferable to keep the early specialized households separate as they did make their breakthrough under different conditions from those of following years.

important role in the household's economy (the hotel and at least one of the restaurants).

The "two studies" initiative is not directed toward aiding women to enter commerce, and local Women's Federation cadres carrying it out share the view widely expressed by rural women and men that commercial activity requires market information, but does not require any training. There is no effort to provide any training related to commerce, although sometimes market information is transmitted through women's movement channels, and this sphere of rural economy that, apart from petty trade, is one of the most profitable, is assumed to be able to attract people spontaneously.[5] Also, the initiative does not appear to be directed toward identifying women who will make a breakthrough into a new area, as many of these initially successful households did. Instead, the "two studies" activities aim to draw in women who have already made a spontaneous breakthrough to economic prosperity, designate such women as models (nü nengshou, or able women), and recruit them to help other women move into a specialized area of production.

For women in a second or subsequent entrepreneurial generation, some of the same requirements of education and entrepreneurship may not hold, and the lack of these may not be such a high barrier. This is especially the case when combined with technical training and some organized support, although it is important to note that there are also informal channels of technical transmission and economic support operating at the same time. Although this initiative is officially represented as adding a missing dimension for rural women, the processes I have observed are a more complex combination of appropriating informal processes and augmenting them through formalized channels. The official women's movement adds resources, organization, and official status, while it acquires the benefit of association with successful rural entrepreneurs.

Attempts to assess a direct relationship between a rural individual's education or training and her economic success are more difficult than

---

[5] Women as well as men were active in Huaili in petty trade, including some women who by 1995 were making the round of local markets selling a small stock (most commonly baby clothes) at a 5% markup. This involved considerable heavy work in taking the goods to market, and the returns were so small that this was not an attractive option. It is possible that there was a trend toward feminization of this type of work, although the numbers involved are too small to be conclusive.

TABLE 12

Specialized Households, Education, and Initial Conditions, Huaili, 1989

| Household | Project(s) | Education | | Initial conditions |
		Wife	Husband	
H89-3	restaurant	some lower middle school; former school teacher	some primary school; army training as a cook	had done some catering as a sideline before decollectivization; as soon as decollectivized, contracted village building on main road; first restaurant in village; used husband's skill and wife's education and entrepreneurship
H89-35	mirror production; restaurant; shop	some lower middle school	some primary school	husband acquired art and mirror-making skill in factory work in NE and elsewhere from 1960; started own mirror production in Huaili in 1983; hired laborers and wife (used as hired labor) work in restaurant; shop minor and being phased out
H89-13	wholesale; factory manager	upper middle school; former teacher	upper middle school	at beginning of decollectivization contracted the unprofitable brigade retail shop, in temporary partnership with another man, and gradually turned it into a profitable wholesale business; sold this early in 1989 and husband became factory manager in county seat while wife became wealthy housewife
H89-24	false teeth	upper middle school; four-year apprenticeship	lower middle school	wife taught the family trade of making false teeth by father (from 1982), until then passed only through male line; husband has learned some dentistry from her father and from self-study and complements her work; this conjugal opportunity caused him to leave his team electrician position

ID	Business	Education 1	Education 2	Notes
H89-14	mushrooms	lower middle school	upper middle school; half-month training course in raising mushrooms	husband responded to advertisement for mushroom training course in Jinan in 1986; developed mushroom business, with assistance of wife, who later became more important as project(s) expanded and diversified
H89-10	hotel, shop	secondary normal	secondary normal	very entrepreneurial couple moved into private enterprise immediately upon decollectivization; started with shop in 1984; hotel with bank loan from 1988; resourceful financial and speculative moves on part of both; only shop in village with reading material
H89-16	restaurant	none	some upper middle school; army training	husband was village political leader who left to set up food store elsewhere in 1985; husband apparently well connected and entrepreneurial; used earnings to establish restaurant for official clientele in Huaili from 1987; illiterate wife learned to be skilled cook from hired cook; wife's younger sister did accounts; husband returned to part-time political work; politics and business combined profitably
H89-11	sewing; cycle repair	lower middle school	lower middle school	wife's sewing skill and good political connections won the couple a prime commercial site in her natal village of Huaili beginning soon after decollectivization; she runs sewing workshop; husband runs cycle repair
H89-8	chickens; pigs	primary school	lower middle school; 2–3 months veterinary training in another township	village's earliest large-scale chicken enterprise, from immediately after decollectivization; wife receives public recognition; husband trained as veterinarian in 1980s and is on staff as Huaili's only veterinarian
H89-17	wholesale	primary school and three years training as a medic; former medic	lower middle school; former team accountant	developed a food wholesaling business from retail beginning in 1984 to two wholesale outlets in 1989; at beginning the couple had been in partnership with the husband's brother, but by 1989 simply a conjugal partnership

they might immediately appear. This situation is not comparable to that of employment, where an individual's qualifications may well be a factor in employability and remuneration. In the case of household enterprises or self-employment, what is essential is that the economic unit in question—here, the household—have access to the essential resources, of which education and training are part. It may be sufficient for one person in the household to have a relatively high level of education, training, or entrepreneurship in order to allow the entire household to run a project. There is no shortage of instances where one person in the household provides the critical human resource, and then, where necessary, trains other members of the household. The data in Table 11 may indicate that a household has an advantage where both members of the core conjugal couple have better than average education, although the leading cases, as presented in Table 12, also show how the ability of one member of the household (either husband or wife) can be key to the project's initiation.

The sharing of economically useful knowledge is therefore critical to strategies for expanding local development. Some types of knowledge, primarily commercial knowledge and household-based financial knowledge, are not readily shared across household boundaries, except perhaps in the case of interhousehold partnerships, but these are not favored in Huaili. Households prefer to maintain firm economic boundaries with other households, the only exception relating to households from which they have recently divided. Sharing the kind of commercial knowledge that is key in commercial and speculative success in the Chinese countryside is done rarely.

Sharing technical knowledge that could result in an increase in local competition is also something that successful households may not greet with enthusiasm. Some forms of technical knowledge are too specialized (such as making false teeth) to be candidates for widespread sharing; and even in that case the skilled woman in this trade in Huaili considered herself obligated to do 60% of her work for free for her father, who had trained her, years after completion of her apprenticeship. Cultural norms have restricted some other skills (such as the traditional process of making sesame oil) within families, even where this skill is more common. A variety of social and political pressures can be exerted on successful households to share some technical (if not commercial) knowledge, and the trend toward larger-scale and more complex forms of rural economic organization is promoting this process. Successful households can share knowledge of some part of a process with other households, where the original household retains a technical and economic advantage and benefits from the relationship. Even already successful households may benefit from access to additional technical advice, especially as rural production becomes rapidly more capitalized.

These considerations are essential in evaluating the relation between education or training and economic success for households that enter a specialized area of production in the second or later generation of economic development. At this point the education or training initially available as a household resource may be less significant than patterns of transmission of technical knowledge and access to technical assistance.

I will address this issue by examining three of the areas of economic activity in Huaili that have involved a number of households in the early 1990s, and that have each required access to technical training of the type advocated in the "two studies": custom seamstress work; large-scale cultivation of mushrooms; and large-scale chicken raising, both for meat and for eggs.[6]

Custom Seamstress Work

Custom seamstress work was both an area of spontaneous economic activity in Huaili and a technical area actively cultivated in the village by the county Women's Federation very early in its efforts to move into economic development work, in 1987. The key person has been one young woman who taught herself to be a skilled seamstress. She worked out of her natal household in Huaili prior to 1984, but at the earliest opportunity built upon good relations she had with the (unrelated) village Party branch secretary of the time to secure a building spot (described as then being a ditch) at the edge of the village adjoining a highway and not far from the periodic market in a nearby village. On that site she devel-

[6]The economic areas with the largest numbers of entrants, apart from agriculture, are actually other ones. Huaili's convenient location has provided marketing opportunities, and many Huaili households engage in very small scale retailing with small markups. I am not addressing this subject, because it is not part of the women's movement strategy under examination. It is also not usually remunerative, unless a specialized area can be effectively cornered, or a household can move to a wholesale level. A second area of importance is motorized transport. I am not including this area because in Huaili it is done only by men. However, it may be worth noting that a few men did have an initial advantage by virtue of being trained as drivers in the collective era, but many other men have acquired some degree of skill and have entered this expanding and relatively remunerative area.

oped a sewing workshop, while her husband moved his cycle repair enterprise to the same site.[7] When I first visited in early 1988, she had six
apprentices working at the year-end peak of activity, although she more
commonly had two apprentices through the year. An apprentice would
work for roughly one year without paying for instruction and without
receiving wages or any other remuneration. At the end of the apprenticeship, each would be able to go out to work on her own, although
some might stay longer to work, or return at peak periods.

The technical and managerial skill required to take on apprentices
appears key to economic success in the custom seamstress field, as the
rate of payment is not high. The field is squeezed at the one end by
women who can sew themselves and have sewing machines, and at the
other end by the increasing availability of fashionable ready-made clothing in local markets. Custom seamstress work is a low-cost alternative
to buying ready-made clothing. It requires the seamstress to go to local
markets to show her skill and receive orders, which she will return to
the customer on the next market day. The self-employed seamstress
can make an income doing this, but it requires developing a clientele in
a competitive marketplace, and doing considerable amounts of work to
a tight schedule in order to make a reasonable income. The more successful seamstresses in the village have taken on apprentices, or have
left the field for unrelated areas of commerce after a few years.

Nevertheless, the field does attract apprentices, and several women
in this village have benefited by being seamstresses for at least a few
years. Most of these women have been connected with this early seam-
stress-entrepreneur. At the time of the most recent field trip in 1995,
she had converted her former workshop into a cycle parts shop run with
her husband, which appeared to be providing a good living with less effort. Seamstress work was being continued by two of her former apprentices. One, her younger sister, was working on her own out of her natal
home and had been doing so since her older sister closed the shop where
she had worked for four years. The other apprentice had also spent a

---

[7] This is not a case of uxorilocal marriage. The couple met while both worked
elsewhere as temporary contract factory workers. The husband is from a village far
from a good commercial site, but has acquired urban registration. The wife moved
her rural registration to his village following marriage, and was for a while allocated
land in that village, although it was always cultivated by a relative of her husband's.
Their living in her natal village is an arrangement that appears to have been made for
purely commercial reasons (good location), and the wife does have a brother. She appears to have been able to enjoy the residential advantages of staying in her natal village without incurring the marital disadvantages of a uxorilocal match.

longer than usual time in the same enterprise, but had left after two years to set up her own business in 1989. By 1995 she had two apprentices (her sister and a matrilateral cousin), and anticipated being able to continue this work after her marriage into a nearby village.

An advantage of work as a seamstress is certainly its mobility in the marketplace and independence of public structures. It can also serve as a means through which women acquire some capital and then can move into areas that may be more remunerative with less effort. The other woman in the village who achieved independent success as a seamstress, also through teaching herself in the early 1980s, made a transition from sewing to running a small food wholesale shop in the 1990s.

Sewing and growing vegetables were the two earliest subjects of training offered through the women's organization in Huaili. In 1987 the county Women's Federation cadre who was attending to the village organized two half-month sewing classes, taught by the leading seamstress, and two one-day vegetable-growing classes. Both built upon skills already present in the community, and the expert seamstress claimed that five or six women who took her class were able to market their work independently by the end of it, although this channel does not seem to have been comparable to a full apprenticeship. Although such technical skills can be spread to some extent through publicly sponsored classes taught by successful women officially recruited to volunteer as teachers, the main channel of transmission appears to have been apprenticeship based upon market conditions. Further, the future offered through such limited training programs may be modest, although possibly important to a small number of women who might not otherwise have had an opportunity to improve their skills.

Mushroom Cultivation

Mushrooms and other forms of edible fungus had distinct potential as cash crops for Ling County, since their marketing did not depend on location close to an urban center. The Ling County Women's Federation selected edible fungus as one of the most promising areas for development in the county and, in 1994, concentrated its energies on making a breakthrough in this area in one of the county's townships. However, Huaili was located elsewhere, and the mushrooms cultivated here were of another variety. The two initiatives shared common considerations of economic potential, but developed independently of each other.

Cultivation of fresh mushrooms was a project associated with one of

Huaili's early women models (*nü nengshou*), and was occasionally the subject of the on-site visits (*xianchang hui*) used by the Women's Federations to demonstrate conspicuous success. This was a household-based enterprise begun by a young married couple in 1986. The husband, an upper middle school graduate, responded to an advertisement by enrolling in a half-month course in the provincial capital, Jinan. Following this, the couple started with a small enterprise in the courtyard, and later expanded to a plasticized greenhouse they constructed on their vegetable plot. The key economic figure in this enterprise was the husband, but the wife was also involved. Her role fluctuated somewhat, partly in connection with the care of the two children she had in the next few years. In the early years she was involved in the planting and the local marketing of the mushrooms, and the household also employed one or two seasonal laborers during the busy season. In 1991, the household used the capital accumulated from the mushroom enterprise to add a recycling enterprise conducted from their courtyard. The wife took care of this business, since it was easier to combine with the care of her younger child than was work in the greenhouses. She continued to do some work growing mushrooms, however, and also went to the greenhouses of three other households that had recently begun growing mushrooms to advise them. Soon thereafter, the couple tried relocating to Tianjin, where they rented land and grew mushrooms to sell in that large city. They found that the cost of renting land and housing outweighed the advantage of being closer to the urban market, and they returned to Huaili. In 1995, the husband bought a large truck and started long-distance hauling, one of the more profitable areas for rural entrepreneurs. The wife gave up recycling and ran the substantial mushroom business herself, with the aid of one hired laborer. The business had expanded to two greenhouses and, in addition, spores were raised in the household that were sold to households within a radius of more than forty *li*. This household had built upon its early start to be the technically most sophisticated and diversified local producer, and one that was able to make a business of supplying other households.

In my first visit to this entrepreneurial household, there had appeared to be some reluctance about sharing their knowledge and crowding the local market, although the husband was preparing to sell spores to an uncle and to help him get started. Subsequently several other households followed as well, although entry to this field was restricted by the capital required and by the risk of plant disease. The market had apparently not become overcrowded even as late as 1995.

The most established of the secondary mushroom-growing households that I visited was one that had been producing mushrooms for six or seven years in 1995. The household was a very modest one of a couple in their sixties living on their own. The main producer was the husband; the wife worked on the mushrooms, and also provided some care for a grandson. The husband said that he had been encouraged to start this project by the original mushroom entrepreneur, who had recommended it as a profitable and physically light undertaking suitable for an older couple. The couple's sons and son-in-law had helped them excavate a pit and erect a greenhouse over it in the household courtyard, and the original mushroom producer provided a source for spores. This household considered mushrooms not to be technically difficult to grow, although they did have some concern about the risk of plant disease. They had had no training to grow mushrooms, but had learned what they needed directly from the first mushroom-producing household.

Another household with several projects (sesame production, a shop, selling clothing in a periodic market) also learned mushroom production from the first household and obtained its spores from the same source. The adult son of the household turned to producing mushrooms in 1992 when he was laid off from his job as a teacher during a period of staff reductions. Three years later he was still producing mushrooms and viewed it as profitable. He had also consulted books on growing mushrooms.

A fourth household had a still more direct connection to the original mushroom producers; the older daughter had been working for that household for three years by 1995, when her household started producing mushrooms itself. This nineteen-year-old woman was one of the few illiterates of her age in the village. She was a member of an exceptional family, the only one in the village that had migrated earlier to the Northeast and returned in the mid-1980s to participate in the division of land to households. The family had evidently been destitute and had returned with no resources or education. The father and mother were illiterate and unskilled. The father worked in the village manual transport team (banyun dui), a village body that provides some hauling work for unskilled men; the mother worked the household's land allocation. Neither of these types of work, strenuous as each is, provides a good income. The mushroom-growing skill of the older of their two daughters (there were no sons) was a significant economic resource for this household. When I visited this household in 1995, it had just started growing mushrooms on a small scale in a dirt-floored room that had been emptied of furniture to provide space. The household had borrowed money from relatives to set up the project, but was still able to begin only on a small scale. The women's head has been in touch with the daughter about technical matters, but not regarding financial help.

The same young woman has also been a significant resource for the neighboring household, which began to grow mushrooms at the same time. This household was also one of the less affluent ones in the village. Prior to growing mushrooms, the husband had sold bean curd made by his wife by the roadside in the village, and they had worked their own and a relative's land. The husband lost his parents at the time of the Great Leap Forward and grew up in an orphanage, but did have a few years of schooling. The wife said she had never wanted to go to school or to literacy class and had not done so. When the opportunity of growing mushrooms appeared they used their savings and borrowed a little to cover the cost of a building, spores, and plastic. They hoped to be able to repay the loan within the year. The critical element for this household was access to the technical knowledge of their neighbor's daughter.

In the case of growing mushrooms, higher degrees of education and entrepreneurship appear to have been essential in starting mushroom cultivation in Huaili, but not to have been necessary on the part of every subsequent household. Transmission of knowledge was taking place through both male and female lines, and there was continuing access to a relatively knowledgeable source within the village.

Chicken and Egg Production

During my earlier visits to the village only one household was engaged in raising more than a few chickens. This household had entered the field early, most likely on the basis of the husband's veterinary training and the wife's hard work. During my initial visit to Huaili in 1988, this household was raising 350 chickens in a room on the side of its courtyard, and the woman was being presented as a model of rural women's success in developing a courtyard economy (tingyuan jingji). This household raised chickens on this level from the time of decollectivization to 1995, with the exception of 1989, when the wife raised some pigs while her husband looked for other economic avenues. They shortly returned to chicken production and in 1992 were planning to rent some dilapidated buildings belonging to the village to raise thousands of chickens. By the end of 1995 they had that space fully utilized by several thousand chickens and thirty-four pigs, and had some more chickens (for a total of six thousand) in a slightly more remote site. They had also rented shop space and were running a feed store, veterinary medicine shop, and egg resale station from those premises. They had the largest egg-producing operation in the village, the only one that had a full range of services, and the only one that was partly moving into the production of chickens for meat. The last feature is especially important because of the township's 1995 project for exporting frozen chickens. This was the one household in Huaili that was positioned to be able to participate in this project, which was targeted primarily for three nearby villages. The wife in this household was very hard working, very careful about revealing any information about their substantial economic success until it had been well consolidated, and did not show signs of providing technical help to other households in the village until the expansion of chicken production in the 1990s. However, at the time of the 1995 visit, they were cited by several other households as a technical resource. Throughout this period, the wife was a model in production and their household was often visited as an example of rural economic success.

It was only after a chicken-raising initiative occurred at the township level that it expanded in Huaili. The original household started raising chickens for meat, in addition to continuing to raise chickens for eggs, and four additional households started to raise chickens for eggs.

The second entry into this area was a partnership between the households of two brothers. The younger brother worked as the chauffeur of the township's Party secretary, and learned of the opportunity through this channel. His household contributed its three *mu* of grain land, while both households contributed labor and took a loan for the initial investment. The older brother became the head of the enterprise, and both wives and one daughter attended classes run by the professor from Tianjin as they started their enterprise in early 1994, and later audited the courses offered by the Rural Correspondence College.[8] They

[8] The five women in Huaili who were reported to be attending the Rural Correspondence College were these three women, the woman in the first chicken-raising household, and the new women's head, who did not raise chickens but was expected to be involved in technical training.

obtained their chicks—more than eight thousand—from the professor and relied upon her and upon the original chicken-raising household for technical assistance. This enterprise appeared to be thriving at the end of 1995, and was beginning to establish ties with a newer chicken-raising household. This household is concentrating on the large-scale production of eggs and will therefore not be involved in the export project, but it is benefiting from access to general chicken-raising instruction offered through the township.

A fourth household started with 360 chickens in the fall of 1994, having heard of the township initiative. This household obtained two-month-old chickens (past their most vulnerable early stage) from the township's top chicken-raising household in an adjacent village, and obtained specialized chicken feed and veterinary care from the first chicken-raising household in Huaili. The household is aware of the specialized nutrients required for good results, but does not need to acquire any technical knowledge in this area because the feed is commercially available from another household within the village. The woman of the household, who is the main chicken-raiser, has a primary school education and missed the training offered by the Tianjin professor, although she did go to her for veterinary assistance while she was in the township. As this household demonstrates, training and expertise are needed for large-scale chicken production, but a household entering the field late can access the necessary technical resources without actually undertaking formal training.

This is even more clearly the case with respect to the fifth household involved in large-scale chicken raising in Huaili. This household also has more than three hundred chickens being raised to lay eggs. But in this case the woman of the household raised chicks bought from the Tianjin professor at their early, vulnerable stage with the loss of only about twenty chicks, and she mixes feed from grain ground in the feed mill owned by the first household and nutrients purchased from the two households in partnership. The woman of the household says she cares for sick chicks herself (as the woman in the preceding household is also beginning to do), and she expressed the view that chickens were not hard to raise. From the point of view of the training initiative, the interesting point here is that this woman has never been to school and has attended no formal training classes. She has, nevertheless, been able to access the necessary technical and material resources from the township and from other households within the village.[9] Although she appears not to have formally benefited from official initiatives, she has actually done so on an informal basis. The links between official initiatives offered through public channels and informal interhousehold ties operating through market relations are central to the practical workings of the emergent "two studies" activities. The Women's Federation is, indeed, very conscious of the dependence of those activities upon early entrepreneurs and informal channels between households, and sees the connection as a source of strength.

OBSERVATIONS

The courtyard economy and "two studies" are continually reviewed by the Women's Federations in the regular, internal channels through which policy and implementation are monitored.[10] Formal statements can appear—to the outsider—deceptively positive, since they are predicated on a shared understanding in China about the power of discourse to shape the future. But while reporting success, it is quite possible to proceed at the same time with identifying and addressing obstacles. This historical process is evident in the adjustments made at short intervals in the initiatives described here. These speak more clearly than any other source about what has been found internally to be successful or effective, and what has been found to require change.

[9] Her husband is a schoolteacher. Although local teachers' hours are long and there was no indication that he was directly involved in raising chickens, his education could have been of some help to his wife.

[10] The Women's Federations have continual reporting mechanisms that generate assessment and reflection on the activities of the women's movement. To the extent that this results in formal written submissions, the accepted framework is that of a comprehensive review of accomplishments in the previous time period (six months or a year), together with a statement of the general direction and specific targets for the next period. I have been permitted to read a considerable number of these reports, and have found them invariably positive. The writing conventions for these and for published reports encourage extensive reporting of numerical achievement of goals and of model cases. These are illustrative and demonstrate specific instances of success, either in implementing policy (by Women's Federation staff) or in the market economy (by individual models). While these documents must serve to promote the Women's Federations' work and policies, it is possible to glean a certain amount of detail from them. In addition, there are regular inspections by personnel from higher levels to lower levels (such as prefecture to county Women's Federation) that can result in days of discussion, both formal and informal. Through these channels, and especially through the verbal channels, problems are identified and policy adjustments formulated.

A few observations may be ventured here, based upon these historical processes, upon discussions with women's heads and Women's Federation staff over the years (they have been generous and patient), and upon what I have been able to see in Huaili during this period.

First of all, mobilization is not simply a relic of the past: it does make a tangible difference. There are more opportunities in the countryside, and some of the barriers to women's participation in public areas of the economy are lower than in the past, including the recent past. Some women have been positioned so that they can readily make use of these opportunities, because of education, skill, household and kinship ties, or entrepreneurial bent. These women are relatively few, however, especially in the less prosperous areas for which the courtyard economy and both phases of the "two studies" initiatives have been designed and targeted. Each of these initiatives has mobilized resources and people to spread opportunity further—through growing vegetables and *xiangchun* in courtyards, establishing small household projects, or following in the path of earlier entrepreneurs. Market openings in themselves would not have led spontaneously to the levels of activity recorded here. This has been accomplished only partly through exhortation, and also through efforts to assist women who did not otherwise have the necessary resources. Women were provided with advice on locally feasible economic opportunities, offered practical training, and in some cases helped with access to funding or linked with a model for mentoring. The degree of success achieved was limited and not always sustained, but mobilization did mean that it reached more women and more disadvantaged women than would otherwise have been the case.

Second, while looking for new and more effective means to mobilize women, the Women's Federations have turned to the idea of competition. Competition existed before, as well, despite the greater emphasis on cooperation, so the change was not simply the introduction of competition, but rather the specific manner in which competition was constructed and used. The formal "competitions" themselves do not appear to have been very competitive or to have fostered competition. The key element was not competition, but rather registration for competition. Through the mechanism of registration, the "two studies" distinguished itself from typical mobilizational campaigns in which everyone was administratively called upon to participate, and instead defined participation in terms of voluntary involvement in a key element of market activity—competition. Even while the content of registration substantively focused on meeting obligations (taxes) and goals (production levels), the "two studies" could, through competition, claim some of the legitimacy newly available through market values.

The criteria of the formal competitions expressly controlled direct competition among registered women; all were to aim to contribute to shared social goals (as officially defined) and to help those in particular need. This demand was especially placed upon those successful women most likely to be in the running for designation as models. A major goal of the formal competitions was to raise the profile of the models and of all participants in the "two studies" through demonstrated and measurable success in the market, a relatively abstract and impersonal medium.

Third, it was this turn toward the market and the embedding of market relations within the "two studies" activities that distinguished this initiative from earlier mobilizational efforts. The earlier campaigns had had goals, models, and competition, as well. In the "two studies," the defining criterion was market success. Women could exclude themselves from success by conspicuous noncompliance with some other element, such as the birth-planning policy, but could only become a model through success in a marketplace quite outside the control of the "two studies," the Women's Federations and, to some extent, any arm of the state.[11] This initiative then became internally defined by market operations, and the women's movement lost decisive control over the criteria for models of success.

A corollary of this departure was the embedding of woman-work in the mainstream of market-oriented economic activity, as women's heads and Women's Federation staff came to play roles resembling economic development officers. This contributed to the legitimacy of their statuses, both in relation to state development plans and in relation to household economic goals. The women's movement was in this respect resolutely in the mainstream of contemporary, officially approved values.

Fourth, in order to operate effectively in the mainstream in the interests of women, there were efforts to develop emergent organizational vehicles for women in the outer domain of rural social life. This was a formidable undertaking, since it implicitly challenged customary gen-

[11] This would seem to have been formally the case, but the state could intervene to assist women, or particular women, as in the case of aiding women's heads in their market projects.

der models that women should remain in the inner domain, and had to transcend the organizational fragility of the rural women's movement. The minimal (and sometimes simply nominal) presence of women's heads in all villages is formal but not necessarily effective. Much of the innovational character of the "two studies" and concurrent institution-building activities addresses this problem. The steps to select women's heads suited for the market, through them to build ties between models and disadvantaged women, to create women's classes in the Rural Correspondence College, and to build new networks through Women's Homes and research associations were all measures to open a space for women and to consolidate it organizationally. These steps could be seen here only in nascent form, but they are potentially significant in providing formal and informal organizational vehicles for women in rural China. The process of creating these is an indication of creative departures in the women's movement's knowledge of effective organization in market conditions.

And finally, this knowledge is expressed through particular practices conceptualized and realized in terms of quality—of the women's movement itself, and of rural women's educational and entrepreneurial abilities. Women doing woman-work at the grass roots have emphatically stressed the importance of quality to me, which is how this study began, and this examination does confirm their view in some significant respects. Women who were able to break through into new areas of economic activity and reap the benefits of doing so do tend to be women with higher levels of education, skill, and economic knowledge. There are a variety of less direct ways in which women can benefit—through household members, the women's organization, helpful models, or informal contacts—but women who achieve increased income through these channels have less success and less control over their lives and futures. They are substantially dependent upon others, however benign or helpful those others might be. Here the women's movement goes beyond simple calculation of increased income or additional household projects, and addresses the roots of the differences between a capacity to initiate activity in the market and a capacity to follow. The approach of focusing on quality is potentially a strategy that, while working through the market, expresses values that transcend the market.

7

Urban Women's Associations

I n the 1980s the official women's movement began a series of
initiatives to extend its scope, and at the same time women
outside the movement began to organize unofficially. Until then, the
traditional focus of the Women's Federations had been the countryside,
and work in the cities had been primarily conducted with women workers and through the official trade unions. But the reinvigorated women's
movement of the late 1980s was expanding and innovating in the cities
as well as in the countryside. I was especially interested in the emergence of new organizational forms beyond the Women's Federations
and made some initial contact in the late 1980s with a form of association (*lianyihui*) women were using in Shandong, an early and active region for this innovation.[1]

These associations were not exactly what I had imagined. They were
primarily organizations of relatively powerful women: high-level officials, factory managers, and senior intellectuals. These women had
their own particular reasons for concern with quality and were active in
placing this issue in debate, in large part because they had experienced
renewed challenges to their roles in the outer domain. These challenges
were complex ones about several aspects of the suitability of women for
leadership positions. Women's responses were also varied, but two were
particularly remarkable and shared a universe of reflection and action
with concurrent initiatives in the countryside: women created new organizational vehicles through which they could support each other, and
they endeavored to move forward on the basis of demonstrated quality.
In this process, privileged urban women were addressing issues similar
to those confronting women in the countryside, but from the opposite

[1] There were also women's associations formed in the countryside, although these
seem to have attracted less attention. I did not directly encounter any of these. For a
brief indication of similar activities in Guangzhou, see Chan (1994).

end of the continuum of power and prestige open to women, just at the time class differences were growing.

The women's associations examined here were formed by senior professional, intellectual, and managerial women toward the end of the 1980s, either independently or in response to initiatives from the Women's Federations.[2] This represented an interesting and innovative departure in China, where the official Women's Federations and structures associated with them had been the only legitimate or even possible channel for organizing women during most of the period since 1949. My own interest in these associations was based on this innovative element, but by the time I was able to make them a priority in fieldwork, the political context had been transformed following June 4, 1989, and the associations could only continue to function in connection with and under the official supervision of the official Women's Federations. The organizational links between the associations and the Women's Federations were important in many cases earlier, and later emerged as critical as women continued to organize in reform China.

The basis for this discussion is an examination of a sample of associations in Shandong in 1990. I spoke with and interviewed leaders and members of several associations in the cities of Jinan (the provincial capital), Qingdao (the leading economic center) and Jining (a city in the less affluent interior). The associations with which I had the most extended contact included two in the arts, two for intellectuals, one for senior officials and enterprise managers, and one for enterprise managers and entrepreneurs.[3] I held group sessions with leaders and organizers of each of these associations and with the Women's Federation to which each was connected, and conducted thirty-four interviews with individual members of these associations, representing a wide range of personal and professional circumstances and degree of involvement in association activity. I also conducted some discussions with scholars in these cities who were concerned with the same issues as the associations (see Liang Xuguang 1989). Earlier explorations were conducted in 1989, some follow-up inquiries were made in 1992 and 1995, and the fieldwork reported here was supplemented by published and unpub-

---

[2] Associations proliferated at this time, and not only in the women's movement. See Bonnin and Chevrier (1991) and Howell (1994).

[3] The research was carried out openly and with official permission; all of the material presented here was provided openly and is public information. Nevertheless, I will not identify the individuals interviewed.

lished reports produced by the Women's Federations, but the core of the data is the 1990 fieldwork.

Two central issues are addressed in the following pages. The first of these is the organizational strategy of building the new women's associations and linking these with the official Women's Federations in order to increase women's participation in the higher strata of public life. The second issue is the discourse of the women involved in shaping this strategy, one of silence or implicit (and sometimes explicit) agreement with the reform Chinese state on most issues regarding women, but the development of a significant emphasis on "quality" (suzhi).

CONTEXT

There are a few particular aspects of the Chinese women's movement that add to the context for its activities in the cities in this period. The middle and late 1980s were years of ferment and experimentation in the women's movement, especially in the cities and especially where Chinese women were able to come in contact with feminists from other cultures and to consider alternative modes of organizing a women's movement.

Earlier in the twentieth century there had been a variety of modes of organizing in the Chinese women's movement, but since the 1950s there had effectively been only the official women's movement, organized through Women's Federations and trade unions. The official women's movement was predicated on a vision of the women's movement that saw it as part of and subordinate to a larger socialist movement. The priority for the official women's movement in China was the interests of the poorest women (especially workers and peasants), and their interests were primarily those of class and nation, not necessarily those of gender. The specific interests of women were addressed in the post-revolutionary period (1949–65) in a variety of ways that targeted poorer women, and that made significant gains in economic and political terms, and also in family and kinship.[4]

The Cultural Revolution (1966–76) surprisingly did not include a revolution against patriarchy, or a strengthening of the women's movement. The early radical years of the Cultural Revolution saw the temporary dissolution of the official Women's Federations, along with

---

[4] See the references cited in Chapter 1.

the other structures of the state, and no emergence of a spontaneous women's movement. Some initiatives were taken to promote the specific interests of women in the final years of the Cultural Revolution era, but these were associated directly or indirectly with the discredited leaders (especially Mao's widow, Jiang Qing) who fell from power in 1976.[5] In the following reform period the organizational and ideological structures of the early post-revolutionary period were reestablished, but without any substantial initiatives being taken in the specific interests of women.

Indeed, as the 1980s proceeded, many women, including those in the Women's Federations, became concerned that women in China were having some of their important economic and political gains eroded. The initiatives presented here are part of Chinese women's organized response as it emerged later in the 1980s and the beginning of the 1990s.[6] These initiatives do not appear revolutionary, but they do address the critical question of effectively organizing for change.

Organizing outside the official framework was politically suspect, most obviously because it might not be socialist in character, but also because it might challenge the Party's interpretation of feminism and its place in the socialist project. The determining factor is the official requirement that Chinese social life should adhere to socialist principles and Marxism–Leninism–Mao Zedong Thought under the guidance of the Chinese Communist Party. These fundamental requirements have been reaffirmed repeatedly during the reform era, and departure or perceived departure from them is not tolerated by the Chinese state, as forcefully demonstrated by the events of June 1989 and their aftermath.

---

[5] The Campaign to Criticize Lin Biao and Confucius was part of the late Cultural Revolution power struggle on the national level, but in the countryside and in the factories was associated with practical steps to reduce patriarchy, especially by confronting and breaking through barriers to women's participation in various forms of (primarily economic) activity previously closed to women, and by promotion of uxorilocal marriage in the countryside. These initiatives did not continue after 1976. These remarks are based upon observations and discussions while I was a student in China, 1974–77.

[6] There were numerous other initiatives pursued by the women's movement during these years, and this larger context should be kept in mind. I have focused on aspects of the women's movement concretely accessible to me during this period in Shandong, where the emphasis was upon economic development and organizational capacity building. There was also work to implement the 1992 Women's Law, protect women's rights in marriage and divorce, organize previously unorganized women in offices and rural industry, and protect women's employment rights and rights to labor benefits, to mention only some of the most active issues.

Although there are some senses in which adherence to these principles may be an abstract or empty matter, they also have a concrete realization in the everyday organizational workings of state power in China. This is directly related to the centrality given to questions of organization in the Marxist-Leninist tradition, including the history of Marxist-Leninist practice in China. Within this tradition, the role of the organized political party is preeminent, and there are high demands for unity within the Party.

One of the most serious crimes a Party member could commit would be to organize a factional grouping within the Party. The prohibition on such organizing extends to the point of not allowing women's caucuses within the Party. There is no intra-Party structure legitimately available to women Party members who might wish to organize on the part of women's specific interests. Because the cause of women's liberation is a component of the Party's inclusive socialist vision and is, in principle, served by the Party as a whole, separate women's caucuses would constitute at least an implicit challenge to the role of the Party as the organizational vehicle for realizing the socialist vision, including the liberation of women.

The sole official vehicle available to women to work officially for the specific interests of women is the network of Women's Federations. The role of the Women's Federations is to mobilize women to carry out the programs of the Party in general. The Women's Federations may also reflect (fanying) the views of women to the Party, but it is not their role to pressure or to criticize the Party. The Women's Federations have substantial responsibilities and their leading members are Party members who sometimes hold other influential posts concurrently. But as mass organizations, the Women's Federations are removed from direct governmental or Party authority and resources. The responsibilities and everyday work of the staff of the Federations have led some of them to develop an informed and critical concern with women's issues, whether or not they had this awareness or interest before being assigned work in a Women's Federation. Some have also become informed and interested about global feminism. However, all work in a structure that is severely limited in what it is capable of doing regarding women's issues. Socioeconomic position and power in China are closely tied to the status and power of one's work unit (danwei), and the Women's Federations are low in status and weak. The staff of the Women's Federations and other women who are assigned similar work in the union structure (the mass organization for workers) are acutely aware of this disadvantage. Most women prefer not be closely associated with woman-work (*funü gong-zuo*), as the work of the Women's Federations is known, because it is a mark of low status and lack of direct power.

Work in the specific interests of women outside this official framework has been difficult to do except on an individual basis. As one Women's Federation cadre expressed it in 1990, "To work outside the official structures is to work against them." The official monopoly upon legitimate organized activity in the interests of women—and the danger clearly implicit in challenging this monopoly—has been a critical factor restricting the active scope of the women's movement in China.

Drawing women into an organized movement is well understood in China to be critical to effective strategies for change. It is a basic tenet of Marxism-Leninism that, once the political line is set, the determining factor is cadres. The interest and significance of the associations discussed here is precisely that they provide an innovative organizational vehicle for the women's movement in China. The women's associations provide a channel through which the Women's Federations can reach powerful women beyond its traditional constituencies. At the same time, links with the Women's Federations give the unofficial women's associations the official legitimacy and connections they need in order to operate in contemporary China. Although the women's movement in China was not active in the popular movements of the early reform period, including the democracy movement, it has been affected by the state's response.

In the wake of June 4, 1989, the Chinese state took a series of measures to attempt to reestablish control and legitimacy in the eyes of the nation's people. Two of these measures were directly significant for the women's movement in China. The first measure was the delegitimation of any organizing outside official channels. This political shift was immediately apparent in June 1989, especially in relation to organizations of students and workers, and in the following months came formally into effect in relation to a wide range of social organizations (*shehui tuanti*). A measure with a direct impact upon nonofficial women's organizations was Order Forty-three (October 25, 1989) of the State Council (Zhonghua 1989) requiring all social organizations to meet a series of formal conditions for officially registering with the government and to submit themselves to governmental review and supervision. Social organizations not so registered were required to disband;

registered organizations were required to limit themselves to their registered and approved activities or face sanction.

As this channel of organization was restricted or closed, there was a parallel effort on the part of the other wing of the central state, the Central Committee of the Communist Party, to reaffirm control over the Party's official mass organizations (*qunzhong tuanti*) for workers, youth, and women and reaffirm their status as the legitimate vehicle for popular political participation in classical Marxist-Leninist terms. In the Central Committee's Notice (December 21, 1989) on "Strengthening and Improving the Party's Leadership Work Regarding Workers, Youth, and Women" (Zhonggong 1990; also see Renmin 1990), the central leadership addressed the role it expected the mass organizations to play in strongly worded terms. The notice explicitly stated that any political advocacy contrary to the Party would absolutely not be permitted, and that the mass organizations would have to become more closely united with the Party Central Committee. Within their own ranks, the mass organizations were to combat tendencies toward "bourgeois liberalism" (*zichanjieji ziyouhua*). The mass organizations were to serve the Party in the classical sense of acting as a "transmission belt" conveying Party policy to the masses and reflecting their views back toward the Party. The notice emphasized the mass organizations as the vehicle through which the masses could participate in the nation's political life.

During the 1990s, the situation for both associations and mass organizations became more relaxed, although the state continued to exercise comprehensive surveillance (see Shehui tuanti 1998; Howell 1994). In the most public events for the Chinese women's movement in the 1990s, the UN World Conference on Women and the NGO Forum held in Beijing and Huairou in 1995, the Women's Federations and the associations worked closely together in the symbiotic manner devised during these years.

WOMEN'S ASSOCIATIONS

Qingdao was one of the earliest and most influential sites for the emergence of a national network of women's associations in the mid-1980s. In 1985 the nation's first association for the advancement of able women (*funü rencai cujinhui*) was initiated by the Qingdao Municipal Women's Federation, and the association was formally established on February 18, 1986. The following year, Qingdao hosted the first national

meeting of associations of women intellectuals (nü zhishifenzi lianyihui), a meeting that sparked the formation of similar associations elsewhere, including Jining, and which led to subsequent national meetings
in Jiangsu in 1988 and in Fujian in early 1989.

Jining formed its association of women intellectuals in 1986, and followed this with an association of women entrepreneurs (its most noted
association) in 1987, an association for the advancement of able women
in 1988, a research association in women's studies theory in 1988, and
an association of women journalists in early 1989. The Jining associations have connections of varying degrees of closeness with the Jining
Municipal Women's Federation, and with similar associations elsewhere. For example, its association of women intellectuals is connected
with an association in Wuhan; the association for the advancement of
women is connected with the national association for the advancement
of women, which is linked with the All-China Women's Federation; and
the association of women entrepreneurs is connected with and represented on the council of the national association of women entrepreneurs, which has been linked to a succession of official bodies, including
the All-China Women's Federation.[7]

In the same atmosphere, but without initial connection to these organizations or to the Women's Federations, some other associations
were also formed. An invitation extended to some women calligraphers
to mount an exhibition in Guilin gave the first impetus toward a provincial association of women artists. This association was formally established in April 1988 in connection with an exhibition with Japanese
artists. It is largely based on the advantage organization has provided for
domestic and international exhibitions. It derives much of its strength
from the personal network of its senior artist, and the association finds
its home in her art institute, but the association has also found it useful
to form connections with the provincial Women's Federation. A fledg-
ling association of women performing artists, initiated by senior
women artists, was moving in the same direction in 1989–90, although
its development was much hampered by the freeze on association approval and growth that followed the events of June 1989.

Each of the associations had a formal structure minimally consisting of a leadership body described as a council (lishihui), and some also

[7] The national association of women entrepreneurs later became involved in an internationally funded training program for women entrepreneurs, facilitated through
the All-China Women's Federation.

had individuals in the role of secretary-general (*mishuzhang*) and vice secretary-general. The latter roles were more marked and significant for the artists' association, where these individuals did much of the concrete organizational work of mounting exhibitions. It was more generally the case that the councils served as markers of prestige, and to some extent of obligation, offered to the leading women in each field, whose involvement with the association gave standing to the association, made it attractive to women of somewhat lesser status, and enhanced its public influence.

Whatever the particular features of any of these or similar associations, all share the practice of restricting membership to include only women of established status, as measured by managerial or professional rank or by formally recognized standards in a given field, and may further require that prospective members be recommended through official channels connected with their work units. Women in associations for the advancement of women are all leading cadres above some specific senior rank, which varies with each association, but which implies significant responsibility. For example, for the Qingdao association for the advancement of women, a member had to be at the level of vice-head of a department (*chu*) in a larger unit, or head of a section (*ke*) in a smaller unit. The provincial women artists' association required a member to have had her work accepted for at least one exhibition, a more open criterion than the three exhibitions required for membership in the mainstream professional association, but one that required a distinct level of achievement and public acknowledgment. Leading women in the relevant fields are actively recruited; membership is largely a matter of invitation, especially when an association is being founded, although women meeting the membership standards do apply. All the associations interviewed in 1990 indicated a recent history of expansion (unless they had just been formed) and the receipt of numerous applications. Many of these applications would have been approved by that date had the growth of the associations not been frozen by restrictions on organizing set in the wake of June 1989, but some limitations would have continued even if that watershed event had not occurred, and these would largely have been gatekeeping in character.

Membership was restricted for several reasons. One fundamental reason, often not mentioned because it was taken for granted, was the norm in China of restricting membership in professional associations. Membership in such an association is always taken as a mark of achieved professional standing. The organizers of these associations were concerned that their associations also be prestigious and influential, since the objectives included publicly demonstrating women's quality. Active recruitment of leading women in each field and restrictions on membership were means to achieve this goal. It is also the case that associations for the advancement of women and the associations of women intellectuals largely operate as a venue where women in relatively isolated leadership positions can compare notes and network with other women in similar situations. The associations could not easily meet some of their specifically elite needs if more junior women, especially those in their own work units, were present.

Class was unquestionably an issue for the associations, although it was one that necessarily remained unspoken. Class appeared both as a historical problem and as a contemporary one. Historically, the older generation of women who emerged or reemerged into prominence in this era largely consisted of women who had come from class backgrounds that were highly unacceptable in revolutionary and post-revolutionary China. The extreme case in this sample was that of the key figure in the artists' group. Her father had been private secretary to a warlord and was imprisoned and executed after 1949. His daughter had nevertheless succeeded in gaining admission to a major art school in the 1950s. Her first husband had been declared a Rightist in 1957, and she had experienced political difficulties from that time. Several of the other members of the artists' association also had somewhat problematic backgrounds, and had been sent to the countryside to work during the Cultural Revolution. The move toward valuing scarce expertise had given these women artists a chance to return to their professions with varying degrees of prominence. Not all of the senior women of this generation had problems with their class background; some of the engineers and other professionals trained during the 1950s and early 1960s were beneficiaries of increased access to education for ordinary working people and for women. The senior managers and entrepreneurs in the associations held positions that placed them in the elite strata of contemporary Chinese society, and their status could well be described in class terms, although that language was not being used within China for managers of state enterprises.

The associations varied in their class composition, and the most elite ones, especially the artists' association, made a point of recruiting and including women from conspicuously nonelite backgrounds. There was an implicit consciousness about class and an effort to address it in the associations, either through membership or through public service, although the structure of the associations meant that the problem persisted. In general, the organizational mechanism for overcoming the class limitations of the associations was their link with the Women's Federations. The Federations were not only primarily concerned with ordinary women, and especially the least privileged rural women, they were composed of women in secondary positions in a mass organization, and of women inclined toward an analysis in terms of both class and gender.

Some of the pressures for controlled membership in the associations were related to organizational problems. The smaller and more academic associations of artists, theorists in women's studies, and even journalists very largely managed their own organizational affairs. The largest of these, the provincial women artists' association, had sixty-three members in 1990, but the artists had the time and the interest (because of the prospect of additional professional opportunities arising from the association) to carry out their own organizational work, with some assistance from their work units and with additional contacts and legitimacy provided through the provincial Women's Federation. Those involved in the smaller associations (the women's studies theory association of forty-six, the journalism association of fifty-four, and the handful of performing artists) faced lighter organizational demands and could manage these themselves, with minimal support from the Women's Federations.

This was not the situation for the larger associations and for those composed of leading cadres from dispersed work units. Scale was definitely a problem for some of the associations, and this was explicitly identified as a practical reason for limiting membership. In Qingdao, the association for the advancement of women had earlier had 470 members who were leading cadres in large and middle-sized work units, but then allowed leading cadres in independent and smaller units to join, bringing the membership to 789 by 1990. Because this was a new organizational form at the time it was established, it experimented with structure. The result was a division into twelve branch associations, with the branches divided along the same lines as the work units of the members, that is, according to which branch of the state (such as a government ministry) supervised each unit. Jining's association for women intellectuals (primarily leading cadres), with 104 members in 1990, was divided into five branches according to the same principles.

Building in this way upon some preexisting structural lines provided a familiar framework, but those involved in doing the organizational work, in both Qingdao and Jining, commented upon problems posed by the association form. As one of the active organizers in Jining phrased the problem, the associations were too "loose" (*songsan*). This might be taken on the surface to refer to the inconvenience of having the members dispersed in numerous different units, in almost as many units as there were members. This would understate the challenge posed, however, if one did not allow for the unfamiliar and difficult problem of organizing outside and across the deep barriers of the work unit (*danwei*), and therefore without access to the normal and heavily used channels built upon the work unit structure.

The work of creating the associations required initiative and influence in order to bring the new entities into existence, and then continued work in recruiting additional members, maintaining contact, and organizing activities. Although the more influential women entrepreneurs and managers could offer the prestige of their names on council lists, pay membership fees, and appear for meetings in their work unit's chauffeured cars, they did not do the organizational work themselves, nor did they provide bases within their work units in which the work could be done. The active base for this work was located instead in the Women's Federations.

In the path-breaking case of Qingdao, the initiative and continuing dynamism of its associations was widely attributed to the woman who became head of the Qingdao Women's Federation in 1984, the year before Qingdao's initiatives in this field began. In 1990 she was still playing a leading and creative role in the work of the associations. The Qingdao Women's Federation was, however, as thinly staffed as any other Women's Federation and did not have the human resources to organize the work of the associations with its own staff. Instead, it turned toward capable women in premature retirement. The vice-head of Qingdao's influential association for the advancement of women was then a fifty-nine-year-old retired Party vice-secretary and national labor hero in the textile sector, a woman who met the criteria for membership, but who was retired because women in such positions retire at fifty-five, while men retire at sixty.[8]

The five-year difference in retirement age, which apparently originated as a preferential benefit for women, is presently one of the major concerns for women leading cadres. Although senior women intellectuals may be able to move to alternative professional work following retirement, women leading cadres are not only faced with a premature end to their careers, but the shortened time frame they face restricts their career opportunities from an earlier age. Qingdao has turned this to an advantage by recruiting retired leading cadres for organizational work. Each of the twelve branch associations of the Qingdao association for the advancement of women has two or three such women, and this is a factor the organizers point to as one of their particular sources of strength.

Jining relies more directly on staff of the municipal Women's Federation. Each of the associations connected with the Women's Federation has a representative of the Women's Federation in the association leadership. The association of women intellectuals and the association of women entrepreneurs have a secretary-general each who does the concrete organizational and logistic work and who is on the staff of the Women's Federation. There is a tendency here, as well as in Qingdao and provincially, to link various associations with different departments within a Women's Federation. The work of liaison and organizing with the associations is consequently dispersed throughout the Women's Federation structure, and does not result in a separate office or personnel within the Women's Federations.

WOMEN'S ASSOCIATIONS AND WOMEN'S FEDERATIONS

The relation between the women's associations and the Women's Federations is symbiotic and critical both to the existence of the associations and to the current strategies of the Women's Federations. The Women's Federations contribute to the associations in several ways. Many of the associations were established on the initiative of the

---

[8] In 1984 this woman had been demoted to the "second line" of responsibility and consequently understood well the concerns of women who experienced professional setbacks at that time.

women in the Women's Federations and, by late 1989, all popular associations required some officially legitimating affiliation, such as one with a Women's Federation, in order to continue to operate at all. Even apart from this requirement, the Women's Federations provided a point of legitimate political access to higher levels of the state for the associations. The Women's Federations were able to arrange public meetings of the associations attended by state leaders, to arrange less formal meetings with local state officials (such as ones on economic issues of concern to managers and entrepreneurs in the economic crisis at the beginning of the 1990s), and to intervene informally with the local state on behalf of the shared interests of association members or the particular needs of individual members. The position of some Women's Federation leading cadres on leading bodies of the state at various levels is an important resource of access to state structures and personnel that the Federations can and do provide to women in the associations. Indeed, the question of restricted access to political power is one of the central problems with which the associations are concerned and to which they are a strategic response. The possibility of addressing political questions through this organizational form defines the elite character of these associations as consisting largely of women leading cadres and as working in affiliation with the Women's Federations on issues affecting women's access to political power. The ties with the Women's Federations are closest for associations of this character. For associations not composed of leading cadres, official ties can still be very useful in a society as statist as China, as apparent, for example, in the usefulness of the provincial Women's Federation in facilitating foreign contacts and foreign travel for leaders of the association of women artists.

Work for women's issues in China has long been viewed as part of the legitimate work of the revolutionary or post-revolutionary state, and is therefore normally expected to be the work of state employees, and not the unpaid vocation of volunteer activists. Many of the leading cadres interviewed in this project made it quite clear that they would never have considered working on women's issues had they not been recruited into these associations by the Women's Federations; in fact, the work was still largely viewed as the work of the Federations.

From the perspective of the Women's Federations, the development of these associations, and especially of the associations of leading cadres and of entrepreneurs and managers, gave the understaffed and underfunded mass organization opportunity to draw upon the abilities and influence of powerful women who would otherwise have no connection with the Federations or their work. This is significant because of the combination of several organizational features that together define the field of work of the Women's Federations. The Women's Federations have an enormous mandate—to organize women for all of the policies of the state and to act as the primary vehicle for addressing all matters of concern to women and, in some regions, including Shandong province, preschool children—but insufficient means to realize this mandate. The high barriers between the different branches of the state (including the lower ranked mass organizations, such as the Women's Federations), linked only by Party structures that do not permit women's caucuses, normally make it very difficult for the Women's Federations to draw upon the resources of even potentially supportive women well placed in the various branches of the state structure. The absence of a recognized pattern of voluntary organization and the definition of "woman-work" as the official work of the staff of the Women's Federations has had the result that most of these women had never previously considered becoming involved in such work. Without the associations, they would have no channel for networking or for organized activity on issues of common concern to them and to the Women's Federations.

Further, the traditional arena of activity for the Women's Federations has been at the grassroots level, directly, in the countryside, or indirectly, through the unions, in urban industrial enterprises. The influential 1989 notice cited earlier in this chapter required mass organizations to focus their activities at the grassroots level. The Women's Federations, at the time of this notice, had been continuing their traditional emphasis upon grassroots work in the countryside without interruption (and with some innovation), but were also taking steps to establish women's committees in urban offices (previously without any form of women's organizations), to form associations of women professionals and women leading cadres, to establish groups engaged in research and writing on women's issues, and to organize women's groups in at least some rural industrial enterprises employing relatively large numbers of women workers.

In short, the Women's Federations were moving in many directions to extend the range of their effective organizing and to organize at middle and higher levels as well as grassroots levels. The move toward organizing senior professional women and women leading cadres in the associations of women intellectuals and associations for the advancement of women have far-reaching importance within this broader strategy because this step directly addresses the question of women's access to state power, which is central to the concerns and strategies of the revitalized Women's Federations.

WOMEN AND STATE POWER

The women initiating the strategy outlined here are all ones whose lives are deeply enmeshed in the workings of the reform era state. The women in the Women's Federations who are involved are obviously concerned because of their direct role as the arm of the state responsible for women and because of the constraints on their effective agency. During the 1980s they also became very much concerned by an erosion of women's positions in state structures, especially at the higher levels, which set the model for further erosion at lower levels during the reform era.

All of the associations encountered in the research were affected by the question of access to state power, and the women active in them were in part pursuing a strategy of improving their professional situations through seeking an adjustment in their relation to the organs of state power. Women entrepreneurs benefit from networking with each other, but also from the opportunity the associations provide for meeting with local leaders and influencing their economic decision-making. It is perhaps for this reason that the entrepreneurs and managers involved in these associations all seem to be in the state and collective spheres, although women are also to be found in important roles in the growing private sector. Women artists can similarly benefit from networking with each other and mounting exhibitions or performances together, but the role of the state in sponsoring and facilitating art leads these associations to be concerned with the state, as does the active role of the state in monitoring the politics of art and of artists.

Either from the perspective of the Women's Federations or from that of the women in the associations, the state in China remains very powerful. The emergence of some form of civil society in China may provide additional channels and opportunities, but the state continues to define life opportunities for very large numbers of women, including the majority of middle-level and higher-level intellectuals and cadres. From the perspective of the women in the Women's Federations creating this strategy, the key factor is that access to state power is essential and that nothing can be accomplished without it. The importance of access to

political and economic decision-making roles has been identified as
critical in anthropology's cross-cultural assessment of women's effective power. China's statist character suggests that the dimensions of
decision-making concentrated in the state assume extraordinary importance in China.

Certainly this is a widely shared view among Chinese women involved in the Women's Federations and the women's associations.
There are several aspects of the political changes in the reform era that
have been disadvantageous to women's political participation at higher
levels, and all of these were a subject of discussion in the summer of
1990. First of all, there was a deep concern that the direction of the
Party's leadership was a retreat from the involvement of women in political leadership. This was made dramatically clear in the formation of
the Thirteenth Congress of the Party in 1987 when women were, in
contrast with recent Congresses, entirely absent from the highest levels
of the Party. This change was associated with the rise of the leading re-
former, Zhao Ziyang, to the position of General-Secretary of the Party
at the same Congress. Zhao Ziyang's open comments against women's
political participation were credited by women within the Women's
Federations and women's associations with effectively causing subsequent losses of positions for women at lower levels of Party leadership.
When Zhao Ziyang fell from power during the crisis of 1989, the influential leader of the Qingdao Women's Federation organized visits to the
capital in support of the authorities, and the Women's Federations were
by 1990 endeavoring to identify and to encourage more positive statements by Jiang Zemin, who succeeded Zhao as General-Secretary in
1989. Neither the Women's Federations nor the women's associations
had been organizationally involved on either side in the political con-
frontations of 1989, but they did hope for some improvement in the
wake of Zhao Ziyang's fall. Whatever other views these women may
have had regarding the reform agenda of the 1980s, they were concerned
about the disadvantages it posed for them as women.

Although only one of the women interviewed spoke positively about
the Cultural Revolution era, and most suffered during those years, the
problems with reform era policies largely appeared through contrast
with earlier policies and practices. Toward the end of the Cultural
Revolution, in 1973–76, when the Cultural Revolution was in other respects in a conservative and authoritarian period, there was a requirement in place that leadership groups (*lingdao banzi*) should have at least

one woman member, or else their composition would not be approved at higher levels. This provided opportunities for a number of women, but many who rose during those years fell around 1978, when the post–Cultural Revolution leadership was restructured. A few of the women who fell then later rose to higher position again, but there was an overall loss in women's representation in political leadership. Reform era policies did not call for women to be represented in leadership, except at the grassroots level. By the early 1990s initiatives were officially underway to accomplish the entry of at least one woman (typically the village "women's head" associated with the Women's Federation network) to village committees and Party branches, and gradually to increase the percentages of township and county leadership bodies with at least one woman member. It was only from organizations such as the Women's Federations and women's associations that there were calls for the entry of women to higher levels of political leadership. Some of the women involved in these initiatives would have preferred clear targets or even quotas for women's participation in leadership bodies at higher levels, although others viewed quotas for women as counterproductive. There was a wider agreement that gender-specific measures were required to address the underrepresentation of women at the higher levels of the state.

Instead, reform policy confronted women with a lack of positive policy on this matter and new practices involving elections, specifically indirect elections and those in which there are more candidates than there are positions to be filled (which had not always been the case). Elections of this description began to be held for the leading positions at each governmental level during the 1980s. Women in both the Women's Federations and the women's associations with whom I spoke in the late 1980s and early 1990s were widely concerned about the associated fall of women from leading positions from 1987, and were able to cite instances from Jiangsu, Jiangxi, and Shandong. The case in Shandong was especially interesting. The head of the Shandong Provincial Women's Federation had been a member of the Provincial Government Standing Committee, which, after the provincial Party committee, was the most important level of decision-making in the province. She had carried this status with her when transferred to the Women's Federation from her earlier post as vice-head of the powerful Organization Department (*zuzhibu*). In the elections of the late 1980s, she was nominated both for the provincial Party committee (to which she was not expected to be elected) and for the provincial standing committee (to which she was expected to be elected).[9] She was not elected to either position and was soon thereafter "promoted" to become vice-head of the All-China Women's Federation in Beijing. This was not viewed as a positive development because of the weakness of the Women's Federations, and indeed of all mass organizations. This was followed by further losses for women at the next governmental level in the municipal elections of early 1989, after which only one relatively minor municipality (Zibo) had a woman vice-mayor remaining in the top leadership at this level of government. In Jining, a woman who had previously been in the municipal standing committee was "promoted" to the powerless municipal People's Congress, another avenue available at each level of government for the marginalization of women.

Qingdao Municipality provides a detailed and influential example of the practices that concerned women so deeply at this time. Prior to the 1989 election the head of the Qingdao Women's Federation had been a member of the municipal standing committee. She was an energetic and effective leader who had been able to do much for women in the municipality through the positions she held. In the election for the municipal standing committee in early 1989 she was nominated as one of eleven candidates for nine positions. This election was, as were the others under discussion here, an indirect election in which only a small number of senior officials had a vote. In this case the electorate consisted of the members of the municipal committee, a body of forty-six leading officials (of whom five were women) in all sectors of municipal government.[10] In any event, the results of this election were determined in advance. The electors were instructed that the following office holders had to be elected to the standing committee: the municipal Party secretary and four vice-secretaries, the mayor and vice-mayor, the head of the organization department, and the head of the propaganda department. The required election of these nine men left no openings for the other candidates. The history of this election, explained in detail by one of the electors and mentioned by many other women interviewed in Qingdao, was public knowledge. The electoral result was viewed as heavily influenced by the fall of women from leading positions at national and provincial levels, and contributed to these women's convic-

---

[9] I do not have the exact date for this election, but it was most likely in 1988.
[10] In the next municipal committee the proportion of women sank further, to one full member and one alternate in a committee of forty-one members.

tion that women's political participation at the highest levels was necessary in order to protect the possibility of their participation at lower levels. Nevertheless, the nonelected candidate possessed sufficient prestige and connections to prevail upon the municipal leadership to take a positive position on the election of women to the leadership of the next governmental level, the district, soon after. She is credited with producing a change in the directions to the electors from a weak "strive to" (*lizheng*) elect women to a stronger "ensure" (*baozheng*) the election of women, and with the subsequent election of women to the leadership bodies of ten of the twelve districts in Qingdao. Similar efforts to involve women in leadership bodies are made at county, township, and even village levels, with somewhat more support from higher political levels, although at these levels the entry of women may require the addition of a position.

Official state policy directs that increases in women's participation in leadership roles in the state should presently occur primarily at lower levels. The difficulty women at all official levels see with this strategy is that it is out of step with the hierarchical practices of the Chinese state, in which it is essential to be mentored, supported, or at least given some opportunity by senior officials. The Women's Federations do have practices of identifying women with promise who can be recommended for advancement, and they make such recommendations. The capacity of the Women's Federations to play this role is hampered by their weakness as a mass organization that, as these elections demonstrated, could be bypassed in elections to the critical governing bodies where the real powers of appointment lie. An advantage of the links with powerful women in the women's associations is that the Women's Federations are able to create useful ties with the handful of women who are in powerful positions outside their own network—women who do not have any other vehicle for coming together, and who cannot legitimately organize as a women's caucus.

Many important positions are filled directly by appointment and, as indicated above, even when there are elections, the results may be wholly or almost wholly predetermined by nonelectoral mechanisms. During the 1980s there was a comprehensive restructuring of the governmental apparatus, which resulted in significant gains and losses in position (see Burns 1987a, 1987b, 1989). By 1990, when a new period of rectification (*zhengdun*) had begun, women in political, managerial, and professional positions were concerned that the setbacks experienced earlier in the reform era not be repeated. Some of these losses could be attributed to the 1980s retreat from policies promoting women in public life, and were the more easily implemented because of the shrinking number of women in the most powerful leadership bodies. Other losses could be at least partly attributed to the workings of policies and practices that were not intended to disadvantage women.

Some of these policies were part of the widespread move toward valuing expertise over politics. This was concretely operationalized by formalizing professional designations and demanding higher degrees of education and expertise on the part of managers and leaders in official positions. One result was the fall from senior position in the mid-1980s of some women (as well as men) who had risen through the ranks on the basis of experience, and some women in this category were interviewed. It was not unusual for such women to find themselves reassigned to woman-work, an assignment universally viewed as demotion and loss of authority. In some other cases, women who had received university education in the 1950s, either in association with relatively privileged backgrounds (in the case of the artists, especially) or in association with the increased access to higher education of that period, found themselves newly advanced to responsible professional positions, in large part because of the relative scarcity of senior professionals. There were striking class reversals as a result of this process. Some of the most qualified women were older women from elite backgrounds educated during the 1940s and 1950s whose fortunes had fallen—in some cases as early as the Anti-Rightist Movement (1957) but more generally during the Cultural Revolution—and who were returning to power and prestige in the reform era. Women of nonelite background who had received a university education in the early 1950s, as in the case of several engineers interviewed, also fared well under this policy, but many women who lost ground at this time did so at least as much by virtue of nonelite background as on grounds of gender. One woman interviewed, a philosopher who became an official in a body that assessed professional designations, was in a position in which she was able to assist a number of women, pointing again to the importance of having women in positions of power.

In addition, there was a problem posed by regulations on retirement age, combined with the state's determination to enforce retirement as a means to bring a younger generation into positions of authority. Women who held sufficiently high professional or bureaucratic rank could postpone retirement beyond the age of fifty-five standard for women in nonmanual work in the state sector (compared with sixty for men). The five-year differential in retirement ages places women at a distinct disadvantage. It not only directly reduces the numbers of women in managerial and professional positions through earlier retirement, it also places women under greater pressure to move ahead in their careers at an earlier stage or find themselves bypassed for advancement on the grounds that they are too close to retirement. Professional women in contemporary China may have attractive alternatives after retirement, but women in primarily official positions, such as those in the Women's Federations and many government offices, do not have this alternative. Policy change with respect to retirement ages for women are one of the active concerns of both Women's Federations and women's associations. More immediate measures to extend retirement age by ensuring that women are granted high-level professional designations or promotions in time to delay their retirement (to the age of sixty-five) have also been taken.

These issues most directly affect the well-being and professional advancement of relatively elite women, but do connect with the concerns of larger numbers of women. The hierarchical nature of the political structures involved means that there are potential advantages to placing women at higher levels, where they may be able to provide protection, nurturance, and opportunity for more women. And the issues that affect elite women may have intrinsic connections with broader concerns affecting the women's movement, especially if the Women's Federations can effectively bring women together in a partial unity across the reemerging class divide.

QUALITY

The views of the women interviewed were diverse, since the women themselves represented a wide range of backgrounds and experiences and had been brought together on the basis of being women in senior positions, and not on the basis of a shared set of ideas. There was also a difference between these women and those who were organizing the associations, primarily Women's Federation staff. Several viewpoints did, nevertheless, emerge as being widely held among one or more segments of the women involved.

Quality was an issue that was discussed prominently. The Women's Federation organizers presented ideas similar to those of their counterparts in the countryside. In effect, they formed a conceptual as well as organizational link between the women in disparate locations. This part of their argument was that the pursuit of quality was a route toward gender equality. Equality is viewed as one of the women's movement's goals, although it is emphasized less in China than in Western feminism. Equality is seen as a limited and partial goal, albeit desirable. The role of quality in the pursuit of equality, in relation to the associations, was primarily one of demonstrating the quality of the women involved. Membership in an association of senior women was a mark of accomplishment, as was designation as a model or other forms of conspicuous success that could be given added publicity through the associations. The actual work of the associations was largely focused upon the achievement of public recognition, for individual women and for the potential of women as leaders in general.

The women involved in the associations commonly presented a slightly different perspective, although this may have been partly because they were presenting their life histories and not only their connections with women's associations. Quality emerged here as something women demanded of themselves. For some, this was connected with coming of age in the 1950s, in an optimistic era in which extraordinary demands were placed on and internalized by people in the interests of a common good. It also appeared to be taken for granted as something women expected of themselves as part of a longer cultural tradition of strong women asking much of themselves whether or not this resulted in recognition or status. As these women reflected on the contemporary conditions for their own recent career success, sustained and disciplined striving was a common theme. The quality in question included professional expertise—many of these women had risen largely due to their professional qualifications—but also adeptness at interpersonal relations in the workplace and at home. The domestic element was essential, since women who were not able to manage their home well would never have the time or support required to succeed in their professions.

While some women were able to point to exceptional personal circumstances or accomplishments, they did not claim to have risen to their positions only or even primarily on the basis of the quality of their work. Some referred to barriers and bias against women that they had experienced and overcome, although there were also women who reported that they had not encountered any such problem. There was a surprising amount of discourse about limitations on women's advancement posed by naturalized gender differences. Some of these consisted of stereotyped ideas, reported by the interviewees and sometimes held by them, of women as being petty and envious, and consequently unsuited for advancement. More widespread arguments were made (or reported as being confronted) about the problem posed by women's roles as mothers. One might suppose that the move to one child, which is widely practiced in the cities, would have reduced this barrier, although none of the women interviewed made that observation.[11] The argument appeared as a statement that women would face a major difficulty posed by the time demands of motherhood at a critical point in their early career development. This was evidently widely cited as grounds for not advancing women, although women managers in some demanding professions did not view this obstacle as insurmountable. It appears to have been harder to manage in situations where work and advancement were more open to subjective assessment.

A critical element in career progress has been the form of mentoring that takes place as a standard practice throughout China, for both women and men. Persons (usually, but not always, men) are noticed as having leadership potential and are targeted for development (*peiyang*). The initiative is taken by the mentor, who is generally a person (usually a man) holding a position in a formal hierarchy for whom developing junior people is an expected or required activity. Junior people cannot easily put themselves forward unless they are so targeted. The key is to have the opportunity to be noticed by someone who will subsequently act as a mentor. There was definitely an element of chance in this, especially at the beginning, although people can strive to be noticed, preferably inconspicuously.

Class, kin and personal ties, and gender can all be factors that affect whether a person gets the chance for these opportunities. Not all the women interviewed were inclined to play the role of mentor for younger women in their work units. Some preferred to be gender-blind in devel-

---

[11] Among women of older generations, who generally had more than one child, it was not unusual to find that mothers had sometimes been separated from their children (usually placed in the care of grandmothers) for prolonged periods and had suffered a variety of familial hardships. These circumstances were related to sacrifices people had been asked to make for national development in the 1950s, or were a result of later political movements, and were not (or not entirely) the result of combining motherhood and work. Younger generations of women are less willing to make these sacrifices, and are less commonly asked to do so. On the issue of generational differences more generally, see Rofel (1999).

oping junior workers, and others specifically preferred men. A male assistant would be more suitable for undertaking some of the networking and negotiating that typically involved drinking or travel, both considered unsuitable for a woman, and for this reason might be convenient for women managers. A few women managers mentioned stereotypical problems with promoting women (such as the interference of family demands) as well as the social barriers to effective networking and negotiating. In any case, a policy or practice of specifically nurturing women would meet resistance in any workplace with limited opportunities.

The solution to these problems was the creation of new and wider organizational mechanisms for the nurturance and promotion of qualified women. The organizations for the advancement of women were one formal network created for this purpose, especially in the wake of women's forced retreat from leadership positions in the late 1980s. A more widely used and widely accessible avenue was the creation of formal "talent pools" (rencai ku) in the Women's Federations. These were established throughout China in this period, and worked for promoting the careers of junior as well as more senior women. The talent pools operated as databases of qualified women whose names could be put forward for opportunities and openings. The network of senior and managerial women in the associations was useful in proposing names and in supporting appointments, although the work appears to have been done primarily by the Women's Federation staff.

The institution of talent pools had several distinct advantages over more diffuse approaches. It addressed the limits posed by the small number of senior women in positions where they could directly nurture junior or mid-career women, even when they were willing to do so. This mechanism also provided an expanded reservoir of suitable candidates, who could be recommended not only to the senior women but also to those men who took a more inclusive approach to management. Since the vast majority of senior managers and officials are men, opening this route further is essential. The talent pools have the additional advantage of including women very early in their careers, as well as those who have already achieved success.

This particular approach does not train women, except in the very important but indirect sense of providing opportunities for women to gain experience and opportunity in new positions. Quality is emphasized, but the strategy is to achieve recognition of the quality women have to offer. In the urban professional context, there is a substantial supply of highly qualified women, and the goal is to expand their opportunities, through a strategy based on the promotion of quality.

Two senior women managers expressed skepticism about the value of this approach, pointing out that urban China in 1990 had a surplus of qualified and un(der)employed men. This argument does point to one of the weaknesses in this approach insofar as it is intended to win support from both men and women in the interests of national development. As Bourque and Warren (1987: 186) earlier argued for education, where men are already finding a shortage of avenues for using their training, there may well be resistance to expanding opportunities for women.

The women's movement in China, nevertheless, remains primarily committed to strategies that use quality rather than employment equity in order to achieve their goals. There was a diversity of views on this subject among these women, revolving around the issue of quotas for women, since this was the available and familiar alternative. The particular form this took in China was modest but, as the example from the Qingdao election indicates, contentious and difficult to achieve. The main instance in the early 1990s was the push to get one woman into each governing body, as in the case of asking each village to put a woman on either its Party branch committee or its village committee. This might simply mean adding one more position in a committee, but the goal was to force open governing bodies that had been closed to women. Quotas generally referred to this low level, and occasionally also to longer-standing Party-sanctioned targets that women should comprise a noticeable portion of delegates to bodies such as people's congresses, where 20% had been a common target level for women. While these were not provocative quotas, many of the women interviewed were ill disposed toward quotas. Their use would put all women at risk of suggestion that they had achieved their positions on the basis of a quota rather than on the basis of their ability.

The women involved in these associations were, whatever their current position, women who had risen to some degree of prominence through ability, hard work, and, as several pointed out, the good fortune to have had exceptional opportunity. None had derived a benefit in her career from being a woman, and even those from particularly privileged backgrounds had strong records of accomplishment. Indeed, while some of the women interviewed had been demoted as insufficiently expert in the mid-1980s, quite a few had risen at the same time precisely because they were experts.

The substance of their qualifications was important for these women. They viewed this in a comprehensive way that included their ability to manage their domestic lives (and often family hardships) and interpersonal relationships with character. In part perhaps as a matter of generation, they considered the ability to bear hardship (*chi ku*) an essential quality for success.

In their work and careers they made significant distinctions between targets or criteria that were hard (*ying*) in contrast with those that were soft (*ruan*), and between work or positions that were real (*shi*) and those that were empty (*xu*). Wherever the hard/soft distinction was made, women found the hard targets or criteria more favorable to them than the soft ones. Faced with hard demands for professional competence (as engineers, physicians, or research scientists) or economic performance (turning a money-losing enterprise around, successfully expanding an enterprise), women had at least the possibility of providing compelling evidence of the quality of their work. Soft criteria (such as managerial ability or political leadership) were viewed as open to subjective judgments that were less likely to be favorable, and that were too vague to be challenged. The key argument is that women preferred to be put to the test and to be judged on their merits.

The argument on real and empty work and positions was conceptually connected with the distinction between hard and soft criteria, and was one also heard from women's movement personnel in the countryside. Here two kinds of distinction were being made. One was between work that consisted of accomplishing something (such as running the production work of a factory) compared with work that might rank more highly but, in this view, had less substance (such as presiding over meetings, negotiating, and networking). The latter was sometimes described as sitting in the office reading newspapers. Indeed, many of the women interviewed had risen to their current position through professional qualifications, and were often vice-heads of work units responsible for professional or productive work while serving under the directorship of a generalist male manager (also see Chen, Yu, and Miner 1997).

The other concern raised about real and empty work recognized that women were sometimes consigned to empty positions. The particular concern here was with women "promoted" from significant responsibilities to an apparently higher position that was in fact empty and relatively powerless. Positions in people's congresses were an instance of this, and such promotions occurred in rural areas, including Ling County, as well as in urban centers. Part of the knowledge women required in navigating the higher reaches of Chinese society consisted of distinguishing real from empty positions, and conversation often turned to the task of discerning where any particular post might fall on this standard. Here again, women's preference was strongly for the real positions; there was no perceptible attraction for the empty positions, even if the title might be attractive or the responsibilities light.

In their pursuit of quality and fulfillment, women were pursuing individual strategies that placed intense demands upon each person. Through the associations, and the official women's movement, they were also working to create mechanisms through which their quality and achievements could be made visible and publicly recognized. In the process new forms of connection between women were forged in informal networks and supported through creative use of the official women's movement. A space was opened in which women could play a larger role in the outer domain.

8

Reflections

The pursuit of quality has been a problematic subject for investigation. The idea of self-cultivation, individual and collective, is an attractive and challenging proposition, and one intrinsic to any project of social transformation. But calls for quality (or purported quality) have all too commonly been used to erect barriers and to exclude people. The women's movement and other democratic movements have been justifiably wary of the resort to quality precisely because of this hidden agenda, and have instead emphasized inclusion and equality.

The official women's movement in China argues, on the contrary, that the pursuit of quality is a means toward achieving equality and the larger goals of women's liberation. In effect, this is an overt denial that the two concepts are in conflict, and it is indeed possible to reconcile them on an abstract level. In practical terms, however, what appears to be underway is a protracted and multifaceted conflict about the actual meanings of quality. All might agree that quality has merit, but what comprises it, how it is assessed, and what it signifies are all in contention.

Briefly stated, one might conclude that the defining issue is positionality. Where striving for quality comes from the person or collectivity itself, it nurtures potential and creates possibilities. Where quality is imposed by others and from outside, its pursuit becomes entangled with practices of exclusion and hierarchy. But self and other, inside and outside, are not sharply separated, and distinguishing them can be complex even with respect to individual persons. The matter is still more complicated in the case of groups, organizations, or movements, and perhaps especially so in the case of those claiming to represent broad interests within and beyond themselves. This makes an understanding of mass organizations (such as the Women's Federations) and of persons associated with them (as women's heads, association members, or others) a challenging proposition.

For the most part, those in the Women's Federations avoid discussing this issue in generalities—except insofar as required by the conventions of modern Chinese political culture—and focus instead on practical strategies. This approach has much to recommend it, and has opened this project to a compatible approach in contemporary anthropology, the ethnography of the particular. That has been attempted in this study through the examination of concrete instances of the pursuit of quality.

THE PURSUIT OF QUALITY

The argument for quality, as I heard it expressed in Shandong, was partially a defensive one: if women's possibilities for participation in economic and political life were questioned in terms of competence, the women's movement was prepared to take up the challenge. Reference here was made to "hard" indicators of the types of quality valued and advocated in the reform mainstream, those that were educational, technical, or professional and those that could be measured by economic success. According to these indicators women were at a tangible disadvantage, but there were ways in which women's existing qualifications and contributions could be made visible, and ways in which they could be demonstrably strengthened. It may have been necessary to engage this issue in China at this time since, despite very significant gains in women's access to all levels of education and employment since the 1950s, there was still a gender gap. In the atmosphere of renewed emphasis on expertise that has characterized the reform era, it would have been difficult for the women's movement to operate with official approval and support unless it had addressed this issue. Arguments in terms of equality were too overtly political and too closely associated with the revolutionary agenda (despite past limitations) to be favored in this climate.

At the same time, the Women's Federations were engaged in a subtle negotiation of the conceptualization of "quality." It was, as much as possible, framed as a set of positive goals for which women were striving, in the same sense in which the entire nation was asked to strive for enhanced quality to achieve material and spiritual civilization. This placed women firmly in the mainstream of contemporary Chinese strategies for developing the national labor force, and enabled the

Women's Federations to make targeted claims on the state's resources. Achievements in the development of quality for women would serve the state's national goals, and simultaneously reduce the gender gap in education and expertise. The Women's Federations operationalized the pursuit of quality primarily in terms of specified objectives, especially literacy, technical training, and income. These were objectives that could be clearly stated and measured, and that facilitated recognition of accomplishments that would remain invisible in less concrete discussion.

Placing the pursuit of quality for women in the mainstream of the Chinese development project made it possible for the Women's Federations to appropriate a dimension of mainstream discourse on quality and to use it in the interests of women. But this implicitly required internalizing the framework of the national development project with both its statist and its market-oriented elements. While both state and market could be used to promote various specific interests of women, the framework remained a limited one. Nevertheless, the concepts of quality and of spiritual civilization were sufficiently ambiguous to be open to interpretations in favor of strengthening a women's movement. A central tension continues between the limits imposed by the internalized mainstream framework and the possibility of a women's movement that could extend beyond those limits.

DIFFERENCES AMONG WOMEN

The author of this strategy and the vehicle for realizing it is the structure of Women's Federations. The Women's Federations have a dual quality in being part of the state apparatus, albeit in a marginal fashion, and also being part of the constituency of women, although at the same time marked off from other women. In conducting their profession of woman-work, the women of the Women's Federations are separate from but connected with the women whose interests they are charged to represent. As the Party's mass organization for women, they share some of its character as a vanguard party that is both of the people and leading the people. Ideally, the relationship should be a close one of shared interests. In actuality, there are significant barriers to this ideal unity, although these take a variety of forms in differing contexts.

In the countryside, where the Women's Federations have historically done most of their work, there is a deep divide because the staff of the Women's Federations are by definition holders of urban registrations, a privileged status that sharply separates them from rural women who hold rural registrations. The rural-urban distinction, reinforced by the registration system, remains a powerful hierarchical division in Chinese society, despite its blurring by unofficial population movements. The Women's Federations are therefore not directly incorporated into the world of rural Chinese women, and they enter the worlds of those women from outside and from above in the status hierarchy. While the grassroots staff of the Women's Federations may (and do) feel disadvantaged and marginal to the core structures of the state, they nevertheless are representatives of the state's women's movement. Their real entry into the rural world is only through women's heads and through other women (models, rural technicians) linked in some fashion to the Women's Federations. The distance of the Women's Federations themselves, and their awareness of this distance, have caused them to emphasize the further development of the base provided by women's heads and of a network of other women who can serve as "backbones" (gugan) for the women's movement in rural China. It is these persons who have the potential to be the organic intellectuals among rural women, rather than the Women's Federation staff directly.

In the cities there are similar situations involving working women and office staff, but with less severe problems of illiteracy and missed education or of such deeply entrenched androcentrism. In addition, the women's movement in the cities encounters women of privileged socioeconomic strata, women who are members of the new elites in both state and private sectors. In moving to extend their reach to these women, the Women's Federations are recruiting powerful women who have resources and social standing higher (and, in some cases, very much higher) than those of the organizers in the Women's Federations. Here the promotion of quality encounters hierarchy, but it is the organizers in the Women's Federations who are at a disadvantage. The object here is to draw the elite women and their resources, prestige, and power into the organized women's movement. Through this mechanism, quality can be demonstrated and networks and mechanisms can be created that will support women's increased participation in the outer domain, including its higher strata.

Both rural and urban contexts offer more varied and complex networks of power relations than can be summarized briefly, but the central point is that building the reform era women's movement has increasingly required dealing with these differences internally. Women are more stratified on their own terms—not simply through derivation from their fathers, husbands, or communities—and the larger society is itself more deeply and openly stratified. Indeed, the particular contemporary pressure for quality is directly related to intensified stratification. The response of the women's movement to this problem is two-sided. One side of the response has been to accommodate and internalize it, as can be seen in its willingness to accept and promote competition, including competition whose terms are decided by external forces and criteria located in the market and beyond the control of the women's movement. Indeed, the entire emphasis on leading women to success in the market economy is dependent upon this accommodation and internalization.

The other side is a muting movement that works against internal differentiation and stratification, even in the process of apparently promoting competition. The formal competitions organized by the women's movement are overtly consistent with the broader spirit of competition prevailing in the society, but are muted. Those who win awards and those who are recognized as models thereby become women expected to contribute to the movement and to help the least advantaged. Women who might otherwise have been under less social pressure for solidarity (although this operates through other channels as well) are drawn into initiatives designed to counter differentiation. If the state's program for development through unleashing market forces were to operate in a less restrained manner, the benefits would be more unevenly distributed. The women's movement's program for spreading training and market involvement more widely is one that attempts to increase the number of women who are included and who benefit from this model of development. The difficulty is that of attempting to counter differentiation through using mechanisms (the market, competition) that are intrinsically producers of inequality.

The official women's movement is insistent and very public about turning toward the market, because the market offers a counter to some of the entrenched forms of androcentrism (especially in rural communities) and because it allows the women's movement to position itself favorably in the mainstream. It is equally insistent about using its own role as part of the state to control and moderate market forces toward more inclusive social goals. This aspect of their strategies is presented somewhat more subtly, in order to maintain a distance from earlier politics and from mobilizational strategies that are now discredited.

However, this role of managing market involvement in the interests of women is the purpose behind these initiatives. Apart from this purpose, the market could be left to operate and there would be no need for the women's movement's development work.

PRACTICAL OBSTACLES AND STRATEGIC RESPONSES

As actually applied through means such as the "two studies," it is possible to trace the concrete processes through which the women's movement strategy is pursued. In the preceding chapters I have outlined what I was able to observe as these activities unfolded in Huaili. If this has any validity as an exemplar of what is possible in a village for the most part favored by the initiative, it indicates that there are substantial practical difficulties in implementing the strategy successfully.

It is a formidable task to identify accurately the educational and technical needs of the women in each particular community, to deliver a program to meet these needs, and to ensure that it is appropriate to the conditions of the local economy. As the case of Huaili indicates, it is even more difficult to identify a program that is economically promising and that a large number of women can simultaneously join. It was, for example, possible to provide local training for sewing, but there is a limit to how many custom seamstresses an area can support, especially when ready-made clothing is becoming increasingly accessible and affordable. Many other economic avenues in the countryside share the same limitation. It is possible to provide technical advice on cultivation of common crops such as grain, cotton, and vegetables, which many women can cultivate, and this was done in Huaili and elsewhere in Ling County. Women in Huaili did not, however, appear to find very much value in such classes, since these were crops they had grown all their lives, and marginal improvements in their productivity could not generate a great deal of additional income. The introduction of training for chicken production offers somewhat more promise, at least in the targeted communities, although the additional expertise is not being widely distributed, and the project is entirely dependent on outside interests and government support.

All of the training and economic development must be provided with very limited material and human resources, even when some instructors and resources can be accessed through "two studies" coordinating committees or other official channels. Although the official women's movement initiated this strategy, it is able to provide only minuscule support, especially when viewed from the village or household levels where microdevelopment occurs. This makes it all the more important to have effective leadership at the grassroots levels, in townships and villages. Organization building—in both formal organizations and informal networks—is critical to the extension of the women's movement's capacity to implement this or any other program.

At present, the official women's movement can and does initiate strategies, but it lacks the local capacity to carry them out effectively except in a limited number of sites. Strengthening the women's movement itself is essential, and this has been a prominent dimension of its pursuit of quality.

Specific problems with the implementation of strategies such as the "two studies" have been addressed through rapid responses on the part of the women's movement. Even in the relatively brief time frame of the present study there have been shifts in direction, from the earlier courtyard economy approach, through the initial "two studies" phase emphasizing literacy and local microstrategies, to the second phase emphasizing more systematic technical training and mainstreaming women into larger-scale local development.

The official women's movement has been flexible and innovative in its efforts to expand networks and draw an increasing number of women into its orbit. This is evident in the creation of Women's Homes and "research associations" in the countryside, and through adjustments of organizational strategies for working with women's associations in a shifting political climate.

The women's movement has been implicitly self-critical and dynamic in making these adjustments. Its responses may, to the extent that resources exist or can be created, permit the women's movement to achieve greater success in its pursuit of quality. Viewed within the context of contemporary reform China, with its particular mix of state and market approaches and the reform political agenda, these strategies offer practical and feasible avenues for improvements for women. Women's qualifications and expertise receive more public recognition and support where they presently exist and, where they are more limited, efforts are made to provide women with literacy, education, and training. Especially where technical training is provided, this can lead to increased income and to more control by women of the economic well-being of themselves and of their households. Women can come together through old structures and new networks that help to create and support a greater presence for women in the outer domain. Where women are in positions of responsibility and leadership, they can be brought within the scope of the women's movement, both to receive and to give support. The presence and role of the official women's movement has continued to mean that it will not only be advantaged women who can benefit from change, but that there will also be strategies to extend the benefits more widely, and especially to target the poorest women. In working toward all of these—and numerous other—goals, there is also the contribution this work makes toward building a women's movement that can survive in the present social context.

This is not a context that is favorable for the women's movement. The turn toward the market was accompanied by a retreat from a transformative political agenda and a move away from mobilization for change. The previous style of direct state intervention was to be replaced by a less direct role for the state that would operate more through the market (see Shue 1988). For an official women's movement that was tied to the state, the choice was between preserving an older style of operation that was now more bureaucratic than transformative, or making an accommodation with emergent market forces. There were perils in both directions. If the women's movement remained dependent upon statist approaches that were no longer socially acceptable, it would risk becoming increasingly irrelevant to the lives of women. But neither the market nor the leading proponents of the market were noticeably supportive of women or the women's movement. The difficulties posed at this juncture were formidable, as can be seen from the experience of Eastern Europe, where post-socialism has been accompanied by a reaction against an official women's movement too closely tied to the former state structures, with resulting setbacks for women (Funk and Mueller 1993; Scott, Kaplan, and Keates 1997). In Eastern Europe this situation has been balanced by the emergence of diverse independent women's movements. In China, independent women's initiatives have been present and may become more influential in the future, but up to the present they have largely worked with or through the official women's movement, especially in the countryside.

The Chinese official women's movement has charted a careful path designed to avoid the perils of state and market but to make use of both. Most obviously, it has openly welcomed the market, and the opportunity it offers to break through the entrenched androcentrism of rural communities. Increased income from women's successful market-oriented activities contributes to household and community income and economic growth. The women's movement sees this as raising women's social as well as economic standing without direct confrontation with androcentric structures, because it increases the size of local economic resources rather than attempting to redistribute them. The extent to which this strategy is effective depends upon women's ability to control the products of their own labor, despite kinship and community mechanisms of gendered appropriation (see Judd 1994, 1997), and this is an issue that has yet to be directly addressed.

The state can be and is used, as well, through its support of the fragile network of federations and associations, and through a variety of legal mechanisms that attempt to entrench and support women's rights, most notably in the Law to Protect the Rights and Interests of Women (Zhonghua 1992), and in steps to increase women's political participation through office holding.[1] In Shandong during these years the emphasis was upon economic development and upon using the state's role in promoting development to mainstream women in this process.

TRANSFORMATIVE POTENTIAL

All of these activities—whether primarily market-oriented, embedded in the state, or both—are reasoned, moderate measures to make practical improvements in the lives of women.[2] Where the project appears to go beyond the immediate, it consists of building organizational capacity and a network with potential for more far-reaching change, but for the present it is closely tied to the current political economy and sociocultural context. Within the available political tradition of women's liberation and socialism, the strategic assumption would be that work for immediate, practical goals would necessarily lead toward transformative social change, because the established social order would not be

[1] I did attempt to extend the present study to explore the implementation of the 1992 Law to Protect the Rights and Interests of Women and of the 1994 Shandong Provincial Measures for Implementing the "Chinese People's Republic Law to Protect the Rights and Interests of Women" (Shandong 1994). While I did have a number of discussions on this topic with the Women's Federations at various levels in Shandong, this proved not to be a feasible route to pursue. I was also not able to connect this set of issues with concrete activities in my field locations, where the overwhelming focus of woman-work remained economic throughout this period, although it was later combined with birth-planning work.

[2] For a slightly different but related set of distinctions between strategic and practical gender interests, see Molyneux (1986).

able to accommodate those goals without such change. Indeed, this perspective might easily seem confirmed by the unfolding of the Chinese revolution in the mid-twentieth century, as the war against the Japanese occupation and for specific, limited changes (such as the land reform) opened the door for socialist transformation.

However, the old order, and perhaps especially those aspects of it that could be described as capitalist, have been more resilient and flexible than earlier revolutionaries anticipated. A result has been that moderate programs for change appear to lack transformative potential, and instead limit people's visions and efforts to what is possible within the present context, rather than challenging its limits. This is a particular problem for the women's movement since its goal of women's liberation requires a fundamental transformation of any of the gender regimes in actual existence.

With the link between immediate goals and transformative vision weakened, work of an immediate, practical nature loses much of its strategic significance. Such work has been widely criticized in those sectors of the women's movement and other movements that retain a transformative commitment. By becoming trapped within the prevailing liberal context (Wallerstein 1995, 1999), immediate work that might have more creative potential in a context-breaking moment instead becomes limited and risks contributing to the flexible accommodation of the status quo.

These limitations are especially acute in the area of quality. The predominant liberal view has been one that emphasizes competence and merit. This approach implies competitive ranking and meritocracy, and also the exclusion of those deemed less competent. Liberal advocates argue for increased education in order to produce (varying degrees of) competence, for liberalism prefers and privileges education over strategies that work more directly for equality. The now commonplace calls for increased education as a major mechanism to resolve social problems, including those of gender inequality, have been identified by critical voices within the women's movement as profoundly problematic (for example, Mies 1986: 20 and Martin 1994).

The contrary position has been one that has refused meritocracy and has argued instead for equality, expressed primarily in terms of civil and political rights. This has been a powerful force against exclusion and for opening the structures of state power to popular forces. Chinese women achieved major historical changes toward equality in this political sense during the twentieth century, through equality-seeking movements for women's liberation and for socialism. Women in China acquired formal political and legal equality, and strove to make formal equality real through continuing political efforts and recurrent campaigns. This work is carried on at present, especially through measures to implement the 1992 Women's Law and to open political office more effectively to women's participation.

Achieving equality in practice involves more than is usually implied by civil and political rights. Especially as the direct scope of the state retreats, and social and economic forces of community and market assert themselves, equality reveals itself as a more complex and subtle matter. As one contemporary proponent of equality strategies has acknowledged, issues of competence necessarily remain important in the workplace and in the world of knowledge (Wallerstein 1999: 103). Increasingly, these are the locations where relations of knowledge and power are generated and contested. Whatever political guarantees might be won for equality and inclusion, if these are not rooted outside the political arena, in the critical areas of everyday life, they risk being fragile or empty. And these are areas in which quality assumes a compelling value.

The forms of knowledge required for equality are multilayered and open-ended. Immediate questions of literacy, education, and training are certainly essential for producing livelihoods and creating a gendered basis for everyday equality. Especially where intellectual labor and economic contribution are valued highly, as they are in China, disadvantages in these areas can be profoundly disabling. There are historical deficits for women in China that continue to generate problems for women, and some of the strategies described here are a response to this problem at the grass roots. More concentrated knowledge in a variety of forms—technical, political, and cultural—is implicated in the generation of inequality, even where socialist experiments have attempted to remove its economic basis.[3] This is a formidable problem to resolve, but breaking down gendered barriers of exclusion or limited access must be part of any solution. And knowledge about how to effect change in gender relations is intrinsically necessary to the project of pursuing equal-

[3] For a theoretical treatment of this problem in relation to Eastern Europe, see Bahro (1978)

ity, as evidenced in the priority given to building a women's movement. This is a knowledge still in the process of creation, with only a portion of its trajectory described here.

The call to raise women's quality is not the spark that will start a prairie fire. That will require a vision that decisively breaks the present context, rather than a set of programs that carefully work within it. But the pursuit of quality may prepare the ground. It allows women to re-move obstacles and position ourselves more favorably in the field of knowledge. And it places the concept of quality in contention, allowing equality-seeking movements to recreate its meaning and to claim it as our own.

Appendix

Appendix

"1994 Town and Township Women's Federation
Post Objectives and Responsibility System
Assessment Standards," Ling County

1 TWO STUDIES, TWO COMPETITIONS WORK (35 POINTS)

1.1 Diversified economic production

Initiate a village focal point for producing edible fungi (a village with more than 20 households producing edible fungi) for 10 points, with 5 points more for another village. Add 5 points for nurturing a large-scale fungi-producing household with an income over RMB 10,000.

Set up a drawnwork processing point (with 20 embroidery workers) for 8 points; add 1 point for each extra 10 workers.

Initiate a model village in another type of courtyard production and achieve county-level model standards and confirmation for 10 points.

1.2 Grain and cotton production

Nurture women models in setting new records in either yield or total production for grain or cotton for 3 points. Add 3 points for women taking on a scientific research project.

1.3 Evaluation of titles

Have a woman receive a government-recognized technical title for .5 point, and .5 point for an additional one.

1.4 Summary, commendation, and standardized management

Produce a summary of "two study, two competitions" activities and receive commendation for 5 points.

Keep registration lists for training, minutes of meetings, summaries of activities, and maintain relevant files for a standardized management system for 2 points.

2 ORGANIZATIONAL WORK (15 POINTS)

2.1 Have a complete village-level women's organization (with heads, committees, and remuneration for heads) for 5 points, and subtract .5 point for each village lacking this.

2.2 Have 80% of women's heads taking the lead in market production and having a specialized productive or commercial project for 5 points, and subtract 1 point for each 10% less.

2.3 Have 50% of women's heads serve concurrently as birth-planning heads for 5 points; subtract 1 point for each 10% less and add 1 point for each 10% more.

2.4 For each town or township Women's Federation cadre who is assessed to be a model Party member or advanced worker add 3 points.

3 RIGHTS WORK (20 POINTS)

3.1 For each case promptly handled within the town or township or referred to higher levels that is reported and resolved, 2 points.

3.2 Have 70% of women's heads enter the "two committees" for 5 points; subtract 1 point for each 10% less and add 1 point for each 10% more.

3.3 Have the remuneration for 70% of women's heads reach the level of 50% of the Party branch secretary's remuneration for 5 points; with no points for not reaching this goal.

3.4 Have women constitute 20% of candidates for Party membership for 3 points.

3.5 Write a report specifically concerning women's questions for 2 points.

3.6 Develop the service sector and establish an economic entity with a yearly income of RMB 1,000 for 5 points; and if it achieves county Women's Federation recognition, add 15 points.

3.7 Act as an advocate for a woman or help a woman resolve an economic dispute for 2 points.

4 WORK WITH CHILDREN AND YOUTHS (11 POINTS)

4.1 For each kindergarten, school, agency, or household heads' school established to standard (with organization, classroom, teacher, teaching materials, system, and files), 6 points.

4.2 Organize one large-scale activity in family education (select and commend good household heads able to teach children, hold family education competitions and family movement meetings) for 5 points.

4.3 Write a worthwhile paper on family education (with use by the prefecture as the standard) for 3 points.

5 FAMILY AND CULTURAL DEVELOPMENT

5.1 For commendation in comparison of "five good family" activities (with commendation as the standard), 5 points.

5.2 For nurturing a "ten star level" family as commended by the county Women's Federation, add 5 points.

5.3 For organizing a collective wedding or engagement activity, add 5 points.

5.4 For calling a family cultural performance or a family cultural construction meeting, add 5 points.

6 OTHER WORK (14 POINTS)

6.1 Organize March 8, June 1, or other festival celebrations and timely report these to higher levels for 1 point for each occasion.

6.2 Submit timely yearly and half-yearly reports, statistical reports, and related materials for 5 points; subtract 1 point for missing one time; for spontaneously submitting material on a model case, add 2 points.

6.3 Run a training class (for more than 50 participants and with the county Women's Federation present as the standard) for 3 points.

6.4 For being visited by the province, prefecture, or county for an on-site inspection, add 10, 8, or 6 points respectively.

6.5 For nurturing a national, provincial, or prefectural model, add 15, 10, or 5 points respectively.

6.6 For writing a news report on women or woman-work that is used by national, provincial, prefectural, or county news units, add 10, 6, 4, or 2 points respectively.

6.7 Attend county Women's Federation meetings as scheduled for 5 points; subtract 1 point for each missed meeting.

6.8 Attend county Women's Federation activities for points as merited by record of attendance.

Works Cited

Abu-Lughod, Lila. 1991. "Writing Against Culture." In Richard G. Fox, ed., *Recapturing Anthropology: Working in the Present*, pp. 137–62. Santa Fe, N.M.: School of American Research Press.

Bahro, Rudolf. 1978. *The Alternative in Eastern Europe*. London: New Left Books.

Bai Lijun. 1991. "Yantao makesizhuyi funüguan zai zhongguo de shijian yu fazhan." *Funü gongzuo* 11: 24–25.

Bao Xinjian. 1995. "Dangdai fazhan lilun xin zouxiang yu woguo shehui wenming xin fazhan." *Wen shi zhe* 4: 3–11.

Barthes, Roland. 1973. *Mythologies*. London: Paladin.

Bonnin, Michel, and Yves Chevrier. 1991. "The Intellectual and the State: Social Dynamics of Intellectual Autonomy During the Post-Mao Era." *China Quarterly* 127: 569–93.

Bourque, Susan C., and Kay B. Warren. 1987. "Technology, Gender, and Development." *Daedalus* 116 (4): 173–97.

Burns, John P. 1987a. "China's Nomenklatura System." *Problems of Communism* 36 (5): 36–51.

———. 1987b. "Civil Service Reform in Contemporary China." *Australian Journal of Chinese Affairs* 18: 47–83.

———. 1989. "Chinese Civil Service Reform: The 13th Party Congress Proposals." *China Quarterly* 120: 739–70.

Central People's Government Council. 1975. *The Marriage Law of the People's Republic of China (1 May 1950)*. Beijing: Foreign Languages Press.

Chan, Cecilia. 1994. "Defending Women's Rights in the Socialist Republic of China: Services of the Guangzhou Women's Federation." *Social Development Issues* 16 (1): 98–106.

Chen, C. C., K. C. Yu, and J. B. Miner. 1997. "Motivation to Marriage: A Study of Women in Chinese State-owned Enterprises." *Journal of Applied Behavioural Science* 33 (2): 160–73.

Compton, Boyd. 1966 [1952]. *Mao's China: Party Reform Documents, 1942–44*. Seattle: University of Washington Press.

Croll, Elisabeth. 1978. *Feminism and Socialism in China*. London: Routledge and Kegan Paul.

———. 1981. *The Politics of Marriage in Contemporary China.* Cambridge: Cambridge University Press.

———. 1983. *Chinese Women Since Mao.* London: Zed Books.

———. 1994. *From Heaven to Earth: Images and Experiences of Development in China.* London: Routledge.

Davin, Delia. 1976. *Woman-Work: Women and the Party in Revolutionary China.* Oxford: Clarendon Press.

———. 1998. "Gender and Migration in China." In Flemming Christiansen and Zhang Junzuo, eds., *Village Inc.: Chinese Rural Society in the 1990s,* pp. 230–40. Richmond, Surrey: Curzon.

Dezhou diqu funü lianhehui. 1989. *Dezhou diqu fulian 1988 nian gongzuo zongjie he 1989 nian gongzuo yaodian.* Dezhou: Dezhou diqu fulian.

Diamond, Norma. 1975. "Collectivization, Kinship, and the Status of Women in Rural China." In Rayna R. Reiter, ed., *Toward an Anthropology of Women,* pp. 372–95. New York: Monthly Review Press.

Erlmann, Veit. 1992. "'The Past Is Far and the Future Is Far': Power and Performance among Zulu Migrant Workers." *American Ethnologist* 19 (4): 688–709.

Fan Ying. 1998. "The Transfer of Western Management to China." *Management Learning* 29 (2): 201–21.

Fox-Genovese, Elizabeth, and Eugene D. Genovese. 1983. "The Ideological Bases of Domestic Economy." In Elizabeth Fox-Genovese and Eugene D. Genovese, eds., *Fruits of Merchant Capital,* pp. 299–336. New York: Oxford University Press.

Funk, Nanette, and Magda Mueller, eds. 1993. *Gender Politics and Post-Communism: Reflections from Eastern Europe and the Former Soviet Union.* New York: Routledge.

Gates, Hill. 1996. *China's Motor: A Thousand Years of Petty Capitalism.* Ithaca, N.Y.: Cornell University Press.

Gilmartin, Christina, Gail Hershatter, Lisa Rofel, and Tyrene White, eds. 1994. *Engendering China: Women, Culture and the State.* Cambridge, Mass.: Harvard University Press.

Han Baozhen. 1995. "Nongcun funü fazhan yu keji peixun." In Li Qiufang et al., eds., *'95 di sici shijie funü dahui zhongguo nongcun funü fazhan luntan lunwenji,* pp. 51–55. Beijing: Zhonghua quanguo funü lianhehui chengxiang gongzuobu.

He Yupeng. 1995. "Nongcun zhengcece; funü jinbu; jingji fazhan." In Li Qiufang et al., eds., *'95 di sici shijie funü dahui zhongguo nongcun funü fazhan luntan lunwenji,* pp. 107–11. Beijing: Zhonghua quanguo funü lianhehui chengxiang gongzuobu.

Honig, Emily, and Gail Hershatter. 1988. *Personal Voices: Chinese Women in the 1980s.* Stanford, Calif.: Stanford University Press.

Howell, Jude. 1994. "Striking a New Balance: New Social Organisations in Post-Mao China." *Capital and Class* 54: 89–111.

Huang Qizao. 1992. "'Shuangxue shuangbi' jiakuai nongcun funü ziqiang zili de bufa." *Funü zuzhi yu huodong* 2: 28.

———. 1993. "Quanguo funü tuanjieqilai, wei jianshe zhongguo tese she-huizhuyi nuli fendou (zai zhouguo funü di qici quanguo daibiao dahui shang de baogao, 1993.9.1)." *Funü zuzhi yu huodong* 5: 15–19.

Jacka, Tamara. 1997. *Women's Work in Rural China: Change and Continuity in an Era of Reform.* Cambridge: Cambridge University Press.

Jenner, Richard A., Len Hebert, Allen Appell, and Jane Baack. 1998. "Using Quality Management for Cultural Transformation in Chinese State Enterprises: A Case Study." *Journal of Quality Management* 3 (2): 193–211.

Jiang Zemin. 1989. "Jiang Zemin tongzhi de jianghua." *Guangming ribao*, 1989.9.30.

Johnson, Kay Ann. 1983. *Women, the Family and Peasant Revolution in China.* Chicago: University of Chicago Press.

Judd, Ellen R. 1994. *Gender and Power in Rural North China.* Stanford, Calif.: Stanford University Press.

———. 1995. "Feminism From Afar or To China and Home Again." In S. Cole and L. Phillips, eds., *Ethnographic Feminism(s): Essays in Anthropology*, pp. 37–51. Ottawa: Carleton University Press.

———. 1997. "Gender and Capital Accumulation in Chinese Village Enterprises." In T. Brook and H. V. Luong, eds., *Culture and Economy: The Shaping of Capitalism in Eastern Asia*, pp. 207–34. Ann Arbor: University of Michigan Press.

———. 1998. "Reconsidering China's Marriage Law Campaign: Toward a De-orientalised Feminist Perspective." *Asian Journal of Women's Studies* 4 (2): 8–26.

———, ed. 1999. "Rural Women in Reform China." *Chinese Sociology and Anthropology* 31 (2).

Korabik, Karen. 1993. "Women Managers in the People's Republic of China: Changing Roles in Changing Times." *Applied Psychology* 42 (4): 353–63.

Li Xiaojiang. 1989. "Zenyang kan dangqian funü wenti he funü yanjiu." *Funü zuzhi yu huodong* 1: 5–9.

Liang Xuguang, ed. 1989. *Funü chengcai lun.* Jinan: Shandong renmin chu-banshe.

Lingxian fulian. 1990. *1990 nian gongzuo yijian.* Lingxian: Lingxian fulian.

———. 1994. *Weirao fazhan mubiao, zuohao jiehe wenzhang, buduan kaichuang funü gongzuo de xin jumian (1994.7.26).* Lingxian: Lingxian fulian.

———. N.d. [1995] *Jianquan zuzhi zengyu huoli wei nongcun liangge wenming de jianshe zuo gongxian.* Lingxian: Lingxian fulian.

Liu Peiying and Huang Jiansong. 1995. "Lingxian shishi lüse yuedong zhongzhi xin jubo guangda funü zhimian reqing zaidu gaozhang." *Funü gongzuo* 7: 23–24.

Liu Shaoqi. 1980 [1939]. "How to be a Good Communist." *Three Essays on Party Building*. Beijing: Foreign Languages Press.

Mann, Susan. 1997. *Precious Records: Women in China's Long Eighteenth Century*. Stanford, Calif.: Stanford University Press.

Mao Zedong. 1977. *Five Essays on Philosophy*. Beijing: Foreign Languages Press.

Martin, Emily. 1994. *Flexible Bodies: The Role of Immunity in American Culture from the Days of Polio to the Age of AIDS*. Boston: Beacon.

Meng Xianfan. 1993. "Nongcun laodongli zhuanyi zhong de zhongguo nongcun funü." *Funü zuzhi yu huodong* 5: 52–59.

———. 1995. "'Nangong nügeng' yu zhongguo nüxing de fazhan." *Funü yanjiu* 4: 48–51.

Mies, Maria. 1986. *Patriarchy and Accumulation on a World Scale in the International Division of Labour*. London: Zed Books.

Mingat, Alain. 1998. "The Strategy Used by High-Performing Asian Economies in Education: Some Lessons for Developing Countries." *World Development* 26 (4): 695–715.

Molyneux, Maxine. 1986. "Mobilization Without Emancipation?: Women's Interests, State, and Revolution." In R. Fagan, C. D. Deere, and J. L. Coraggio, eds., *Transition and Development: Problems of Third World Socialism*, pp. 280–302. New York: Monthly Review Press

Munro, Donald T. 1977. *The Concept of Man in Contemporary China*. Ann Arbor: University of Michigan Press.

Ng, Rita Mei Ching. 1998. "Culture as a Factor in Management: The Case of the People's Republic of China." *International Journal of Management* 15 (1): 86–93.

Parish, William L., Xiaoye Zhe, and Fang Li. 1995. "Nonfarm Work and Marketization of the Chinese Countryside." *China Quarterly* 143: 697–730.

Pei Xiaolin. 1998. "Rural Industry—Institutional Aspects of China's Economic Transformation." In Flemming Christiansen and Zhang Junzuo, eds., *Village Inc: Chinese Rural Society in the 1990s*, pp. 83–102. Richmond, Surrey: Curzon.

Porter, Marilyn, and Ellen Judd, eds. 2000. *Feminists Doing Development: A Practical Critique*. London: Zed Books.

The Program for the Development of Chinese Women (1995–2000). 1995. Beijing: All- China Women's Federation.

"Quarterly Chronicle and Documentation (July–September 1994)." 1994. *China Quarterly* 140: 1219–45.

"Quarterly Report and Documentation (April–June 1995)." 1995. *China Quarterly* 143: 923–58.

Rai, Shirin M., and Zhang Junzuo. 1994. "Competing and Learning: Women and the State in Contemporary Rural Mainland China." *Issues and Studies* 30 (3): 51–66.

Renmin ribao. 1990. "Gongqingfu gongzuo yao you yige xin fazhan" (she-lun). *Renmin ribao*, Feb. 1.

Rofel, Lisa. 1999. *Other Modernities: Gendered Yearnings in China After Socialism*. Berkeley: University of California Press.

Scott, Joan W., Cora Kaplan, and Debra Keates, eds. 1997. *Transitions, Environments, Transitions: Feminisms in International Politics*. New York: Routledge.

The Second Report of the People's Republic of China on the Implementation of the Nairobi Forward-looking Strategies for the Advancement of Women. 1994. Beijing

Shandongsheng fulian. 1989. *Yong kexue jishu wuzhuang nongcun funü zai zhenxing shandong zhong fahui shenglijun zuoyong*. Jinan: Shandongsheng fulian.

―――. 1993. "Weirao quanju zhanlüe jiji tansuo shijian, nuli shixian liang da jingsai huodong xin feiyue." *Funü gongzuo* 12: 7–11, 15.

[Shandong]sheng fulian xuanchuanbu. 1989. "Wosheng kaizhan 'shuang-xue shuangbi' jingsai huodong qingkuang zongshu." *Funü gongzuo* 12: 12–14.

Shandongsheng shishi 'Zhonghua renmin gongheguo funü quanyi baozhang fa' banfa. 1994. Jinan: Shandongsheng funü lianhehui.

"Shehui tuanti dengji guanli tiaoli (1998)." 1998. *Zhonghua renmin gongheguo guowuyuan gongbao* 919: 1018–35.

Shue, Vivienne. 1988. *The Reach of the State: Sketches of the Chinese Body Politic*. Stanford, Calif.: Stanford University Press.

Smil, Vaclav. 1995. "Who Will Feed China?" *China Quarterly* 143: 801–13.

Stacey, Judith. 1983. *Patriarchy and Socialist Revolution in China*. Berkeley: University of California Press.

Stalin, Joseph. 1947 [1939]. "Report on the Work of the Central Committee to the Eighteenth Congress of the C.P.S.U. (B.)." In *Problems of Leninism*, pp. 596–642. Moscow: Foreign Languages Publishing House.

"Statistical Communique of the State Statistical Bureau of the People's Republic of China on 1993 National Economic and Social Development—28 February 1994." 1994. British Broadcasting Corporation, *Summary of World Broadcasts: Weekly Economic Report*. FEW/0326 WS 1/1.

Taussig, Michael. 1992. *The Nervous System*. New York: Routledge.

Walker, Kathy LeMons. 1993. "Economic Growth, Peasant Marginalization, and the Sexual Division of Labor in Early Twentieth Century China: Women's Work in Nantong County." *Modern China* 19 (3): 345–65.

Wallerstein, Immanuel. 1988. "The Bourgeois(ie) as Concept and Reality." *New Left Review* 167: 91–106.

―――. 1995. *After Liberalism*. New York: New Press.

―――. 1999. *The End of the World as We Know It: Social Science for the Twentieth-first Century*. Minneapolis: University of Minnesota Press.

Wolf, Margery. 1985. *Revolution Postponed: Women in Contemporary China*. Stanford, Calif.: Stanford University Press.

———. 1992. *A Thrice Told Tale: Feminism, Postmodernisation and Ethnographic Responsibility*. Stanford, Calif.: Stanford University Press.

Wu Aiying. 1991. "Buduan tigao 'shuangxue shuangbi' jingsai huodong shuiping renzhen zongjie jingyan qianghua peitao cuoshe." *Funü gongzuo* 5: 6–15.

Xiao Wen. 1995. "Shiying shichang jingji shenhua 'shuangxue shuangbi' huodong—quanguo nongcun funü 'shuangxue shuangbi' huodong yantaohui lundian gaishu." *Funü yanjiu luncong* 1: 36–38.

Yan Guirong. 1992. "Xin xingshi xia jiceng fulian mianlin wenti zhongzhong." *Funü gongzuo* 5: 16–17.

Yang Yanyin. 1991. "Shuangxue shuangbi qidongyuan, fazhan nongye zuo gongxian." *Funü gongzuo* 3: 6–10.

Yang Yu'e. 1988. "Shangpin jingji de fazhan qianghua le funü de zhuti yishi." *Funü gongzuo* 10: 5–6.

Yao Zhongda. 1984. "Development of Productive Forces Promotes the Advancement of Adult Education in China." *Convergence* 17 (3): 11–15.

Ye Lin. 1989. "Quanguo fulian guowuyuan babuwei deng shier danwei xietiaohui jueding kaizhan quanguo nongcun funü 'shuangxue shuangbi' jingsai." *Funü zuzhi yu huodong* 2: 13.

Zhao Yulan. 1994a. "Jiji toushen gaige nuli canyu fazhan quansheng funü tuanjieqilai wei shixian shandong shehuizhuyi xiandaihua jianshe de hongwei mubiao jiangong liye." *Funü gongzuo* 4: 8–15.

———. 1994b. "Zai quanguo youxiu nü nongmin qiyejia mingming biaozhang dahui shang de jianghua." *Funü gongzuo* 7: 4–8.

———. 1994c. "Zai quango 'shuangxue shuangbi' 'jinguo jiangong' jingsai huodong yantaohui shang de jianghua." *Funü gongzuo* 10: 1, 4–9.

Zhonghua renmin gongheguo renmin daibiao dahui. 1992. *Funü quanyi baozhang fa (1992.4.3)*. Beijing: n. p.

Zhonggong zhongyang. 1990. "Jiaqing gaishan dang dui gongqingfu gongzuo lingdao" (1989.12. 21). *Renmin ribao*, Feb. 1.

Zhonghua renmin gongheguo guowuyuan. 1989. "Shehui tuanti dengji guanli tiaoli." *Renmin ribao*, Nov. 9.

Index

In this index an "f" after a number indicates a separate reference on the next page, and an "ff" indicates separate references on the next two pages. A continuous discussion over two or more pages is indicated by a span of page numbers, e.g., "57–59."